The Essentials of Mysticism
and Other Essays
By Evelyn Underhill
Edited by Anthony Uyl

Devoted Publishing
Woodstock, Ontario, 2017

The Essentials of Mysticism
and Other Essays
By Evelyn Underhill (1875-1941)
Edited by Anthony Uyl

Originally Printed in 1920

What kind of philosophies do you have?
Let us know!

Contact us at: devotedpub@hotmail.com
Visit our shop on Facebook: @DevotedPublishing
Published in Woodstock, Ontario, Canada 2017

For bulk educational rates, please contact us at the above email address.

ISBN: 978-1-77356-012-0

Table of Contents

PREFACE 4

The Essentials of Mysticism 5

The Mystic and the Corporate Life 14

Mysticism and the Doctrine of Atonement 21

The Mystic As Creative Artist 28

The Education of the Spirit 38

The Place of Will, Intellect and Feeling in Prayer 43

The Mysticism of Plotinus 49

Three Mediæval Mystics 58

   1: The Mirror of Simple Souls 58

   II 60

   2: The Blessed Angela of Foligno 64

   3: Julian of Norwich 72

Mysticism in Modern France 78

   1. Soeur Thérèse de l'Enfant Jésus 78

   2. Lucie-Christine 83

   3. Charles Péguy 87

PREFACE

The essays collected in this volume have been written during the past eight years. They deal with various aspects of the subject of mysticism: the first half-dozen with its general theory and practice, and special points arising within it; the rest with its application as seen in the lives and works of the mystics, from the pagan Plotinus to the Christian contemplatives of our own day. Most of them have already appeared elsewhere, though all have been revised and several completely rewritten for the purposes of this book. "The Essentials of Mysticism" and "The Mystic as Creative Artist" were first printed in The Quest; "Mystic and the Corporate Life," "Mysticism and the Doctrine of Atonement," and "The Place of Will, Intellect, and Feeling in Prayer" in The Interpreter; "The Education of the Spirit" in The Parents' Review; "Mysticism of Plotinus" in The Quarterly Review; "The Mirror of Simple Souls" and "Sreur Therese de I' Enfant Jesus" (under the title of "A Modern Saint") in The Fortnightly Review; "The Blessed Angela of Foligno" in Franciscan Essays; "Julian of Norwich" in The St. Martin's Review and Charles Martin's Review; "Peguy" in The Contemporary Review. All these are now republished by kind permission of the editors concerned.

E.U.
August 1920.

The Essentials of Mysticism

What are the true essentials of mysticism? When we have stripped off those features which some mystics accept and others reject -- all that is merely due to tradition, temperament or unconscious allegorism -- what do we find as the necessary, abiding and essential character of all true mystical experience? The question is really worth asking. For some time, much attention has been given to the historical side of mysticism, and some -- much less -- to its practice. But there has been no true understanding of the difference between its substance and its accidents; between traditional forms and methods, and the eternal experience which they have mediated. In mystical literature words are frequently confused with things, and symbols with realities; so that much of this literature seems to the reader to refer to some self-consistent and exclusive dream world, and not to the achievement of universal truth. Thus the strong need for re-statement which is being felt by institutional religion, the necessity of re-translating its truths into symbolism which modern man can understand and accept, applies with at least equal force to mysticism. It has become important to disentangle the facts from ancient formulae used to express them. These formulae have value, because they are genuine attempts to express truth; but they are not themselves that truth; and failure to recognise this distinction has caused a great deal of misunderstanding. Thus, on its theological and philosophical side, the mysticism of Western Europe is tightly entwined with the patristic and mediaeval presentation of Christianity; and this presentation, though full of noble poetry, is now difficult if not impossible to adjust to our conceptions of the universe. Again on its personal side mysticism is a department of psychology. Now psychology is changing under our eyes; already we see our mental life in a new perspective, tend to describe it under new forms. Our ways of describing and interpreting spiritual experience must change with the rest if we are to keep in touch with reality; though the experience be unchanged.

So, we are forced to ask ourselves, what is the essential element in spiritual experience. Which of the many states and revelations described by the mystics are integral parts of it; and what do these states and degrees come to, when we describe them in the current phraseology and strip off the monastic robes in which they are usually dressed? What elements are due to the suggestions of tradition, to conscious or unconscious symbolism, to the misinterpretation of emotion, to the invasions of cravings from the lower centres, or the disguised fulfilment of an unconscious wish? And when all these channels of illusion have been blocked, what is left? This will be a difficult and often a painful enquiry. But it is an enquiry that ought to be faced by all who believe in the validity of man's spiritual experience; in order that their faith may be established on a firm basis, and disentangled from those unreal and impermanent elements which are certainly destined to destruction, and with which it is at present too often confused. I am sure that at the present moment we serve best the highest interests of the soul by subjecting the whole mass of material which is called "mysticism" to an inexorable criticism. Only by inflicting the faithful wounds of a friend can we save the science of the inner life from mutilation at the hands of the psychologists.

We will begin then with the central fact of the mystic's experience. This central fact, it seems to me, is an overwhelming consciousness of God, and of his own soul: a consciousness which absorbs or eclipses all other centres of interest. It is said that St Francis of Assisi, praying in the house of Bernard of Quintavalle, was heard to say, again and again, "My God! My God! what art Thou, and what am I?" Though the words came from St Augustine, they well represent his mental attitude. This was the only question he thought worth asking; and it is the question which every mystic asks at the begining and sometimes answers at the end of his quest. Hence we must put first among our essentials the clear conviction of a living God as the primary interest of consciousness; and of a personal self capable of communication with Him. Having said this, however, we may allow that the widest latitude is possible in the mystic's conception of his Deity. At best, this conception will be symbolic; his experience, if genuine, will far transcend the symbols he employs. "God," says the author of The Cloud of Unknowing, "may well be loved but not thought." Credal forms, therefore, can only be for the mystic a scaffold by which he ascends. We are even bound, I think, to confess that the overt recognition of that which orthodox Christians mean by a personal God is not essential. On the contrary, where it takes a crudely anthropomorphic form the idea of personality may be a disadvantage; opening the way for the intrusions of disguised emotions and desires. In the highest experiences of the greatest mystics the personal category appears to be transcended. "The light in the soul which is increate," says Eckhart, "is not satisfied with the three persons, in so far as each subsists in its difference ... but it is determined to know whence this Being comes, to penetrate into the Simple Ground, into the Silent Desert within which never any difference has lain." The all-inclusive one is beyond all partial apprehensions though the true values that those apprehensions represent are conserved in it. However pantheistic the mystic may be on the one hand, however absolutist on the other, his communion with God is always personal in this sense: that it is communion with a living Reality, an object of love capable of response, which demands and receives from him a total self-donation. This sense of a double movement, a self-giving on the divine side answering to the self-giving on the human side, is found in all great mysticism. It has, of course, lent itself to emotional exaggeration, but in its pure form seems an integral part of man's apprehension of Reality. Even where it conflicts with the mystic's philosophy -- as in Hinduism and Neoplatonism -- it is still present. It is curious to note, for example, how Plotinus, after safeguarding his Absolute One from every qualification, excluding it from all categories, defining it only by the icy method of negation, suddenly breaks away into the language of ardent feeling when he comes to describe that ecstasy in which he touched the truth. Then he speaks of "the veritable love, the sharp desire" which possessed him, appealing to the experience of those fellow mystics who have "caught fire and found the splendour there.. These, he says, have "felt burning within themselves the flame of love for what is there to know -- the passion of the lover resting on the bosom of his love."

So we may say that the particular mental image which the mystic forms of his objective, the traditional theology, is not essential. Since it is never adequate, the degree of its inadequacy is of secondary importance. Though some creeds have proved more helpful than others to the mystic, he is found fully developed in every great religion. We cannot honestly say that there is any wide difference between the Brahman, Sufi, or Christian mystic at their best. They are far more like each other than they are like the average believer in their several creeds. What is essential is the way the mystic feels about his Deity, and about his own relationship with it; for this adoring and all-possessing consciousness of the rich and complete divine life against the self's life, and of the possible achievement of a level ofbeing, a sublimation of the self, wherein we are perfectly united with it, may fairly be written down as a necessary element of all mystical life. This is the common factor which unites those apparently incompatible views of the universe which have been claimed at one time or another as mystical. Their mystical quality abides wholly in the temper of the self who adopts them. He may be a transcendentalist: but, if so, it is because his intuition of the divine is so lofty that it cannot be expressed by means of any intellectual concept, and he is bound to say, with Ruysbroeck, "He is neither this nor that." He may be a unanimist; but if he is it is because he finds in other men -- more, in the whole web of life -- that mysterious living essence which is a mode of God's existence, and which he loves, seeks, and recognizes everywhere. "How can I find words for the beauty of my Beloved? For He is merged in all beauty," says Kabir. "His colour is in all the pictures of the world, and it bewitches the body and the mind." He may be -- often is -- a sacramentalist; but if so, only because the symbol or the sacrament help him to touch God. So St Thomas [Aquinas]:

Adoro te devote, latens Deitas,
Quæ sub his figuris vere latitas
[O Godhead hid, devoutly I adore Thee, Who truly art within the forms before me]

The minute the mystic suspects that any of these things are obstacle instead of means, he rejects them; to the scandal of those who habitually confuse the image with reality.

Thus we get the temperamental symbolist, quietist, nature mystic or transcendentalist. We get Plotinus rapt to the "bare pure one"; St Augustine's impassioned communion with Perfect Beauty; Eckhart declaring his achievement of "the wilderness of God"; Jacopone da Todi prostrate in adoration before "the Love that gives all things form"; Ruysbroeck describing his achievement of "that wayless abyss of fathomless beatitude where the Trinity of divine persons possess their nature in the essential Unity"; JacobBoehme gazing into the fire-world and there finding the living heart of the Universe; Kabir listening to the rhythmic music of Reality, and seeing the worlds told like beads within the Being of God. And at the opposite pole we have Mechthild of Magdeburg's amorous conversations with her "heavenly Bridegroom", the many mystical experiences connected with the Eucharist, the Sufi's enraptured description of God as the "Matchless Chalice and the Soveregn Wine", the narrow intensity and emotional raptures of contemplatives of the type of Richard Rolle. We cannot refuse the title of mystic to any of these; because in every case their aim is union between God and the soul. This is the one essential of mysticism, and there are as many ways from one term to the other as there are variations in the spirit of man. But on the other hand, when anybody speaking of mysticism proposes an object that is less than God -- increase of health, of knowledge, of happiness, occultism, intercourse with spirits, supernormal experience in general -- then we may suspect that we are off the track.

Now we come to the next group of essentials: the necessary acts and dispositions of the mystic himself, the development which takes place within him -- the psychological facts, that is to say, which are represented by the so-called "mystic way". The mystic way is best understood as a process of sublimation, which carries the correspondences of the self with the Universe up to higher levels than those on which our normal consciousness works. Just as the normal consciousness stands over against the unconscious, which, with its buried impulses and its primitive and infantile cravings, represents a cruder reaction of the organism to the external world; so does the developed mystical life stand over against normal life with its preoccupations and its web of illusions encouraging the animal will-to-dominate and the animal will-to-live. Normal consciousness sorts out some elements from the mass of experiences beating at our doors and constructs fromthem a certain order; but this order lacks any deep meaning or true cohesion, because normal consciousness is incapable of apprehending the underlying reality from which these scattered experiences proceed. The claim of the mystical consciousnes is to a closer reading of truth; to an apprehension of the divine unifying principle behind appearance. "The One," days Plotinus, "is present everywhere, and absent only from those unable to perceive it"; and when we do perceive it, we "have another life ... attaining the aim of our existence, and our rest." To know this at first hand -- not to guess, believe or accept, but to be certain -- is the highest achievement of human consciousness, and the ultimate object of mysticism. How is it done?

There are two ways of attacking this problem which may conceivably help us. The first consists in a comparisons of the declarations of various mystics and a sorting out of that which they have in common; a careful watch being kept, of course, for the results of conscious or unconscious imitation, of tradition and theological preconceptions. In this way we get some firsthand evidence of factors which are at any rate usually present, and may possibly be esential. The second line of enquiry consists in a re-translation into psychological terms of those mystical declarations; when many will reveal the relation in which they stand to the psychic life of man.

Reviewing the first-hand declarations of the mystics, we inevitably notice one prominent feature: the frequency with which they break up their experience into three phases. Sometimes they regard these objectively, and speak of three worlds, or three aspects of God of which they become successively aware. Sometimes they regard them subjectively and speak of three stages of growth through which they pass, such as thos of Beginner, Proficient and Perfect; or of phases of spiritual progress in which we first meditate upon reality, then contemplate reality, and at last are unitedwith reality. But among the most widely separated mystics of the East and West this threefold experience can nearly always be traced. There are, of course, obvious dangers in attaching absolute value to number-schemes of this kind. Numbers have an uncanny power over the human mind; once let a symbolic character be attributed to them, and the temptation to make them fit the facts at all costs becomes overwhelming. We all know that the number "three" has a long religious history, and are therefore inclined to look with suspicion on it's claim to interpret the mystic life. At the same time there are other significant numbers -- such as "seven" and "ten" -- which have never gained equal currency as the bases of mystical formulae. We may agree that the mediaeval mystics found the threefold division of spiritual experience in Neoplatonism; but we must also agree that a formula of this kind is not likely to survive for nearly two thousand years unless it agrees with the facts. Those who us it with the greatest conviction are not theorists. they are the practical mystics who are intent on making maps of the regions into which they have penetrated.

Moreover, this is no mere question of handing on one single tradition. the mystics describe their movement from appearance to reality in many different ways, and use many incompatible religious symbols. the one common factor is the discrimination of three phases of consciousness, no more, no less, in which we can recognise certain common characteristics. "There are," says Philo, "three kinds of life: life as it concerns God, life as it concerns the creature, and a third intermediate life, a mixture of the former two." Consistently with this, Plotinus speaks of three descending phases or principles of Divine Reality: the Godhead or absolute and unconditioned One; its manifestation as Nous, the Divine Mind or Spirit which inspires the "intelligible" or eternal world; and Psyche, the Life or Soul of the physical universe. Man, normally in correspondence with this physical world of succession and change, may by spiritual intuition achieve first consciousness of the eternal world of spiritual values, in which, indeed, the apex of his soul already dwells; and in brief moments of ecstatic vision may rise above this to communion with its source, the Absolute One. There you have the mystic's vision of the universe, and the mystic's way of purification, enlightenment and ecstasy bringing new and deeper knowledge of reality as the self's interest, urged by its loving desire of the Ultimate, is shifted from sense to soul, from soul to spirit. There is here no harsh dualism, no turning from a bad material world to a good spiritual world. We are invited to one gradual, undivided process of sublimation, penetrating ever more deeply into the reality of the Universe, to find at last "that One who is present everywhere and absent only from those who do not perceive him." What we behold, that we are: citizens, according to our own will and desire, of the surface world of the senses, the deeper world of life, or the ultimate world of spiritual reality.

An almost identical doctrine appears in the Upanishads. At the heart of reality is Brahma, "other than the known and above the unknown". His manifestation is Ananda, that spiritual world which is the true object of aesthetic passion and religious contemplation. From it, life and consciousnes are born, in it they have their being, to it they must return. Finally there is the world process as we know it, which represents Ananda taking form. So, too, the mystic, Kabir, who represents an opposition to the Vedantic philosophy, says, "From beyond the Infinite, the Infinite comes, and from the Infinite, the finite extends." And again: "Some contemplate the formless and others meditate on form, but the wise man knows that Brahma is beyond both." Here we have the finite world of becoming, the infinite world of being, and Brahma, the unconditioned absolute, exceeding and including all. Yet as Kabire distinctly declares again and again, there are no fences between these aspects of the Universe. When we come to the root of reality we find that "conditioned and unconditioned are but one word"; the difference is in our degree of awareness.

Compare with this three of the great mediaeval Catholic mystics: that acute psychologist, Richard of St Victor, the ardent poet and contemplative Jacopone da Todi, and the profound Ruysbroeck. Richard of St Victor says that there are three phases in the contemplative consciousness. the first is called dilation of mind, enlarging and deepening our vision of the world. the next is elevation of mind in which we behold the realities which are above themselves. the third is ecstasy, in which the mind is carried up to contact the truth in its pure simplicity. this is really the universe of Plotinus translated into subjective terms. So, too, Jacopone da Todi says in the symbolism of his day that three heavens are open to man. he must climb from one to the other; it is hard work but love and longing press him on. First, when the mind has achieved self-conquest, the "starry heaven" of multiplicity is revealed to it. Its darkness is lit by scattered lights; points of reality pierce the sky. Next, it achieves the "crystalline heaven" of lucid contemplation where the soul is conformed to the rhythm of divine life, and by its loving intuition apprehends God under veils. Lastly, in ecstasy, it is lifted to that ineffable state which he calls the "hidden heaven" where it enjoys a vision of imageless reality and "enters into possession of all that is God". Ruysbroeck says that he has experienced three orders of reality: the natural world, theatre of our moral struggle; the essential world, where God and Eternity are indeed known, but by intermediaries; and the super-essential world, where, without intermediary and beyond all separation, "above reason and without reason", the soul is united to "the glorious and absolute One".

Take again, a totally different mystic, Jacob Boehme. he says that he saw in the Divine Essence three principlesor aspects. The first he calls "the deepest Deity, without and beyond nature", and the next its manifestation in the Eternal Light-world. The third is that outer world in which we dwell according to the body, which is a manifestation, image or similitude of the Eternal. "And we are thus", he says, "to understand reality as a threefold being, or three worlds in one another." We observe once again the absence of watertight compartments. the whole of reality is present in every part of it; and the power of correspondence with all these aspects of it is latent in man. "If one sees a right man," says Boehme again, "he may say, I see here three worlds standing."

We have now to distinguish the psychological element in all this. How does it correspond with psychological facts? Some mystics, like Richard of St Victor, have frankly exhibited its subjective side, and so helped us translate the statements of their fellows. Thus Dionysius the Areopagite says in a celebrated pasage: "Threefold is the way to God. the first is the way of purification, in which the mind is inclined to learn true wisdom. the second is the way of illumination, in which the mind by contemplation is kindled to the burning of love. the third is the way of union, in which the mind, by understanding, reason and spirit is led up by God alone." This formula restates the Plotinian law; for the "contemplation" of Dionysius is the "spiritual intuition" of Plotinus, which inducts man into the intelligible world; his "union" is the Plotinian ecstatic vision of the One. It profoundly impressed the later Christian mystics, and has long been accepted as the classic description of spiritual growth, because it has been found again and again to answer to experience. It is therefore worth our while to examine it with some care.

First we notice how gentle, gradual and natural is the process of sublimation thaty Dionysius demands of us. According to him, the mystic life is a life centred on reality; the life that first seeks reality without flinching, then loves andadores the reality perceived, and at last, wholly surrendered to it, is "led by God alone." First, the self is "inclined to learn true wisdom." It awakes to new needs, is cured of its belief in sham values, and distinguishes between real and unreal objects of desire. that craving for more life and more love which lies at the very heart of our selfhood, her slips from the charmed circle of our senses into a wider air.. When this happens abruptly, it is called "conversion"; and may then have the character of a psychic convulsion, and be accompanied by various secondary psychological phenomena. But often it comes without observation. Here the essentials are a desire and a disillusiuonment sufficiently strong to overcome our natural sloth, our primitive horror of change. "The first beginnings of all things is a craving," says Boehme; we are creatures of will and desire." The divine discontent, the hunger for reality, the unwillingness to be satisfied with the purely animal or the purely social level of consciousness is the first essential stage in the development of mystical consciousness.

So the self is either suddenly or gradually inclined to "true wisdom"; and this change of angle affects the whole character, not only or indeed specially the intellectual outlook, but the ethical outlook too. This is the meaning of "purgation." False ways of feeling and thinking, established complexes which have acquired for us an almost sacred character, and governed though we knew it not all our reactions to life -- these must be broken up. that mental and moral sloth which keeps us so comfortably wrapped in unrealities must go. This phase in the mystics growth has been specially emphasised and worked out by the Christian mystics, who have made consuiderable additions to the philosophy and natural history of the soul. The Christian sense of sin and conception of charity, the Christian notion of humility as a finding of our true level, an exchanging of the unreal standards of egoism for the disconcerting realities of life seen from the angle of Eternity;the steadfast refusal to tolerate any claim to spirituality which is not solidly based on moral values, or which is divorced from the spirit of tenderness and love -- all this has immensely enriched the mysticism of the West, and filled up some of the gaps left by Neoplatonism. It is characteristic of Christianity that, addressing itself to all men -- not, as Neoplatonism tended to do, to the superior person -- and offering to all men participation in Eternal Life, it takes human nature as it is; and works from the bottom up instead of beginning at a level which only a few of the race attain. Christianity perceived how deeply normal men are enslaved by the unconscious; how great a moral struggle is needed for their emancipation. Hence it concentrated on the first stage of purgation, and gave it a new meaning and depth. the monastic rule of poverty, chastity and obedience -- and we must remember that the originasl aim pf monasticism was to provide a setting in which the mystical life could be lived -- aims at the removal of those self-centred desires and attachments which chain consciousness to a personal instead of a universal life. He who no longer craves for personal possessions, pleasures or powers, is very near to perfec t liberty. His attention is freed from its usual concentyration on the self's immediate interests, and at once he sees the Universe in a new, more valid because disinterested, light.

> *Povertate e nulla avere*
> *e nulla cosa poi volere*
> *ed omne cosa possedere*
> *en spirito de libertade*

Yet this positive moral purity which Christians declared necessary to the spiritual life was not centred on a lofty aloofness from human failings, but on a self-giving and disinterested love, the complete abolition of egoism. this alone, it declared, couyld get rid of that inward disharmony --one aspect of the universal conflict between the instinctiveand the rational life -- which Boehme called the "powerful contrarium" warring with the soul.

Now, this "perfect charity in life surrendered," however attained, is an essential character of the true mystic; without it contemplation is an impossibility or a sham. But when we come to the means by which it is to be attained, we re-enter the region of controversy; for here we are at once confronted by the problem of asceticism, and its connection with mysticism -- perhaps the largest and most difficult of the questions now facing those who are concerned with the re-statement of the laws of the spiritual life. Originally regarded as a gymnastic of the soul, an education in those manly virtues of self-denial and endurance without which the spiritual life is merely an exquisite form of hedonism, asceticism was identified by Christian thought with the idea of mortification; the killing out of all those impulses which deflect the soul from the straight path to God. For the true mystic, it is never more than a means to an end; and is often thrown aside when that end is attained. Its necessity is therefore a purely practical question. fasting and watching may help one to dominate unruly instincts, and so attain a sharper and purer concentration on God; but make another so hungry and sleepy that he can think of nothing else. Thus Jacopone da Todi said of his own early austerities,, that they resulted chiefly in idigestion, insomnia and colds in the head; whilst John Wesley found in fasting a positive spiritual good. Some asctic practices again are almost certainly disguised indulgences of those very cravings which they are supposed to kill, but in fact merely repress. Others -- such as hair shirts, chains, and so forth -- depended for their meaning on a mediaeval view of the body and of the virtuers of physical pain which is practically extinct, and now seems to most of us utterly artificial. No one will deny that austerity is better than luxury for the spiritual life; but perfect detachment of the will and senses can be achievedwithout resort to merely physical expedients by those living normally in the world, and this is the essential thing.

The true asceticism is a gymnastic not of the body but of the mind. It involves training in the art of recollection; the concentration of thought, will, and love upon the eternal realities which we commonly ignore. The embryo contemplative, if his spiritual vision is indeed to be enlarged, and his mind kindled, as Dionysius says, to "the burning of love" must acquire and keep a special state of inward poise, an attitude of attention, which is best described as "the state of prayer"; that same condition which George Fox called "keeping in the Universal Spirit." If we do not attend to reality we are unlikely to perceive it. The readjustments which shall make this attention natural and habitual are a phase in man's inward conflict for the redemption of consciousness from its lower and partial attachments. This conflict is no

9

dream. It means hard work; mental and moral discipline of the sternest kind. the downward drag is incessant, and can be combatted only by those who are clearly aware of it, and are willing to sacrifice lower interests and joys to the demands of the spiritual life. In this sense, mortification is an integral part of the "purgative way". Unless the self's "inclination to true wisdom" is strong enough to inspire those costing and heroic efforts, its spiritual cravings do not deserve the name of mysticism.

These, then, seem essential factors in the readjustment which the mystics call "purgation". We go on to their next stage, the so-called "way of illumination". Here, says Dionysius, the mind is kindled by contemplation to the burning of love. there is a mental and an emotional enhancement, whereby the self apprehends the reality it has sought; whether under the veils of religion, philosophy, or nature-mysticism. may mystics have made clear statements about this phase in human transcendence. thus the Upanishads invite us to "know everything in the Universe as envelopedin God." "When the purified seeker," says Plato, "comes to the end, he will suddenly perceive a nature of wondrous beauty. . . . Beauty absolute, separate, simple, and everlasting." His follower, Plotinus, says that by spiritual intuition man "wrought into harmony with the Supreme," enters into communion with Nous, the "intelligible world" of eternal realities -- that splendour yonder which is his home: and further, that this light, shining upon the soul, enlightens it, makes it a member of the spiritual order, and so "transforms the furnace of this world into a garden of flowers." Ruysbroeck declares that this eternal world "is not God, but it is the light in which we see Him." Jacopone da Todi says that the self, achieving the crystalline heaven, "feels itself to be a part of all things," because it has annihilated its separate will, and is conformed to the movement of the Divine Life. Kabir says, "The middle region of the sky, wherein the spirit dwelleth, is radiant with the music of light." Boehme calls it the "light-world proceeding from the fire-world"; and says it is the origin of that outward world in which we dwell. "This light," he says, "shines through and through all, but is onlyapprehended by that which unites itself thereto." It seems to me clear that these, and many other descriptions I cannot now quote, refer to an identical state of consciousness, which might be called an experience of Eternity, but not of the Eternal One. I say "an experience", not merely a mental perception. Contemplation, which is the traditional name for that concentrated attention in which this phase of rreality is revealed, is an activity of all of our powers; the heart, the will, the mind. Dionysius emphasizes the ardent love which this revelation of reality calls forth, and which is indeed a condition of our apprehension of it; for the cold gaze of the metaphysician cannot attain it, unless he be a lover and a mystic too. "By love he may be gotten and holden, by thought never," says the author of The Cloud of Unknowing.

It is only throughthe mood of humble and loving receptivity in which the artist perceives beauty, that the human spirit can apprehend a reality which is greater than itself. the many declarations about noughting, poverty, and "holy nothingness" refer to this. The meek and poor of spirit really are the inheritors of Eternity.

So we may place the attitude of selfless adoration, the single-hearted passion of the soul, among the essentials of the mystic in the illuminated way. A very wide range of mystical experiences must be attrributed to this second stage in man's spiritual growth. Some at least of its secrets are known to all who are capable of aesthetic passion; who in the presence of beauty, know themselves to stand on the fringe of another plane of being, where the elements of common life are given new colour and value, and its apparent disharmonies are resolved. So, too, that deep sense of a divine companionship which many ardent souls achieve in prayer is a true if transitory experience of illumination. We shall probably be right in assuming that the enormous majorityof mystics never get beyond this level of consciousness. Certainly a large number of religious writers on mysticism attribute to its higher and more personal manifestations the names of "divine union" and "unitive life", thereby adding to the difficulty of classifying spiritual states, and showing themselves unaware of the great distinction which such full-grown mystics as Plotinus, Jacopone da Todi, or Ruysbroeck describe as existing between this "middle heaven" and the ecstatic vision of the One which alone really satisfies their thirst for truth. Thus Jacopone at first uses the styrongest unitive language to describe that rapturous and emotional intercourse with Divine Love which characterises his middle period; but when he at last achieves the vision of the Absolute, he confesses that he was in error in supposing that it was indeed the Truth Whom he thus saw and worshipped under veils. Or, parme fo fallanza

> *non se' quel che credea*
> *tenendo non avea*
> *verta senza errore*

Thus Ruysbroeck attributes to the contemplative life "the inward and upweard-going ways by which one may pass into the Presence of God," but distinguishes these from that superessential life wherein "we are swallowed up, beyond reason and above reason, in the deep quiet of the Godhead which is never moved."

All the personal raptures of devotional mysticism, all the nature-mystics joyous consciousness of

God in creation, Blakes's "world of imagination and vision," the "coloured land" of AE., the Sufi's "tavern on the way" where he is refreshed by a draught of supersensual wine, belong to the way of illumination. For the Christian mystic the world into which it inducts him is, pre-eminently, the sphere of the divbine Logos-Christ, fount of creation and source of all beauty; the hidden Steersman who guides and upholds the phenomenal world:

> *Splendor che dona a tutto 'l mondo luce,*
> *amor, Iesu, de li angeli belleza,*
> *cielo e terra per te si conduce*
> *e splende in tutte cose tua fattezza.*

Here the reality behind appearance is still mediated to the mystic under symbols and forms. The variation of these symbols is great; his adoring gaze now finds new life and significance in the appearances of nature, the creations of music and art, the imagery of religion and philosophy, and reality speaks to him through his own credal conceptions. But absolute value cannot be attributed to any of these, even the most sacred; they change, yet the experience remains. thus an identical consciousness of close communion with God is obtained by the non-sacramental Quaker in his silence and by the sacramental Catholic in the Eucharist.The Christian contemplative's sense of personal intercourse with the Divine as manifest in the incarnate Christ is hard to distinguish from that of the Hindu Vaishnavite when we have allowed for the differeny constituents of his apperceiving mass:

> *Dark, dark, the far Unknown and closed the way*
> *To thought and speech; silent the Scriptures; yea,*
> *No word the Vedas say.*
> *Not thus the Manifest. How fair! how near!*
> *Gone is our thirst if only He appear--*
> *He, to the heart so dear.*

So, too, the Sufi mystic who has learned to say: "I never saw anything without seeing God therein;" Kabir exclaiming: "I have stilled my restless mind, and my heart is radiant; for in Thatness I have seen beyond Thatness, in company I have seen the Comrade Himself;" the Neoplatonist rapt in contemplation of the intelligible world "yonder"; Brother Lawrence doing his cooking in the presence of God, reveal under analysis an identical type of consciousness. this consciousness is the essential; the symbols under which the self apprehends it are not.

Among these symbols we must reckon a large number of the secondary phenomena of mysticism: divine visions and voices, and other dramatisations of the self's apprehension and desires. The best mystics have always recognised the doubtful nature of these so-called divine revelations and favours, and have tried again and again to set up tests for discerning those which really "come from God" -- ie, mediate a valid spiritual experience. Personally I think very few of these phenomena are mystical in the true sense.

Just as our normal consciousness is more or less at the mercy of invasions from the unconscious region, of impulses which we fail to trace to their true origin; so too the mystical consciousness is perpetually open to invasion from the lowercentres. These invasions are not always understood by the mystic. Obvious examples are the erotic raptures of the Sufi poets, and the emotional, even amorous relations in which many Christian ascetics believe themselves to stand to Christ or Our lady. The Holy Ghost saying to Angela of Foligno, "I love you better than any other woman in the vale of Spoleto"; the human raptures of Mechthild of Magdeburg with her Bridegroom; St Bernard's attitude to the Virgin; the passionate love songs of Jacopone da Todi; the mystical marriage of St Catherine of Siena; St Teresa's wound of love; these and many similar episodes, demand no supernatural explanation, and add nothing to our knowledge of the work of the Spirit in man's soul. So, too, the infantile craving for a sheltering and protective love finds expression over and over again in mystical literature, and satisfaction in the states of consciousness which it has induced. The innate longings of the self for more life, more love, an ever greater or fuller experience, attains a complete realisation in the loifty mystical state called union with God. But failing this full achievement, the self is cap[able of offering itself many disguised satisfactions; and among these disguised satisfactions we must reckon at least the majority of "divine favours" enjoyed by contemplatives of an emotional type. Whatever the essence of mysticism may turn out to be, it is well to recognise these lapses to lower levels as among the least fortunate of its accidents.

We come to the third stage, the true goal of mystic experience; the intuitive contact with that ultimate reality which theologians mean by the Godhead and philosophers by the Absolute, a contact in which, as Richard of St Victor says, "the soul gazes upon Truth without any veils of creatures -- not in a mirror darkly, but in its pure simplicity." The claim to this is the loftiest claim which can be made by human consciousness. There is little we can say of it, because there is little we know; save that the vision or experience is alwaysthe vision or the experience of a Unity which reconciles all opposites, and fulfils all man's highest intuitions of reality. "Be lost altogether in Brahma like an arrow that has completely penetrated its target," say the Upanishads. This self-loss, says Dionysius the Areopagite, is the Divine Initiation: wherein we "pass beyond the topmost altitudes of the holy ascent, and leave behind all divine illumination and voices and heavenly utterances; and plunge intoi the darkness where truly dwells, as Scripture saith, that One which is beyond all things." Some recent theologians have tried to separate the conceptions of God and of the Absolute; but mystics never do this, though some of the most clear sighted, such as Meister Eckhart, have separated that unconditioned Godhead known in ecstasy from the personal God who is the object of devotional religion, and who represents a humanisation of reality. When the great mystic achieves the "still, glorious and absolute Oneness" which finally satisfies his thirst for truth -- the "point where all lines meet and show their meaning" -- he generally confesses how symbolic was the object of his earlier devotion, how partial his supposed communion with the Divine. Thus Jacopone di Todi -- exact and orthodox Catholic though he was -- when he reached "the hidden heaven," discovered and boldly declared the approximate character of all his previous conceptions of, and communion with, God; the great extent to which subjective elements had entered into his experience. In the great ode which celebrates his ecstatic vision of Truth, when "ineffable love, imageless goodness, measureless light" at last shone in his heart, he says, "I thought I knew Thee, tasted Thee, saw Thee under image: believing I held Thee Thy completeness I was filled with delight and unmeasured love. But now I see I was mistaken -- Thou art not as I thought and firmly held." So Tauler says that compared with the warm colour and multiplicity of devotional experience, the vey Godhead is a "rich nought," a "bare, pure, ground"; and Ruysbroeck that it is "an unwalled world," "neither this nor that." "This fruition of God," he says again, "ios a still and glorious and essential oneness beyond the differentiation of the Persons, where there is neither an indrawing or an outpouring of God, but the Persons are still and one in fruitful love, in calm and glorious unity.... There is God our fruition and His own, in an eternal and fathomless bliss."

"How, then, am I to love the Godhead?" says Eckhart. "Thou shaly love Him as He is: not as a God, not as a spirit, not as a Person, not as an image, but as a sheer, pure One. And in this One we are to sink from nothing to nothing, so help us, God." "This consciousness of the One," says Plotinus, "comes not by knowledge, but by an actual Presence superior to any knowing. To have it, the soul must rise above knowledge, above all its wandering from its unity." He goes on to explain that all partial objects of love and comtemplation, even Beauty and Goodness themselves, are lower than this, springing from the One as light from the sun. To see the disc, we must put on smoked glasses, shut off the rays and submit to the "radiant darkness" which enters so frequently into mystical descriptions of the Absolute.

It is an interesting question whether this consummation of the mystic way need involve that suppression of the surface consciousness which is called ecstasy. the majority of mystics think that it must; and probably it is almost inevitable that so great a concentration and so lofty an intuition should for the time it lasts drive all other forms of awareness from the field. Even simple contemplation cannot be achieved without some deliberate stilling of the senses, a deliberate focussing of our vagrant attention, and abolishes self-consciousness while it lasts. this is the way that our mental machinery works; but this should not make us regard trance states as any part of the essence of mysticism. The ecstatic condition is no guarantee of mytic vision. It is frequentlypathological, and is often found along with other abnormal conditions in emotional visionaries whose revelations have no ultimate characteristics. It is, however, just as uncritical to assume that ecstasy is necessarily a pathological symptom as it is to assume that it is necessarily a mystic state. We have a test that we can apply to the ecstatic; and which separates the results of nervous disorder from those of spiritual transcendance. "What fruit dost thou bring back from this thy vision?" is the final question which Jacopne da Todi addresses to the mystic's soul. And the answer is: "An ordered life in every state." The true mystic in his ecstasy has seen, however obscurely, the key of the Universe: "la forma universal di questo nodo." hence he has a clue by which to live.. Reality has become real to him; and there are no others of whom we can fully say that. So, ordered corresondence with each level of existence, physical and spiritual, successive and eternal -- a practical realization of the proportions of life--is the guarantee of the genuine character of that sublimation of consciousness which is called the mystic way; and this distinguishes it from the fantasies of psychic illness or the disguised self-indulgences of the dream-world. The real mystic is not a selfish visionary. He grows in vigour as he draws nearer and nearer the sources of true life, and his goal is only reached when he participates in the creative energies of the Divine Nature. The perfect man, says the Sufi, must not only die into God in ecstasy (fana), but abide in and with Him (baqa), manifesting his truth in the world of time. He is called to a life more active, because more contemplative, than that of other men: to fulfil the monastic ideal of a balanced carreer of work and prayer. "Then only is our life a whole," says Ruysbroeck, "when contemplation and work dwell in us side by side, and we are perfectly in both of them at once."

Plotinus speaks in the same sense under another image in one of his most celebrated passages:

"We always move round the One, but we do not always fix our gaze upon It. We are like a choir of singers standing round the conductor, who do not always sing in time because their attention is diverted to some external object. When they look at the conductor, they sing well and are really with him. So we always move around the One. If we did not, we should dissolve and cease to exist. But we do not always look towards the One. When we do, we attain the end of our existence and our rest; and we no longer sing out of tune, but form in truth a divine choir about the One." In this conception of man's privilege and duty we have the indestructible essence of mysticism.

The Mystic and the Corporate Life

One of the commonest of the criticisms which are brought against the mystics is that they represent an unsocial type of religion; that their spiritual enthusiasms are personal and individual, and that they do not share or value the corporate life and institutions of the church or community to which they belong. Yet as a matter of fact, the relation that does and should exist between personal religion and the corporate life of the church frequently appears in them in a peculiarly intense, a peculiarly interesting form; and in their lives, perhaps, more easily than elsewhere, we may discern the principles which do or should govern the relation of the individual to the community.

In the true mystic, who is so often and so wrongly called a "religious individualist" we see personal religion raised to its highest power. If we accept his experience as genuine, it involves an intercourse with the spiritual world, an awareness of it, which transcends the normal experience, and appears to be independent of the general religiouis consciousness of the community to which he belongs. The mystic speaks with God as a person with a Person, and not as a member of a group. He lives with an immediate knowledge far more than by belief; by a knowledge achieved in those hours of direct, unmediated intercourse with the Transcendent when, as he says, he was "in union with God". The certitude then gained -- a certitude which he cannot impart, and which is not generally diffused -- governs all his reactions to the Universe. It even persists and upholds him in those terrible hours of darkness when all his sensee of spiritual reality is taken away.

Such a personality as this seems to stand in little need of the support which the smaller nature, the more languid religious consciousness, receives from the corporate spirit. By the very term, "mystic", we indicate a certain aloofness from the crowd, suggest that he is in possession of a secret which the community as a whole does not and cannot share; that he lives at levels to which they cannot rise. I think that much of the distrust with which he is often regarded comes from this sense of his independence of the herd; his apparent separation from the often clumsy and always symbolic methods of institutional religion, and the further fact that his methods and results cannot be criticised or checked by those who have not shared them. "I spake as I saw," said David; and those who did not see can only preserve a respectful or an exasperated silence.

Yet this common perception that the mystic is a lonely soul wholly absorbed in his vertyical relation with God, that his form of religious life represents an opposition to and an implicit criticism of tghe corporate and institutional form of religious life; this is decisively contradicted by history, which shows us, again and again, the great mystics as the loyal children of the great religious institutions, and forces us to admit that here as in other departments of human activity the corporate and the individual life are intimately plaited together.Even those who have broken away from the churches that reared them, have quickly drawn to themselves disciples, and become the centres of new groups. Surely, therefore, it is worthwhile to examine, if we can, the nature of the connection between these two factors: to ask, on the one hand, what it is that the corporate life and the group consciousness which it develops give the mystic; on the other, what is the treal value of the mystic to the corporate life of his church?As to the first question: What is it that the corporate life does for the geat spiritual genius?--for I think that we may may allow the mystic to be that. First and most obviously, it gives him a favourable environment. he must have an environment: he must be affected by it. That is a certainty in the case of any living thing; a certainty so obvious that it would be hardly worth stating were it not that those who talk about the mystic craving for solitude -- his complete aloofness from human life -- seem often to ignore it. The idea of solitude in any complete sense is, of course, an illusion. We are bound, if we live at all, to accept the fact of a living world outside ourselves, to have social relations with something; and it only remains to decide what these relations shall be. The yogi or the hermit who retreats to the forest in order to concentrate his mind more utterly upon the quest of God, only exchanges the society of human beings for the society of other living things. Did he eliminate all else, the parasites of his own body, the bacterial population of his alimentary system, would be there to remind him that man cannot live alone. He may shift his position in the web of life, but its strands will enmesh him still. So, too, the monk or nun, "buried alive" in the cloister is still living a family life that is governed by special ideals.

Now it is plainly better for the mystic, whose aim is the establishment of special relations with the spiritual order, that the social consciousness in which he is immersed, and from which he is taking colour all the time, should have a spiritual and religious tendency; that the social acts in which he takes

14

part should harmonise rather than conflict with his own deep intuition of reality. The difference in degree between that deep intuition and the outward corporate acts -- the cult -- which he thus shares may be enormous; for the cult is an expression of the crowd consciousness, and manifests its spiritual crudity, its innate conservatism, its primitive demands for safety and personal rewards. The inadequacy or unreality of the forms, the low level of the adoration that they invoke, may distress and even disgust him. Yet, even so, it is better that he should be within a church than outside it. Compared with this one fact -- that he is a member of a social group which recognises spiritual values, and therefore lives in an environment permeated by religious concepts -- the accuracy in detail of the creed which the group professes, the adequacy of its liturgical acts, is unimportant.

Next, the demands made and the restrictions imposed by the community on the individual are good for the mystic. Man is social right through; in spirit as well as in body and mind. His most sublime spiritual experiences are themselves social in type. Intercourse of a person with a Person, the merging of his narrowe consciousness in a larger consciousness, the achievement of a divine sonship, a spiritual marriage: these are tghe highest things that he can say concerning his achievement of Divine Reality. And they all entail, not a narrow self-realisation, but the breaking down of barriers, the setting up of wider relationships. It followes that self-mergence in the common life is an education for that self-mergence in the absolute life at which the mystic aims. Such self-mergence, and the training in humility, self-denial, obedience, suppleness, which is involved in it, is held by all ascetic teachers to be essential to the education of the human soul. Union with, and to a certain extent submission to, the church, to the family -- to life, in fact -- an attitude of self-giving surrender: this is the best of preparations for that total self-naughting of the soul which is involved in union with God; that utter doing away ofthe I, the Me, and the Mine, till it becomes one will and one loive with the divine will and love.

On these two counts alone -- harmonious environment and salutary discipline -- we shall expect, other things being equalthat the richest and most fruitful types of mystical experience will arise within religious institutions rather than outside them; and as a matter of fact, this is what we do find. The Hindu ascetic has his recognised place in the Hindu system. He has but reached the summit of a pyramid which is firmly based on earth. The Sufi is a good Moslem, and commonly a member of a religious confraternity which imposes a strict rule of life. The Christian mystic too grows up from the Christian society. His roots strike deep down into that favouring soil. Though his branches may shoot up to the heavens, and seem to draw thence all the light and heat by which he lives, yet he is really fed from below as well as from above. When he refuses to acknowledge this principle, when he abjures the discipline, the authority, the support of the corporate life and regards himself as a separate individual, dependent on direct inspiration alone; how quickly he becomes unbalanced and eccentric, how difficult it is for him to avoid the disease of spiritual megalomania. Refusing the support and discipline of organised religion, he becomes likea poet who refuses to be controlled bhe laws of prosody; which seem to limit, but really strengthen and beautify his work.

It is true that right through the history of Christian mysticism there has been a line of insurgent mystics who have made this refusal; whose direct vision of spiritual perfection has brough with it so overwhelming a sense of the imperfection, formalism, unreality, the dreadfulness of religious institutions, that it has forced them into a position of more or less acute revolt from the officioal church. So clear has been their own consciousness of the spiritual world that the soul's life and growth, its actual and individual rebirth, have shone out for them as the only things that matter. Hence the dramatisation of these things in ceremonial religion, the effort to give spiritual values a concrete form, has seemed to them like a blasphemous parody. Unable to harmonise the inward and the outward -- the all-penetrating reality of religion as they understand it, with its crude expression in the external cult, where formal acts and intellectual assents so often seem to take the place of inward changes -- in the end they solve the problem by repudiating the external and visible church. this rebel-type, victims of exaggerated individualism, which would make the special experiences of a few the standard for a whole race, has persisted side by side with the law-abiding type; who have preserved, if not always a perfect balance between liberty and obedience, at any rate a more reasonable proportion between them. Often the corruption of the times in which he lived has seemed to the mystic to make rebellion inevitable. This is particularly true in the case of George Fox, whose ragings were directed less against organised religion than against unreal religion; and who might, had he lived in 14th century Germany, have found a congenial career as one of the Friends of God. Yet, even so, the careers of these rebels have been on the whole unfruitful compared with those who remained within the institutional framework and effected their reforms from inside. They seldom quite escape the taint of arrogance. There is apt to be a touch of self-consciousn ess in their sanctity. We have only to compare the influence exerted by the outstanding figures of the two groups, to realise which type of spiritual life has had the best and most enduring influence on the spiritual history of the race; which, in fact, best stands the pragmatic test.

On the rebel side we have of course the leaders of many dead heresies and sects. The Montanists of the second century, with their claim to direct inspiration, their cult of ecstatic phenomena and prophetic speech; the numerous mystical heretics and illuminati of the Middle Ages, often preachingthe most extravagant doctrines and always claiming for them divine authority -- for instance, the Brethren of the Free Spirit, who claimed the possession of the Holy Ghost as an excuse, not only for theological but also for moral aberrations. later, there are the Quietists, a particularly poisonous brand of unbalanced contemplatives; and contemporary with their revolt against Catholic forms andauthorities, innumerable mystical revolts against Protestant forms and authorities, the very names of whose originators are now almost forgotten. Amongst these two mighty figures stand up: Jacob Boehme and George Fox. But wejmust remember as regards Boehme that, although he certainly spoke with great violence against the rror of confusing external acceptance of religion with internal adherence to God, "historical Christians" with "new men", he never disowned the Lutheran Church within which he was born. On the contrary it ws that church that persecuted and finally disowned him. As to that great and strange genius, George Fox, who aimed at nothing less than a world religion of a mystical type, the free and conscious contact of every soul with the Spirit of God, I believe that any unbiassed student of his Journal must allow that, enormous as his achievement was, it might have been far greater had his violent sense of vocation, his remarkable spiritual gifts, been disciplined and controlled by the corporate consciousness as expressed in institutional religion. then, some of the energy which he expended in denunciations of steeple-houses might have been employed in healing the disharmony between the visible and invisible church; helping that vision of the Eternal by which he was possessed to find concrete expression within traditional forms. here, as elsewhere, the Inner Light would have burned with a better and truer flame had it submitted to the limitations of a lamp.

I do not suggest that these people, even the most extravagant of them, were not truly spiritual or truly mystical. The sort of criticism that divides mysticism into two groups -- the orthodox, who are inspired by God, and the heretical, who are inspired by Satan -- of course belongs to the darkages of theology. On the contrary, these rebel-mystics most often possessed -- sometimes in a highly-developed form -- the sharp, direct consciousness of the Divine Life which is the essential quality of the mystic. this was to them the central fact; by comparison with it they judged all other things. What they did not possess was the balancing, equivalent consciousness of, and reverence for, corporate human life; that group-personality which is the church, and its value and authority. they lacked the sense that the whole organism, the whole herd, with all its imperfections, is yet interdependent, and has got to move together, urged from within by it's more vivid spirits, not stung from without, as if by some enthusiastic spiritual mosquito. To a greater or lesser extent they failed in effect because they tried to be mystical in a non-human instead of a human way; were "other-worldly" in a bad sense of the word. They have not always remembered that Christ Himself, the supreme pattern of all mystics, lived a balanced personal life of clear personal vision, unmediated intercourse with God on the one hand, and gentle and patient submission to the corporate consciousness on the other hand. Though severely critical of the unrealities and hypocrisy of current institutionalism, he yet sought to form the group, the "little flock" in which His ideas should be incorporated within, and not over against, the official Jewish Church; and thus gradually to leaven the whole.

Put now against these vigorous individualists the names of the mystics who have never felt that their passionate correspondences with the Eternal Order -- their clear vision of the adorable Perfection of God and the imperfection, languor and corruption of man -- need involve a break with the corporate religious life. Observe how these have continued for centuries to be fruitful personalities, often not merely within their own communion, but outside it too; how they have ascted as salt, as leaven, permeating and transmuting the general consciousness of the Body of Christ. Often, too, these have been reformers -- drastic, unrelenting disturbers of the established order of things. St Bernard, St Hildegarde, Mechthild, Jacopone da Todi, St Catherine of Siena, Tauler were passionate in their denunciations of slackness, corruption, and disorder. But they made their protests, and brought back the general consciousness to a closer contact with reality, from within, and not from without, the Christian Church. Consider St Bernard and Richard of St Victor, whose writings influenced for centuries the whole of the religious literature of Europe; St Hildegarde, St Gertrude, Mechthild of Magdeburg, great mystics, good churchwomen, but severe denouncers of formalism and unreality; St Francis of Assisi who removed evangelical poverty from the sphere of notion to the sphere of fact; Sty Catherine of Siena, who changed Italian politics; St Joan of Arc, who altered European history; the soaring transcendentalism of Ruysbroeck, who was yet content to be a humble parish priest; the great mystical movement of the Friends of God, ardent Catholics and ardent reformers too. Even our own great mystical poets, Donne, Crashaw, Vaughan, Herbert, Traherne, Coventry Patmore, and Francis Thonpson, were one and all convinced institutionalists. Finally, look at some of the great cloistered mystics, of whom St Teresa and St John of the Cross are types; and see how, though they seem in the eyes of the world to be "buried alive" they are and remain the ardent centres of a spreading light, which perpetually stimulates and revivifies not only members of their own order or communion, but spiritually sensitive souls outside.

Perhaps it is in those contemplatives who lived within and were obedient to the rule of the great monastic orders that we can see most easily the nature of the link between the individual soul and the religious group within which it does or should develop; the enormous value to it of traditionthat huge accumulation of tendencies, ideals, systems, wisdom both speculative and practical, which is preserved in the corporate consciousness. Here the influence of the religious family, the rule of life, the ideal held out, the severe education in self-control administered to every novice, can always be traced; conditioning, and, I believe, helping and bracing the character of that communion with the Transcendent which the individual mystic enjoys. As the baby at birth enters into a civilisation prepared for him, and is at once supported, educated, even clothed by a tradition prepared by countless generations of the past; so the novice whose spiritual childhood begins within a great monastic family receives -- supposing, of course, that the order is true to its ideals -- the support and benefits of a tradition evolved during previous generations in response to the needs of other similar souls; and he is by so much the better off than he would be were he a solitary, or a deliberate rebel who refuses to accept the heritage of the past. he finds a life beautifully adjusted to his needs; yet, which being greater and older than his own, keeps his rampant individualism in check, nurtures and cultivates his growing spiritual consciousness, and opposes -- by its perpetual demands on humility, obedience, and unselfishness -- the vice of pride which the mystical individualist seldom escapes. Such a mystical consciousness would not necessarily die without the support of this corporate tradition, any more than the bay would necessarily die did it emerge into the conditions of the paleolithic cave instead of into those of the modern nursery. But in both cases the environment would be unfavourable, and the effort required to attain that position into which the child of tradition enters at birth would be an enormous drain upon the powers of the organism.

The instinct of many mystics for a certain measure of solitude is no contradiction of this. the hermits and the anchorites, even such rare and extreme types as St Anthonyof Egypt, who is said to have lived in perfect solitude for twenty years, did not withdraw from the Christian society; nor did they disown the validity of its external and institutional life. They sought to construct or find within the Christian church an environment in which their special tendencies could develop in a normal way; and this not merely for themselves, but also for the sake of other souls. Such a period of withdrawal was felt by them to be a necessary condition of their full effectiveness for life. So, too, the poet or the artist must retreat from his fellows if he is to commune with the eternal loveliness and interpret her to other men: for a total concentration on reality is the condition under which it is revealed. the Catholic Church has always recognised, and does still in the continued existence of the cloistered orders, the reasonableness of this demand. We do not as a rule say bitter things when a person od artistic or speculative genius leaves his family group and goes to Paris or Oxford in order that his special powers may become educated and more effective for life; nor should we feel resentment because the mystical genius sometimes feels that the life of the home circle, or even the normal life of the community, cannot give the special training which he requires. In a few cases the mystics have felt a long period of complete isolation to be necessary to them; but most often they have been accessible to those who really needed them, and helped these all the more because of the long periods of silence in which they listened to the Voice of God, too often inaudible for them, as for us, in the general bustle of the world. Their point of view has been beautifully stated by a young French mystic, Elizabeth de la Trinité, who died a few years ago. "I want," she says, "to be all silence, all adoration, that I may penetrate more and more deeply into God; and become so full of Him that I can give Him in my prayers to those poor souls still ignorant of His gift." She wants to be a channel, a duct, by which the loive and power of God, of which she is so strongly conscious, can flow out to other souls. It is not for herself that she is working; it is for the world. Do we not find expressed there both the individual longing and the corporate responsibility of the mystic? And do we not touch here the intimate connection which should exist between the separate life of the great mystics and the corporate life of the church? On the one hand, the highly organised society, making it possible for the contemplative to develop his special powers in a harmonious environment, and preventing the frittering of his energies; on the other, that contemplative, like a special organ developed by the Body of Christ, gaining for the whole community contacts and certitudes, which it could not gain in any other way. News of God can only enter the temporal order through some human consciousness. Is it unreasonable that for so great an office certain individuals should be set apart -- within the community, not over against it -- and should live in a special way?

As a matter of fact, the church has gained a thousandfold by her acquiescence in the specvial vocation of the mystics; for the treasures they won were never kept for themselves but always showered upon her. True, she has not hesitated to scrutinise and control them; sometimes her attitude has seeemed to the enthusiast for liberty to be deliberately obscurantist and tyrannical. Yet, even here -- an although in many cases there has clearly been ignorance, injustice and persecution -- the mystic gains more than he loses by submission to the collective judgement. Even in their harshest form, discipline and tradition are still priceless for him. First they school him in the virtue of humility, the very foundation of the Christian character; which is seldom possessed by the spiritual genius who always leads and never submits, and whose triumphant formula, "God and myself!" too often winds up becoming "Myself and God!"

O caritate, vita, ch' ogn' altro amor e morto non vai rompendo legge; nante l'observe tutto.said Jacopone da Todi; that natural rebel who deliberately submitted himself to an uncongenial religious authority and there found perfect freedom.

Next, the solid sense of community, the mere fact that it always lags behind the more vivid spirits, that the forward moving shepherd who sees new pastures has got to take account of the slowest sheep -- all this is a valuable safeguard against the notorious extravagances of a mysticism unfettered by authority. It is significant that the greatest mystics in all communions have ever raised up their voices most earnestly against spiritual licence; have been most eager to submit their soaring intuitions to the witness of their Scriptures or the corporate feeling of their church. They realise the fact that they owe to this church the huge debt which every individual owes to the tradition of his art or of his trade. The church represents a complete spiritual civilization, a conserver of values; were it not for her, every new spiritual genius who arose would have to begin at the beginning, at the Stone Age of the soul. Instead of that he finds himself placed within a social order enriched by all the contributions of his great predecessors. The bridges are built; the roads are made and named; his own experiences and discoveries are made more valid, less terrifying, more comprehensible to him, because othewrs have been this way before. Compare the clarity, the sure-footedness as one may say, of Ruysbroeck, of St Catherine of Siena, of St Teresa, with the entanglements, the sense of wandering in beautiful but trackless places, which one feels when reading even Boehme, Fox, or Blake; and others are far less coherent than they. man needs a convention, a tradition, a limitation, if he is not to waste his creative powers; and this convention the mystics find best and most easily in the forms of the church to which they belong.

So we see that the corporate life of his church gives the mystic a good deal. What does he, on his part, give to it.Those who see in the mystic chiefly one who rebels against, or has no use for the corporate religious life, and acknowledges no authority but that of his own spiritual intuitions, usually conceive of his experiences as having value for himself alone. he cannot, they say, communicate them or teach others to share them. Often, therefore he is spoke of as useless, selfish, other-worldly: a "lonely soul." These phrases suggest that those who use them have a very narrow view of usefulness, a very materialistic view of the Body of Christ, and a very unevangelical view of the relative positions of Mary and Martha. As a matter of fact, the mystic, instead of being useless, selfish, and other-worldly is useful, unselfish and this-worldly. he is a creative personality, consecrated to the great practical business of actualising the eternal order within the temporal; and although the pursuit of this business brings him hours of exquisite joy, it brings him hours of great suffering, too -- suffering which is gladly and patiently endured. he does it, or tries to do it, not because he seeks the joy, but solely for love -- love of God, love of his fellow men -- for he is perpetuating in a certain sense the work of Christ, mediating between his brethren and Divine Reality. Hence, where he is fuilly developed, he will, as Ruysbroeck tells us, swing like a pendulum between contemplation and action, between adoration of God and service of man. In him life has evolved her most powerful spiritual engine; and she uses it not for the next world, but for this world, for the eternalisation of the here and now, the making of it more real and more divine, more fully charged with the grandeur of God. Often the mystics special work is done in a positiveand obvious fashion which should satisfy the most practical mind, and which is not yet wholly actuated by his central intention, that of raising up -- as he sometimes says -- new children of the Eternal Goodness, bringing back the corporate life to a closer contact with God. "My little children, of whom I travail," says St Paul to his converts.There is a typical mystic speaking of his life work. Can we call St Francis of Assisi, the most devoted and original of missionaries; St Joan of Arc, remaking the consciousness of France by the most active of methods; St Catherine of Siena, purifying the Italian Church, St teresa, regenerating the whole Carmelite order, and leaving upon it a stamp it has never lost; "lazy contemplatives"? Or St catherine of Genoa, the devoted superintendent of a great hospital, who never permitted her hours of ecstatic communion with God to interfere with her duty to the sick?

Taken as a class, the Christian mystics are distinguished by nothing so much as their heroic and unselfish activities; by their vasried and innumerable services to the corporate life of the church. From their ranks have come missionaries, preachers, prophets, social reformersm poets, founders of institutions, servants of the poor and the sick, patient guides and instructors of souls. We sometimes forget that even those knowen chiefly by the writings they have left behind them have sacrifice to the difficult task of reducing their transcendent experience to words, hours in which -- were the popular idea of a mystic the true one -- they might have been idly basking in the Divine Light. But these practical activities, though often great, are only a part of the mystics contribution to the corportate life. If his special claims about communication with the Transcendent be true at all -- and this argument is based on the assumption that there is at least some truth in it -- then he really does tap a source of vitality higher than that with which other men have contact. In the language of theology, he has not merely "efficient" but also "extraordinary" grace; a larger dower of life, directly dependent on his larger, more generous love. This is a claim to which his strange triumphs over circumstance, his conqwuests over ill-fortune, ill health, oppositions and deprivations of every kind, give weight. Not many strong and normal persons would willingly face, or indeed endure,the hardships which St paul, St Francis, St Joan of Arc,

St Teresa, gladly and successfully embraced.

This larger and intenser vitality the mystic does not and cannot keep to himself. He infects with it all with whom he comes in contact, kindles the latent fire in them: for the spiritual consciousness is caught, not taught. Under his influence -- sometimes from the mere encounter with his personality -- other men begin to lead a more real, a more eternal life. Ruysbroeck says that the Spirit of God, when it is truly received into a soul, becomes a spreading light; and history confirms this. Corporate experience of God always begins in personal experience of God. The rise of Christianity is the classic illustration of this truth, but Hindu and Moslem religious history also declare it. Round each of the great unitive mystics little groups of ardent disciples, of spiritual children, have grown up. This is true both of those who remained within and those who seceded from the official Church -- for instance, St Bernard, Eckhart, Yauler, Ruysbroeck, St Catherine of Siena, St Catherine of Genoa, St Teresa, Boehme, Fox. Nor did their influence cease with death.

Further, in reckoning up the value of the mystics to the church as a whole we sometimes forget the extent top which that church is indebted to mystical intuition for the actual data upon which her corporate life is based. Christianity, it is true, is fundamentally a historical religion; but it is also a religion of experience, and its very history deals quite as much with the events which attend human intercourse with the Transcendent and Eternal as with concrete and visible happenings in space and time. The New Testament is thick with reports of mystical experiences. The Fourth Gospel and the Epistles of St Paul depend for their whole character on the soaring mystical genius their writers possessed. Had St paul never been caught up in the third heaven, he would have had a very different outlook on the world, and Christianity would have been a very different religion in consequence. had the Fourth Evangelist never known what it was to feel the sap of the Mystic Vine flow through him, his words would have lacked their overwhelming certitude. So, too, the liturgies bear the stamp of mystical feeling, and most of the great religious concepts which the church has gradually added to her store come from the same source. If we ask ourselves what the history of the world would be without the history of her mystics, then we begin to see how much of her light and colour emanates from them; how much of their doctrine represents their experience translated into dogmatic form. That communion with -- that feeding on -- the Divine Life which she offers to every believer in the Eucharist is the central fact of their existence. From Clement of Alexandria downwards, again and again they appeal to Eucharistic images in order to express what it is that really happens to the soul immersed in contemplative prayer. "I am the food of the full grown," says God to St Augustine. "Every time we think with love of the Well-beloved, He is anew our meat and drink," says Ruysbroeck. So, too, the church's language concerning new birth, divine sonship, regeneration, union with Christ, and the whole concept of grace, regarded as a transcendent life and love perpetually pressing in on humanity -- all this is of mystical origin, and represents not the speculations but the concrete experience of the great mystics. They are pushed out, as it were, by the visible church like tentacles, to explore the unseen world which surrounds her, and drawn back again to her bosom that they may impart to the whole body the more abundant life which they have found. Were it not for the unfailing family of the mystics, thus perpetually pushing out beyond the protective edges of the organism, and bringing back official Christianity into direct touch with the highest spiritual values, and so constantly reaffirming the fact -- by them felt and experienced --of the intimate correspondence, the regenerating contact of God with the soul, the church would long ago have fallen victim to that tendency to relapse into the mechanical which dogs all organised groups. Then the resistance which she has sometimes offered to the freshness and novelty, the adventurous quality of the mystical impulse, where it has appeared without preparation and sought to correct by its own overwhelming certitude the spiritual conventions of the day, would have become that hopeless inertia which is the precursor of death.

So we may best look upoin the great Christian mystic as a special organ developed within the Christian body for a special use. His particular sensibilities, like those which condition artistic genius, are the gates through which messages from the Transcendent come to man.. he is findi ng and feeling the ilnfinite; not for himself, but for us. His achievement, bridging the gap which lies between the normal mind and the supersensuous world, makes more valid and more actual to us the assumptions on which external religion is built; vindicating the church's highest claim, and hence the soul's highest claim -- the claim that achievement of Eternal Life, communion with ultimate reality, is possible to the spirit of man. More, since all human lives interpenetrate, and isolation is impossible save in death, the more we, the social group, are willing to accept the claim of the mystic, and receive what he tells us in a spirit of humility instead of a spirit of criticism; the more completely he will be able to share his treasure with us, the more deeply we shall be able to enter into that consciousness which he represents, which he brings in his own person into the human scheme.

This, of course, the Christian church has said far more beautifully in her doctrine of the Communion of Saints; and that doctrine, rightly understood, is indeed the connection between the great mystics and the corporate life within which they arise. Were the activities of these more vital spirits whoolly hidden from us, wholly silent and supersensual -- as they are not -- it would be a grossly

19

The Essentials of Mysticism

materialistic and violently un-Christian jusdgement which concluded from this that their lives were useless save to themselves. How can a life which aims at God be useless, if we believe that achievement of Him is the final destiny and only satisfaction of every soul? It would be an implicit debnial of the efficacy of prayer, of the "prevailing merits" of sanctity, its value to the society which produces it -- the power of a great and loving spirit to help, infect, and reinforce more languid souls -- did we agree that the life of the most strictly enclosed contemplative was wasted. Christians, who believe that the world was redeemed from within the narrow limits of Palestine, should not thus confuse space with power, or character with the manner of its self-expression. Without the ardent prayers of the mystics, the vivid spiritual life they lead, what would the sum of human spirituality be? How can we tell what we owe to the power which they liberate, the currents which they set up, the contacts which they make? The land they see and of which they report to us, is the land towards which humanity is going. They are like the lookout men upon the cross-trees, assuring us from time to time that we are still upon our course. Tear asunder their peculiar power and office from the office of the whole, and you will have on one side a society deprived of the guides which God has raised up for it; on the other an organ deprived of its real perfection and beauty, because severed from the organism which it was intended to serve.

Mysticism and the Doctrine of Atonement

AMONGST the problems which have to be met by those who incline to a mystical view of Christianity -- that view which lays special emphasis on the growth and experience of the individual soul, its ascent to union with God, as the very aim and object of religion -- one of the most pressing is that which centres on the doctrine of the Atonement. It is clear that many people feel that such a mystical and empirical view of religion leaves no room for this doctrine, or for the idea which it represents; that they are convinced that there is here a real conflict between two incompatible views of the Christian faith. On the one hand, they see orthodox Christianity still centred on the "atoning act" of Christ, with its implications of reconciliation and vicarious suffering, of the divine life humiliating itself, in order to do within the temporal order something for man which man cannot do for himself; a doctrine which retains its attraction and value, because so full of hope and mercy for the sinful and the weak. On the other hand, they see that demand of personal and individual growth, purification, life-enhancement, progressive union with God -- helped doubtless by grace, but no less dependent on will -- as the condition of attaining Eternal Life, which seems to be made by mystical theology. The opposition, in fact, is supposed to be between a concept of spiritual life in which each man must himself do and be, achieve and actualize in his own person, and not merely as the acceptor of a creed or themember of a Church -- must not only accept the gift, but must set himself to be an imitator, so far as he may, of the Giver -- and one in which a special manifestation in time and space of the divine power and love, for Christians the sacrifice of Christ on the Cross, does something for the man accepting it, which he cannot do for himself. In the one case, we are saved one by one, by effort, response, growth; in the other, we are saved as members of a group. Here the individual and the corporate ideals in their most intense forms face one another.

It does, then, seem at first as though we had here an irreconcilable opposition. Yet before we discard either of these ideas, it is worth while to enquire whether they need really entail conflict, or can be regarded as two sides of a greater whole. It is true that there are certain extreme views of the Atonement which do appear to be hopelessly irreconcilable with the mystical view of religion: especially those which lay peculiar stress, not on the latent powers, but on the essential impotence of man; centring the soul's salvation on " imputed righteousness," and finding the whole meaning and reason of the Incarnation in the one historical "propitiatory act" of Calvary. There is real conflict between such a creed, centred on the idea of something done once for all to the soul -- to the world -- from outside, and that which is centred on the idea of a life perpetually welling up in the soul, on growth, movement, organic change. Yet, on the other hand, is there not a curious similarity between these two apparently opposite views of salvation? Is not the drama of the divine life incarnate, humbling and limiting itself to the human life to save it, essentially a dramatic representation of that other experience, of the divine life limiting itself and mysteriously emerging within each soul, to transmute, regenerate, infinitize it, which the mystics describe to us? Is not what theologians call "grace" -- that essential factor of the mystic life-process -- a makinggood by the addition of a new dower of transcendent vitality, of the shortcomings of the merely human creature regarded as an " inheritor of Eternal Life"; just as the historical surrender of Calvary is conceived by orthodox Christianity to make good the shortcomings of the whole race, regarded as heirs of the Kingdom? And if this be so, then can the opposition between these two ideas of salvation -- the vital and the theological -- be as real as it sometimes appears? Are they not both plans in which atonement plays a part?

After all, both these views of the Christian scheme have emerged and diverged from the same source. St. Paul, the greatest of all Christian mystics -- soaked, too, in the idea of grace and of growth in grace, and deeply impressed with the fact of the soul's individual responsibility -- is also supremely the theologian of the Atonement. Though no doubt his teaching on the subject was first called forth by the practical need of finding some meaning in the tragedy wf the crucifixion, it is yet a development of that profound conception of His own death as a filling up to the brim of the cup of sacrifice and surrender, which seems to have inspired Christ Himself. If there were indeed a fundamental inconsistency between these two ideas in their pure and original form, then St. Paul would be inconsistent; for he certainly held them both. We all know that the usual way of studying St. Paul's "doctrines" for purposes of edification has been to isolate each of his ardent and poetic utterances, place it, as it were, in cold storage till it is no longer reminiscent of the living mobile body from which it came, and then subject it to analysis. We are also beginning to know that this method is not quite fair to a man who was a poet, an artist, a lover, as well as a constructive genius of unequalled power. The Pauline utterances are mostly impassioned efforts to express something which Paul knows in his own person; descriptions of the way in which the Christian revelation has met his own needs, regenerated his own nature. They are closely connected with the interioradventures which have attended on his new spiritual existence "in Christ." To adopt a well-known phrase of St. Bonaventura, they come "of grace, not of doctrine; of desire, not of intellect; of the ardours of prayer, not of the teaching of the schools." To put it in another way, they are the fruits of his mystical consciousness, which he is trying to express in artistic or intellectual terms. If we accept this statement then the fact of Paul's mystical experience and all that it means to him must never be absent from our minds when we are trying to understand his declarations. He lives in that supernal atmosphere which he calls " Christ-Spirit "; he speaks to us from that sphere. Nothing outside of it is real to him. Whatever its other bearings may be, his doctrine of Atonement is solidly real on that plane -- the mystic's plane, the plane of union -- or not at all. When he says he is "crucified with Christ," "hid in God with Christ," he means these things. They are not vaguely pious utterances, but desperate attempts towards the communication of a real state, really felt and known. Paul does feel himself welded together with that Transcendent Life, at once so intimate and personal, so infinite and universal, which he identifies with the glorified Jesus. Because of this union -- and only because of it -- the acts, powers, holiness, adventures of that life avail for him, Paul. He is a bit of its Body, in his own bold metaphor. So that the first great factor of salvation, as he sees it, is the essentially mystical factor of the "union" of the soul with Christ; the "doing away of the flame of separation." The Atonement follows, as it were almost logically, from this.

The general content of his letters makes us feel that St. Paul had an extremely rich, deep view of life; so great, indeed, that it refuses to be hammered into a consistent system, and we can never manage to embrace it all at once. Always bits get left out, and hence there is apt to be a certain distortion in all our views of the Pauline universe. There was a wonderful wholeness, a strongly affirmative qualityabout his sense of existence; subtractions and negations were unnatural to him. Any paradoxes and inconsistencies which we find in his statements are the inevitable result of an effort to express the enormous sweep, the living multiplicity, and (to borrow a word from William James) the thickness of his vision of Reality. Hence it follows that he was able to see and treat the soul of man, both as intensely individual and responsible, and at the same time as a part of the body of all life; that "mystical body of many members" of which the head is Christ-Spirit, the Divine Humanity which appeared in Jesus -- a corporation actualized in the Christian Church, but potentially co-extensive with the whole of mankind. These two -- the separate and the corporate -- are aspects of one whole. They seem to us to conflict, only because the totality to which they contribute is beyond the focus of the mind. Thus Paul could and did demand of the individual, on the one hand the self-mergence of faith, the corporate sense, the humble acknowledgment of personal impotence; and on the other hand, could demand of that same man the personal industry and self-dependence which "works out its own salvation," "runs for an imperishable garland," and "presses on towards the goal."

All through those passages in the Epistle to the Romans on which the doctrine of the Atonement was afterwards built, Paul seems to be trying to express -- often by the use of traditional images, which of course revenge themselves upon his free handling of them, as imagery so often revenges itself upon poets -- his vision of something supreme, some enormous uplift to eternal levels, some fundamental change, achieved by, for, in the human race. He has this vision just because, and in so far as, this supreme thing has been achieved by, for, in him, the mystic Paul. Behind the formula, we feel the first-hand experience. What is this crucial change? Surely it is the fundamental mystical achievement, the fundamental religious fact; the humansoul's conscious attainment of God. At bottom, atonement is wanted simply and solely to help man to do that; to enable the spirit of life to reach its goal. If we did not want God, we should be very well satisfied as we are: but we are not satisfied -- "Thou hast made us for Thyself, and our hearts shall find no rest save in Thee." No doubt Paul's eschatological views, the whole tendency of his time, made him connect this achievement, which he knew at first hand, with the imminent coming of a Liberator. For him, it was part of the preparation, the new vitality already given to those who were destined to live the new life. Achieved in one, it permeated the whole "new race" of spiritual men; but this is only the interpretation which a complex of causes made him put upon the transcendent fact. The prominence given to Paul's legal imagery, its isolation from the general trend of his life and thought, has made us inclined to forget all this. But if we try to see Reality from his angle, to catch the wild accents of his enthusiasm and his love, the theory that he seriously held anything approaching what would be called a "commercial" theory of atonement falls to the ground at once. That he should sometimes have argued in this sense when cornered by Judaizing opponents, is likely enough: and it is characteristic of the mystical temperament to ignore the discrepancy between such intellectual exercises and the fundamental intuition by which it lives. Life and love are as much the key-words of Paul's system as they are of the Fourth Gospel itself. He was the noblest of souls; and we cannot imagine a soul with a spark of nobility wanting atonement as a buying-off of penalty incurred, as a paying by another of a debt which it owes, a mere saving of it from pain or any other retribution. The living, loving soul can only want atonement as a road-making act; a bridge thrown out to the infinite, on which man can travel to his home in God. Now, Paul had made that journey in the spirit. He knew already, at first hand, that Divine Reality was accessibleto him, and that this contact was the greatest thing in life. But he knew and felt, too, that however much he, Paul, had really achieved this new state, this fruition of Eternity, by difficult growth from within; yet first, he could never have done it at all without the enormous uplift of enhancing-grace, that new dower of energy which was poured in on him from beyond the confines of his own nature; and secondly, great though the change had been, yet it was nothing compared with the immeasurable human possibilities achieved in Christ.

For Paul, these two achievements -- the victory of Christ and the victory of the Christian soul -- are intimately connected. True, one is infinitely great, the other very little. Except Christ, "all have fallen short of the glory"; have failed to grow up to the "fullness of the stature," to actualize the immense spiritual possibilities of man. Still, we are all in the same line; partakers of the same kind of life, "grace" or immanent Spirit, and aiming, consciously or unconsciously, at the same goal -- union with God. Now, total dependence on God, the centring of our whole interest and attention on

the Spiritual Order, is the very essence of union with Him. Everything short of that total dependence, that supreme rightness of relation, is trespass; a backing of the finite against the infinite. In the death of Jesus, that total dependence, that perfect relation, was completely achieved at last: the supreme mystic act, the self-donation of love, was done perfectly, and in this sense "once for all." Aleph, it is enough. The spirit of man, in this "new man," had overcome its limitations, the downward drag of instinct, and had leapt to the heights. This was the "redemption that is in Christ Jesus." In this unique vindication of humanity, this exhibition of regnant spirit overcoming the world, Christ-Spirit crowned with splendour all the tentative efforts of man, and, because of the corporate nature of humanity, conferred that splendour on the race.

But there is far more in it than this. And first, theChristian's achievement of God, such as it is -- from that of the least of believers to that of the greatest of the mystical saints -- is really and practically conditioned by the known fact and known character of the achievement of Christ. It is the addition of this fact, this distinct historic happening, to the racial consciousness, which makes possible the specially Christian apprehension of God; differentiates it, say, from that of a Hindu or a Neoplatonic saint. A reference to the phenomena of apperception will help us to understand this. As in the world of nature or art our perception of each new object is governed by the images and ideas already dominant within the mind, so, too, in the religious sphere. If Christians had not got the idea of Calvary in their consciousness -- if the image of the surrender of Jesus, His sublime exhibition of love and faith, were not there first as a clue, something about which to group and arrange their spiritual intuitions -- it would make a vital difference to their interpretation of the relation of the soul to God; and this means that the relation itself would be quite different for the conscious self, other elements would be stressed, and different results would flow from it. It is only because the sacrifice of Jesus is now part of the Christian's "apperceiving mass" -- because, coming to the contemplation of the spiritual world, he inevitably brings the Cross with him -- that he is able to make the characteristically Christian contact with God. That Christian contact is a direct gift to him, from the historic Person and the historic act. We approach the Transcendent Order with that, or, as Paul tersely puts it, "in Christ"; and our fruition of Reality results, not, as some extreme mystics have liked to think, from any "naked apprehension" -- for naked apprehension has no meaning, no content, for the mind -- but from a fusion of that which we bring with us and that to which we ascend: tradition and experience, the past and the present. Through love of Christ the Christian comes to the Cross, and through the Cross he enters a spiritual region he could notreach in any other way. So we find that even for the most transcendental of Christian contemplatives, still "in the Cross all doth consist." It has for him a terror and a rapture which the judicious philosopher can never know; and reveals to him strange secrets beyond the province of philosophy.

" Vocce legendo, en croce legendo nel libro che c'è ensanguinato
Ca essa scrittura me fa en natura ed en filosofia conventato;
O libro signato che dentro se' aurato, e tutto fiorito d'amore!"

That Cross gives the Infinite a colour which it did not have before. So, even from the point of view of the most hardened and thorough-going psychologist, Paul's statement that "through one act of righteousness, the free gift came unto all men" is literally accurate. It is true -- and that not in any conjuring-trick sense, but in a sense which fulfils on highest levels life's basic laws -- that "by the grace of one man" "the gift has abounded to the many," entincturing and altering the whole universe, and hence the whole experience, of every receptive soul; atoning for the faulty attitude, the imperfect love, of average man.

But still this is not all. There are other laws of life gathered up in, and redistributed from, this great lens. Essentially the idea which the Christ of the Gospels seems to have had of His own death is the idea of a making good of some general falling-short on life's part: a "filling-up of the cup" of sacrifice and surrender, to balance the other overflowing cup of error and sin. It is not only man's unaccomplished aim, but God's unaccomplished aim in life, which He is represented as fulfilling; and the fact that this conception owes a good deal to Old Testament prophecy need not invalidate its mystical truth. If we accept this idea, then, as well as showing individual man the way to perfect union with God -- "building the bridge and reforming the road which leads to the Father'sheart," as St. Catherine of Siena has it -- Christ in His willing death is somehow performing the very object of life, in the name of the whole race. The true business of an atoner is a constructive one. He is called upon to heal a disharmony; bridge a gap between two things which, though separate, desire to be one. Even the sacrificed animal of primitive religions seems most often to be a reconciling victim, the medium of union between the worshipper and his deity. In religions of a mystical type, then, the Atoner or Redeemer will surely be one who makes patent those latent possibilities of man which are at once the earnests of his future blessedness and the causes of his present unrest. He will achieve the completion and sublimation of our vague instinct for sacrifice and love, and thus bridge the space between that which is most divine in humanity and that which is most human in divinity; filling up the measure of that "glory," that real and divine life, of which we all fall short, yet without which we can never be content. Is not this again what St. Paul feels that Christ did? What he seems, at bottom, to see in the Passion -- though the imagery by which he tries to communicate it often sounds harsh in our ears -- is, the mysterious fulfilment of all cosmic meanings; the perfect surrender to infinite ideals of Man, the compound inhabitant of two possible orders of reality, who by this painful self-loss achieves perfect identifica- tion with the Divine will. This fulfilment was, as he distinctly tion with the Divine will. This fulfilment was, as he distinctly says, the duty and destiny of the human soul. All creation looks for it "with outstretched neck." But all have fallen short. Christ, the perfect man, does it, does what man was always meant to do; and because of the corporate character of humanity, in His utter transcendence of self-hood and of all finite categories He inevitably lifts up, to share His union with God, all who are in union with Him. The essence of the Atonement, then, would not lie so much in the sacrificial act as in the lift-up of the human spirit which that act guarantees; the new levels of life which it opens for therace. "Much more, being reconciled, shall we be saved in his life," says Paul.

"In his life" a new summit has been conquered by humanity. But are we to stop there? Is not the attainment of that same summit, the achievement of that life-giving surrender to the Universal Spirit -- "a life-giving life," Ruysbroeck calls it -- just what the great mystics, following as well as they can the curve of the life of Christ, try to do according to their measure? Theirs, after all, is the vision which sees that "there is no other way to life but the way of the Cross," and that the human life of Christ is "the door by which all must come in." Thus the spiritual victory of the Cross is for them not so much a unique, as a pioneer act. It is the first heroic cutting of a road on which they are to travel as far as they can; not merely the vicarious setting-right of the balance between God and man, upset by man's wilful sin. In their ascent towards union with God, are not they road-makers, or at any rate road-menders, too? Are they not forging new links between two orders of reality, which are separate for the once-born consciousness? If so, then we may regard each one of them as a bit of the slowly achieved atonement of the race; that gradual pressing-on of humanity into the heart of the Transcendent Order. For Christians, this movement was initiated by Christ. But surely it is continued and helped by every soul in union with Him, even those who knew not His Name; and Julian of Norwich was right when she said that she knew she was "in the Cross with Him."

Two things are perpetually emphasized in modern presentations of religion. First, the stress tends more and more to be upon experience. Nothing which authority tells us is done for us truly counts, unless we feel and realize it as done in us. In so far as this is so, the tendency is to a mystical concept of religion; and, speaking generally, to just the concept of religion which is supposed to conflict with the idea of atonementas usually understood. But, secondly, the social and corporate character of Christianity is strongly emphasized; and, where this corporate character is admired more than it is understood, mysticism is harshly criticized as the religion of the spiritual individualist, a "vertical relation," the "flight of the alone to the Alone." St. Paul's "completing opposites," in fact, are still in the foreground of our religious life; and so perhaps some re-statement of the solution by which he found room for both of them, and hence both for personal responsibility and atonement, may be possible and fruitful for us, too.

And first we notice that those enthusiasts for the corporate idea who condemn the mystics as religious egoists seem to forget that they are contradicting themselves; that if their vision of the Church of Christ as a mystical body be true, then the mystic's ascent to God cannot be a flight of the Alone. The poisonous implication of that phrase -- true in its context but always misunderstood -- has stuck like mud to the white robes of the saints. But the mystic is not merely a self going out on a solitary quest of Reality. He can, must, and does go only as a member of the whole body, performing as it were the function of a specialized organ. What he does, he does for all. He is, in fact, an atoner pure and simple: something stretched out to bridge a gap, something which makes good in a particular direction the general falling-short. The special kind of light or life which he receives, he receives for the race; and, conversely, the special growth which he is able to achieve comes from the race. He depends on it for his past; it depends on him for its future. All are part of life's great process of becoming; there are no breaks. Although there is perfect individualization, there is interpenetration too. His attainment is the attainment of the whole, pressing on behind him, supporting him. Thus -- to take an obvious example -- the achievement of peculiar sanctity by the member of a religious order is the achievement of that order in him; and this not in a fantastic and metaphoricalsense. The support of the Rule, the conditions of the life, the weight of tradition, the special characters which each religious family inherits from its Patriarch, have all contributed something to make the achievement possible; and are factors governing the type which that achievement assumes. We recognize the Cistercian stamp upon St. Bernard, the Dominican on Suso and Tauler, the Carmelite on St. John of the Cross. Each such case vindicates once more the incarnational principle; it is the true spirit of the community, flowering in this representative of theirs, which we see. Thus, as we may regard Christ from one point of view as supremely ideal Man incarnate -- the "heavenly man " as Paul calls Him -- summing up, fulfilling, lifting to new heights all that came before, and therefore actualizing all that humanity was ever intended to do, and changing for ever more the character of its future achievements; so, in a small way, we may regard St. Teresa as Carmel, the ideal Carmel, incarnate. Each is a concrete fact which atones for the falling-short of a whole type, and yet is conditioned by that type. The thought of what the Carmelite life was meant to do, the pressure of that idea seeking manifestation, did condition Teresa's achievement. Are we not also bound to say that the thought of the Jewish visions of an ideal humanity, of the Son of Man and the Suffering Servant, did condition the external accidents of the life and death of Christ?

So as to the past. Still more as to the future are the corporate and individual aspects of spiritual life inextricably twined together. As that done by one is an outbirth of the whole, so that done to one may avail for the whole. Only by staying within the circle of this thought -- a thought which surely comes very close to the doctrine of Atonement -- can we form a sane and broad idea of what the mystic, and the mystic's experience, mean for the race. Consider again the case of Teresa. As, even in a time and place of considerable monastic corruption -- for no one who has read her life andletters can regard the Convent of the Incarnation as a forcing house of the spiritual life -- still the idea of her order conditioned her great and Godward-tending soul, and her dedicated life filled up the measure of its glory; yet more has Teresa's own, separate, unique achievement conditioned the spirit of her order ever since. All the saints which it has nourished have been salted with her salt. All that she won has flowed out from her in life-giving streams to others. She has been a regenerator of the religious life, has achieved the ideal of Richard Rolle, and become a "pipe of life" through which the living water can pass from God to man. Is not this, too, rather near the idea of Atonement, a curiously close and faithful imitation of Christ; especially when we consider the amount of unselfish suffering which such a career entails?

The objective of the Christian life, we say, is union with God: that paradoxical victory-in-surrender of love which translates us from finite to infinite levels. Most of us in this present life and in our own persons fall short of the glory of this. We are not all equally full of grace; we do not all grow up to the full stature of the Sons of God; and it is no use pretending that we do. But the mystical saint does achieve this, and by this act of mediation -- this "vicarious" achievement, if you like to put it so -- performed by a member of our social organism, the gift does really "abound unto the many." For what other purpose, indeed, are these apparently elect souls bred up? What other social value can we attribute to them than that which we see them actually possessing in history -- the value, that is, of special instruments put forth by the race, to do or suffer something which the average self cannot do, but which humanity as a whole, in its Godward ascent, must, can, and shall do; ducts, too, whereby fresh spiritual energy flows in to mankind; eyes, open to visions beyond the span of average sight; parents of new life. Carlyle said that a hero was "a man sent hitherto make the divine mystery more impressively known to us" -- to atone, in fact, for the inadequacy of our own perception of Reality, our perpetual relapses to lower levels of life; to make a bridge between us and the Transcendent Order. And when the hero as mystic does this, is he not in a special sense a close imitator of Christ?

We seem to have here the highest example of a principle which is operative through the whole of the seething complex of life, for there is a sense on which every great personality fulfils the function of an atoner. On the one hand he does something towards the making good of humanity's "falling short" in one direction or another; on the other hand, he gives to his fellow-men -- adds to their universe -- something which they did not possess before. Burke, speaking of the social contract, has said that society is a partnership in all science, all art, every virtue, and all perfection; and, since the ends of such a partnership cannot be obtained but in many generations, it is a partnership between the living, the dead, and the unborn. "Each contract of each particular state," he says, "is but a clause in the great primæval contract of eternal society, linking the lower with the higher natures, connecting the visible and the invisible world, according to a fixed compact sanctioned by the inviolable oath which holds all physical and all moral natures each in their appointed place." In such a partnership -- linking higher and lower, visible and invisible worlds in one -- the creative spirits in every department of life may properly be called "atoners," for they have a corporate and racial value which is in exact proportion to their individual achievement of reality. Thus the great artist, or the great musician, really redeems his fellows from slavery to a lower level of colour, form, sound. He atones for their dullness towards that which has always been there, and endows them with new possibilities of vision and hearing; gives them, in fact, more abundant life; is the Door, the Way, to a wider universe. His creative actsopen new gates to the whole race. The fact that he has lived and worked has effected a permanent change in the stream of life, which can never again be that which it was before. If we were more accustomed, on the one hand, to look at the achievements of religious genius from the artistic and creative point of view, and on the other hand, to discern the work of the Holy Spirit in the artistic as well as the religious field, I believe that we should find a close parallel between the work of supreme personality redeeming spirit, and the work of the great artist redeeming sense, from servitude to old imperfections and disharmonies.

We might almost make it the test of true greatness, this wonderful power of flinging out the filaments of life in all directions; this way in which noble and creative personalities of every type seem to be so much more than themselves -- to count for so much more than themselves -- to be, in their generous activities, the servants of all life. They appear to be the sum of tendencies which preceded them; and to gather those tendencies to a focus and distribute them again, enhanced and re-directed, to succeeding generations of souls. Such a personality has to the full the divine power of giving and of taking. Whilst he seems specially original, it is always true that the past, the race, nourishes him to an enormous extent. Christ Himself conformed to this law. The great man is rooted in history, plaited up in the life of his own time: absorbs from the human as well as from the spiritual. His feet are in Time, though his head is in Eternity. He is never isolated and ring-fenced. Where he seems so, that appearance is found on examination to be deceptive, as Dr. Rufus Jones has shown in the case of Jacob Boehme, and Baron von Hugel in that of George Fox. So, again, the special act, vision, or experience of the spiritual genius never ends with him. He is a centre of divine fecundity -- it is the mystics' own phrase. The touch of the divine life stimulates him to creation. He is a regenerator, a whirlpool of new forces, aparent of new things. It seems that life's "tendency to lag behind," its tendency not to do its best, receives its corrective in all such great spirits; and the Christian atonement becomes the supreme, the divine manifestation of a vital law which we find operative on every level of existence.

If we acknowledge the extent to which Grace, Spirit, God, works on man through personality, through specific men -- as a communication of transcendent vitality to certain souls ("elect," if you like) in order that they may bring forth new life, new vision, new goodness, may fertilize the race afresh--- then shall we not expect to find that Christianity, being a vital, dynamic system, has exhibited and emphasized these facts throughout the whole of her great career? This outward thrust of great personalities from the social organism, these fresh unique saving contacts made by the individual in the name of the All, these sudden, incalculable, upward leaps of life, these changes in the national consciousness which the hero, poet, prophet can produce -- we shall expect to find all this operative in the highest degree in the Christian Church. We shall expect to find her claiming for her greatest and most God-achieving spirits, not only special honour, but a special value, a special redeeming power in respect of the corporate body to which they belong; and this, of course, is exactly what we do find. The mystical saints, in fact, seem to provide us with a link between the doctrine of the Atonement -- of the special racial value of the utterly surrendered life in God, which was once, and once only, perfectly achieved -- and the doctrine of the Communion of Saints, or interpenetration and mutual help of all souls "in Christ." From these two ideas there follows of necessity that further doctrine of the "prevailing merits" of the saints, their special "atoning" value for other men, the corporate social work done by heroic virtue flowering in individual souls, which the Catholic Church has always deduced from them. At the back of both ideas we find the same fact; that Life andLove, when supremely evoked within the temporal order, cannot keep themselves to themselves. Such life and such love have, in spite of their marked individuality, a profoundly social character; they are violently contagious; they spread, they interpenetrate, they transmute all selves that will receive them. They entincture the whole stream of duration, make good its shortcomings, make widening circles of splendour within the flux.

So, if we want to think of a Celestial Hierarchy, actual to us, founded in history, related with us by a thousand links, it is surely of the saints and the mystics that we ought to think; rising as it were in graduated orders, according to the strength and purity of their union with God, the fullness of their possession of Eternal Life, towards the Cross in which their tendencies are perfected and gathered up. These are amongst the highest values which life has given to us. The apostolic type; the men of action, dynamic manifestations of the Spirit. The prophetic type; men of supreme vision, enlarging the horizons of the world. The martyr-type; men of utter sacrifice and complete interior surrender. These are the three ways in which the mystical passion for God breaks out through humanity. These three types make good -- atone for -- our corporate spiritual shortcomings; redeem the dead level of that race which has thrust them forth towards the Infinite.

Perhaps it seems to us that their difference from us is too great; that they are cut off, divided by a chasm from the common experience of man to form an exclusive, "other-worldly" type. Their life rises up like a great mountain, full of beauty and strangeness; and ours is like the homely plain. But there is no break between the plain and the mountain. It is pushed out from us, it is part of us; its value is bound up with the value of the whole -- with our value, as struggling, growing men. It, every inch of it, atones for our flatness and enhances the average level of therace. We have all seen in Catholic countries how a sudden hill with a Calvary on its summit can glorify and atone for the whole landscape -- so poor without it, so noble with it -- from which it is lifted up. Now the Cross is, and remains, the central feature in the Christian landscape too: but is it not the long slope of that hill, going from the common level to the heights, which makes it so homely to us, so accessible to us, so supremely a part of us, and completes its task of linking humanity and divinity?

These are some of the reasons why the doctrine of Atonement seems to be closely bound up with the mystical vision of life, and hard to understand -- whether we mean by it a spiritual principle or a historic event -- without that mystical vision. We have Christianity saying to us, on the one hand, that the utmost ideal of humanity, the ideal of perfect self-donation to the purposes of Spirit, perfect self-surrender to the interests of the All, was completely and transcendently achieved in Jesus. In Him man leapt to the heights; and this unique attainment counts for the whole race. But, on the other hand, it says that all who can are called to go as far as they are able on the same road; to "fill up the measure of the sufferings," to "grow to the full stature," to "press on to the high calling" of the human soul. Through these more vital personalities -- the mystics, the twice-born, the saints -- the radiance of the spiritual streams out on the race; God speaks to man through man. Such personalities act as receivers and transmitters; they really and practically distribute the flashes of the Uncreated Light. Their activities are vicarious; they do atone for the disabilities of other men. Therefore the social value of the mystics, their place in the organism, is intimately connected with the atoning idea. Were it not for the principle which the doctrine of Atonement expresses, the mystics would be spiritual individualists, whose life and experience would be meaningless except for themselves. And were it not for the continuance of the mysticallife, the perpetual renewal of the mystical self-donation in love, its known value for the race, then the historic Atonement of Jesus would be an isolated act, unrelated to the great processes of the Spiritual World, of which it should form the crown.

The Mystic As Creative Artist

HOSTILE criticism of the mystics almost invariably includes the charge that their great experiences are in the nature of merely personal satisfactions. It is said that they stand apart from the ruck of humanity, claiming a special knowledge of the supersensual, a special privilege of communion with it; yet do not pass on to others, in any real and genuine sense, the illumination, the intuition of Reality, which they declare that they have received. St. Bernard's favourite mistranslation from Isaiah, "My secret to myself," has again and again been used against them with damaging effect; linked sometimes with the notorious phrase in which Plotinus defined the soul's fruition of Eternity as "a flight of the alone to the Alone." It is true that these hints concerning a solitary and ineffable encounter do tally with one side of the experience of the mystic; do describe one aspect of his richly various, many-angled spiritual universe, one way in which that divine union which is his high objective is apprehended by the surface-consciousness. But that which is here told, is only half the truth. There is another side, a "completing opposite," to this admittedly indescribable union of hearts; a side which is often -- and most ungraciously -- forgotten by those who have received its benefits. The great mystic's loneliness is a consecrated loneliness. When he ascends to that encounter with Divine Reality which is his peculiar privilege, he is not a spiritual individualist. He goes as the ambassador of the race. His spirit is not, so to speak, a"spark flying upwards" from this world into that world, flung out from the mass of humanity, cut off; a little, separate, brilliant thing. It is more like a feeler, a tentacle, which life as a whole stretches out into that supersensual world which envelops her. Life stretches that tentacle out, but she also draws it in again with the food that it has gathered, the news that it has to tell of the regions which its delicate tactile sense has enabled it to explore. This, it seems to me, is the function of the mystic consciousness in respect of the human race. For this purpose it is specialized. It receives, in order that it may give. As the prophet looks at the landscape of Eternity, the mystic finds and feels it: and both know that there is laid on them the obligation of exhibiting it if they can.

If this be so, then it becomes clear that the mystic's personal encounter with Infinite Reality represents only one of the two movements which constitute his completed life. He must turn back to pass on the revelation he has received: must mediate between the transcendent and his fellow-men. He is, in fact, called to be a creative artist of the highest kind; and only when he is such an artist, does he fulfil his duty to the race.

It is coming to be realized more and more clearly that it is the business of the artist not only to delight us, but to enlighten us : in Blake's words, to "Cleanse the doors of perception, so that everything may appear as it is -- infinite." Artists mediate between the truth and beauty which they know, and those who cannot without their help discern it. It is the function of art, says Hegel, to deliver to the domain of feeling and delight of vision all that the mind may possess of essential and transcendent Being. In this respect it ranks with religion and philosophy as "one of the three spheres of Absolute Spirit." Bergson, again, declares that it is the peculiar business of art to brush aside everything that veils reality from us, in order to bring us face to face with thereal, the true. The artist is the man who sees things in their native purity. "

"Could reality," he observes in a celebrated passage, "come into direct contact with sense and consciousness, could we enter into immediate communion with things and with ourselves -- then, we should all be artists. . . . Deep in our souls we should hear the uninterrupted melody of our inner life: a music often gay, more often sad, always original. All this is around and within us : yet none of it is distinctly perceived by us. Between nature and ourselves -- more, between ourselves and our own consciousness -- hangs a veil: a veil dense and opaque for normal men, but thin, almost transparent, for the artist and poet." He might have added, for the mystic too.

This veil, he says again, is woven of self-interest: we perceive things, not as they are, but as they affect ourselves. The artist, on the contrary, sees them for their own sakes, with the eyes of disinterested love. So, when the mystics declare to us that the first conditions of spiritual illumination are self-simplification, humility and detachment, they are demanding just those qualities which control the artist's power of seeing things in their beauty and truth. The true mystic sees Reality in its infinite aspect; and tries, as other artists, to reveal it within the finite world. He not only ascends, but descends the ladder of contemplation; having heard "the uninterrupted music of the inner life," he tries to weave it into melodies that other men can understand.

Bergson's contemporary, Eucken, claims -- and I think it is one of his most striking doctrines -- that man is gradually but actually bringing into existence a spiritual world. This spiritual world springs up from within through humanity -- that is, through man's own consciousness -- yet at the same time humanity is, as it were, growing up into it; finding it as an independent reality, waiting to be apprehended, waiting to be incorporated into our universe. In respect of man'snormal universe, this spiritual world is both immanent and transcendent: "Absent only from those unable to perceive it," as Plotinus said of the Nous. We are reminded of the Voice which said to St. Augustine, "I am the Food of the Full-grown."

This paradox of a wholly new order of experience thrusting itself up through the race which it yet transcends, is a permanent feature in the teachings of the higher religions and philosophies, and is closely connected with the phenomena of inspiration and of artistic creation. The artist, the prophet, the metaphysician, each builds up from material beyond the grasp of other souls, a world within which those other souls can live and dream: a world, moreover, which exhibits in new proportions and endows with new meanings the common world of daily life. When we ask what organ of the race -- the whole body of humanity -- it is, by and through which this supernal world thus receives expression, it becomes clear that this organ is the corporate spiritual consciousness, emerging in those whom we call, pre-eminently, mystics and seers. It is, actually and literally, through them that this new world is emerging and being built up; as it is through other forms of enhanced and clarified consciousness, in painters, musicians, philosophers, and the adepts of physical science, that other aspects of the universe are made known to men. In all of these, and in the mystic too, the twin powers of a steadfast, selective attention and of creative imagination are at work. Because of their wide, deep, attention to life they receive more news from the external world than others do; because of the creative cast of their minds, they are able to weave up the crude received material into a living whole, into an idea or image which can be communicated to other men. Ultimately, we owe to the mystics all the symbols, ideas and images of which our spiritual world, as it is thought of by the bulk of men, is constructed. We take its topography from them, at second-hand; and often forget thesublime adventures immortalized in those phrases which we take so lightly on our lips -- the Divine Dark, the Beatific Vision, the Eternal Beauty, Ecstasy, Union, Spiritual Marriage, and the rest. The mystics have actually created, from that language which we have evolved to describe and deal with the time-world, another artistic world; a self-consistent and spiritually expressive world of imaginative concepts, like the world of music or the world of colour and form. They are always trying to give us the key to it, to induct us into its mysterious delights. It is by means of this world, and the symbols which furnish it, that human consciousness is enabled to actualize its most elusive experiences; and hence it is wholly due to the unselfish labours of those mystics who have struggled to body forth the realities by which they were possessed, that we are able, to some extent, to enter into the special experiences of the mystical saints; and that they are able to snatch us up to a brief sharing of their vision, to make us live for a moment "Eternal Life in the midst of Time."

How, then, have they done this? What is the general method by which any man communicates the result of his personal contacts with the universe to other minds ? Roughly speaking, he has two ways of doing this, by description and by suggestion; and his best successes are those in which these two methods are combined. His descriptions are addressed to the intellect, his suggestions are appeals to the imagination, of those with whom he is trying to communicate. The necessities which control these two ways of telling the news -- oblique suggestion and symbolic image -- practically govern the whole of mystical literature. The span of this literature is wide. It goes from the utterly formless, yet infinitely suggestive, language of certain great contemplatives, to the crisply formal pictorial descriptions of those whose own revelations of Reality crystallize into visions, voices, or other psycho-sensorial experiences. At one end of the scale is thevivid, prismatic imagery of the Christian apocalypse, at the other the fluid, ecstatic poetry of some of the Sufi saints.

In his suggestive and allusive language the mystical artist often approaches the methods of music. When he does this, his statements do not give information. They operate a kind of enchantment which dilates the consciousness of the hearer to a point at which it is able to apprehend new aspects of the world. In his descriptive passages, on the other hand, he generally proceeds, as do nearly all our descriptive efforts, by way of comparison. Yet often these comparisons, like those employed by the great poet, are more valuable for their strange suggestive quality than for any exact parallels which they set up between the mystic's universe and our own. Thus, when Clement of Alexandria compares the Logos to a "New Song,"when Suso calls the Eternal Wisdom a "sweet and beautiful wild flower,"when Dionysius the Areopagite speaks of the Divine Dark which is the Inaccessible Light, or Ruysbroeck of "the unwalled world,"we recognize a sudden flash of the creative imagination; evoking for us a truth far greater, deeper and more fruitful than the merely external parallel which it suggests. So too with many common metaphors of the mystics: the Fire of Love, the Game of Love, the Desert of God, the Marriage of the Soul. Such phrases succeed because of their interior and imaginative appeal.

We have numerous examples of this kind of artistic language -- the highly charged imaginative phrase -- in the Bible; especially in the prophetic books, and the Apocalypse.

The Essentials of Mysticism

Ho, every one that thirsteth, come ye to the waters.
I will give thee treasures of darkness and hidden riches of secret places.
The Lord shall be a diadem of beauty.
He showed me a pure river of the water of life.
I heard a voice from heaven, as the voice of many waters.
I saw a new heaven and a new earth.

Whereas the original prophetic significance of these phrasesis now meaningless for us, their suggestive quality -- their appeal to the mystic consciousness -- retains its full force. They are artistic creations; and have the enormous evocative power proper to all great art. Later mystics use such passages again and again, reading their own experiences into these traditional forms. The classic example of this close alliance between poetic readings of life and practical mysticism is of course the mystical interpretation of the Song of Songs, which appears in Christian mysticism at least as early as the fourth century. But there are many other instances. Thus St. Macarius finds in Ezekiel's vision of the Cherubim a profoundly suggestive image of the state of the deified soul, "all eyes and all wings,"driven upon its course by the Heavenly Charioteer of the Spirit. Thus in The Mirror of Simple Souls, another of Ezekiel's visions -- that of the "great eagle, with great wings, long wings, full of feathers, which took the highest branch of the cedar"becomes the vivid symbol of the contemplative mind, "the eagle that flies high, so right high and yet more high than does any other bird, for she is feathered with fine love, and beholds above other the beauty of the sun."

When we pass to the mystical poets, we find that nearly all their best effects are due to their extraordinary genius for this kind of indirect, suggestive imagery. This is the method by which they proceed when they wish to communicate their vision of reality. Their works are full of magical phrases which baffle analysis, yet, as one of them has said :

"Lighten the wave-washed caverns of the mind
With a pale, starry grace."

Many of these phrases are of course familiar to every one. Vaughan's

"I saw Eternity the other night
Like a great ring of pure and endless light."Blake's
"To see a world in a grain of sand
And a heaven in a wild flower,
Hold infinity in the palm of your hand,
And eternity in an hour."

Whitman's

"Light rare, untellable, lighting the very light."

Thompson's

"Ever and anon a trumpet sounds
From the hid battlements of Eternity."

These are artistic, sidelong representations of the mystic's direct apprehension of the Infinite on, so to speak, its cosmic and impersonal side. Others reflect the personal and intimate contact with the Divine Life which forms the opposite side of his complete experience. Thus Francis Thompson :

"With his aureole
The tresses of my soul
Are blent
In wished content."

So, too, St. John of the Cross:

"All things I then forgot,
My cheek on him who for my coming came;
All ceased, and I was not,
Leaving my cares and shame
Among the lilies, and forgetting them."

Best of all, perhaps, Jalaluddin Rumi:

> *"In a place beyond uttermost place,*
> *in a tract without shadow of trace,*
> *Soul and body transcending I live,*
> *in the soul of my loved one anew."*

Sometimes the two aspects, personal and impersonal, are woven together by the poet: and then it is that we come nearest to an understanding of the full experience he is trying to express. A remarkable example of this occurs in GerardHopkins, perhaps the greatest mystical poet of the Victorian era:

> *"Thou mastering me*
> *God! giver of breath and bread;*
> *World's strand, sway of the sea;*
> *Lord of the living and dead;*
> *Thou hast bound bones and veins in me, fastened me flesh,*
> *And after it almost unmade, what with dread,*
> *Thy doing: and dost thou touch me afresh?*
> *Over again I feel thy finger and find thee."*

> *"I kiss my hand*
> *To the stars, lovely-asunder*
> *Starlight, wafting him out of it; and*
> *Glow, glory in thunder;*
> *Kiss my hand to the dappled-with-damson west:*
> *Since, though he is under the world's splendour and wonder,*
> *His mystery must be instressed, stressed;*
> *For I greet him the days I meet him, and bless when I understand."*

So much for the poets. In the prose writings of the mystics we find again the same characters, the same high imaginative qualities, the same passionate effort to give the ineffable some kind of artistic form. This effort includes in its span a wide range of literary artifices; some endeavouring to recapture and represent in concrete symbols the objective reality known; some, like one dominant art movement of the present day, trying to communicate it obliquely, by a representation of the subjective feeling-state induced in the mystic's own consciousness. At one end of the scale, therefore, we have the so-called negative language of mysticism, which describes the supersensuous in paradox by refusing to describe it at all; by declaring that the entry of the soul upon spiritual experience is an entry into a Cloud of Unknowing, a nothing, a Divine Darkness, a fathomless abyss. The curious thing is, that though here, if anywhere, the mystic seems to keep his secret to himself, as a matter of fact it is just this sort of language which has been proved to possess the highest evocative power. For many types of mind, this really does fling magic casements wide; does give us a momentaryglimpse of the perilous seas. I am inclined to think that, many and beautiful as are the symbolic and pictorial creations of mystical genius, it is here that this genius works most freely, produces its most magnificent results. When Ruysbroeck speaks of the boundless abyss of pure simplicity, that "dim silence where all lovers lose themselves"; when he assures us that, "stripped of its very life," the soul is destined to "sail the wild billows of that Sea Divine," surely he effects a true change in our universe. So, too, the wonderful series of formless visions -- though "vision" is a poor word for intuitive experience of this sort -- experienced by Angela of Foligno, far exceed in their suggestive power her vividly pictured conversations with Christ, when she declares that she beheld "those eyes and that face so gracious and so pleasing."

"I beheld," she says of her ultimate experience of the Absolute, "a Thing, as fixed and stable as it was indescribable; and more than this I cannot say, save what I have often said already, namely, that it was all good. And though my soul beheld not love, yet when it saw that ineffable Thing it was itself filled with unutterable joy, and it was taken out of the state it was in, and placed in this great and ineffable state. . . . But if thou seekest to know that which I beheld, I can tell thee nothing, save that I beheld a Fullness and a Clearness, and felt them within me so abundantly that I cannot describe it, nor give any image thereof: for what I beheld was not bodily, but as though it were in heaven. Thus I beheld a beauty so great that I can say nothing of it save that I saw the Supreme Beauty, which contains in itself all goodness." In the end, all that Angela has said here is, "Come and see! "but in saying this, she tells us far more than many do who go about to measure the City of Contemplation. Here words suggest, they do not tell; entice, but do not describe. Reminding us of the solemn declaration of Thomas a Kempis,that "there is a distance incomparable between those things that imperfect men think, and those that men illumined by high revelation behold," they yet extend to other minds a musical invitation to intercourse with new orders of reality.

This sort of language, this form of paradoxical, suggestive, allusive art is a permanent feature in mystical literature. It is usually supposed to be derived through Dionysius the Areopagite from the Platonists, but is really far older than this. As it comes down the centuries, it develops in depth and richness. Each successive mystic takes up the imagery of negation where the last one leaves it -- takes it, because he recognizes that it describes a country where he too has been -- and adds to it the products of his own most secret and august experiences. As in the torch-race of the antique world, the illuminating symbol, once lit, is snatched from hand to hand, and burns ever brighter as it is passed on.

I take one example of this out of many. Nearly all the great mystics of the later Middle Ages speak of the Wilderness or Desert of Deity; suggesting thus that sense of great, swept spaces, "beyond the polar circle of the mind" -- of a plane of experience destitute of all the homely furniture of thought -- which seems to characterize a certain high type, or stage, of contemplation. It represents the emergence of the self into a real universe -- a "place beyond uttermost place" -- unrelated to the categories of thought, and is substantially the same experience which Dionysius the Areopagite and those mystics who follow him call the Divine Ignorance or the Dark, and which his English interpreter names the Cloud of Unknowing, where the soul feels itself to be lost. But each mystic who uses this traditional image of amazement -- really the description of a psychological situation, not of an objective reality -- gives to it a characteristic touch; each has passed it through the furnace of his own passionate imagination, and slightly modified its temper and its form. This place, or state, says Eckhart, is "a still wilderness where no one is at home,"It is "the quiet desert of the Godhead," says Tauler; "So still, so mysterious, so desolate! The great wastes to be found in it have neither image, form, nor condition." Yet, says Richard Rolle -- suddenly bringing the positive experience of the contemplative heart to the rescue of the baffled contemplative mind -- in this same wilderness consciousness does set up an ineffable correspondence with Reality.

"[There] speaks the loved to the heart of the lover; as it were a bashful lover, that his sweetheart before men entreats not, nor friendly-wise but commonly and as a stranger kisses . . . and anon comes heavenly joy, marvellously making merry melody."

Here the mystic, with an astonishing boldness, weaves together spatial, personal and musical imagery, positive and negative experience, in order to produce his full effect.

Finally, St. John of the Cross, great thinker, manly and heroic mystic, and true poet, effects a perfect synthesis of these positive and negative experiences -- that apparent self-loss in empty spaces which is also, mysteriously, an encounter of love.

"The soul in dim contemplation (he says) is like a man who sees something for the first time, the like of which he has never seen before . . . hence it feels like one who is placed in a wild and vast solitude where no human being can come; an immense wilderness without limits. But this wilderness is the more delicious, sweet and lovely, the more it is wide, vast and lonely; for where the soul seems most to be lost, there it is most raised up above all created things."

All this language, as I have said, belongs to the oblique and paradoxical side of the mystic's art; and comes to us from those who are temperamentally inclined to that pure contemplation which "has no image." Psychologically speaking, these mystics are closer to the musician than to any other type of artist, though they avail themselves when they wish of material drawn from all the arts. But there is another kind of mystic, naturally inclined to visualization, who tendsto translate his supersensual experience into concrete, pictorial images; into terms of colour and of form. He uses, in fact, the methods of the painter, the descriptive writer, sometimes of the dramatist, rather than those of the musician or the lyric poet. He is, I think, as a rule much less impressive than the artist of the illusive kind, and is seldom so successful in putting us into communion with reality. On the other hand -- and partly because of his more concrete method -- he is the more generally understood. For one person to whom Plotinus or Ruysbroeck communicates his sublime intuition of reality, a hundred accept at their face-value, as true "revelations," the visions of St. Gertrude or St. Teresa.

The picture-making proceedings of this type of mystical artist are of two kinds. Sometimes they are involuntary, sometimes deliberate. Often we find both forms in the same individual; for instance, in Mechthild of Magdeburg and in Suso, where it is sometimes extremely difficult to find the dividing line between true visionary experience entirely outside the self's control, and the intense meditation, or poetic apprehension of truth, which demands a symbolic and concrete form for its literary expression. In both cases an act of artistic creation has taken place; in one below, in the other above, the normal threshold of consciousness. In

true visionaries, the translation of the supersensual into sensual terms is uncontrolled by the surface intellect; as it is indeed in many artists. Without the will or knowledge of the subject, intuitions are woven up into pictures, cadences, words; and, by that which psychologists call a psycho-sensorial automatism, the mystic seems to himself to receive the message of Reality in a pictorial, verbal, dramatic or sometimes a musical form -- "coming in to his body by the windows of the wits," as one old writer has it.

Thus the rhythmic phrases in which the Eternal Wisdom speaks to Suso, or the Divine Voice to St. Catherine of Siena, verge on poetic composition; but poetic composition of theautomatic type, uncontrolled by the mystic's surface-mind. Thus, too, the great fluid visions of the prophets, the sharply definite, often lovely, pictures which surge up before the mind of Suso, the Mechthilds, St. Gertrude, Angela of Foligno, of the great St. Teresa herself, are symbolic pictures which represent an actual interior experience, a real contact with the supersensual; exhibiting the interpretative power inherent in the mystical imagination. These pictures are seen by the mystic -- sometimes, as he says, within the mind, sometimes as projections in space -- always in sharp definition, lit by that strong light which is peculiar to visionary status. They are not produced by any voluntary process of composition, but loom up, as do the best creations of other artists, from his deeper mind, bringing with them an intense conviction of reality. Good instances are the visions which so often occur at conversion, or mark the transition from one stage of the mystic way to another: for example, the mystic marriage of St. Catherine of Siena, or that vision of the Upper School of True Resignation, which initiated Suso into the "dark night of the soul." I believe that we may look on such visions as allied to dream-states; but in the case of the great mystics they are the richly significant waking-dreams of creative genius, not the confused and meaningless dreaming of normal men. Suso himself makes this comparison, and says that none but the mystic can distinguish vision from dream. In character they vary as widely as do the creations of the painter and the poet. The personal and intimate, the remote and metaphysical, sides of the spiritual life are richly represented in them. Sometimes the elements from which they are built up come from theology, sometimes from history, legend, nature, or human life. But in every case the "glory of the lighted mind" shines on them.

Often a particularly delicate and gay poetic feeling -- a faery touch -- shows itself in the symbolic pictures by which these mystics try to represent their encounter with thespiritual world. Coventry Patmore once spoke of a "sphere of rapture and dalliance" to which the great contemplatives are raised; and it is from such a sphere that these seem to turn back to us, trying, by direct appeals to our sense of joy, the most stunted of our spiritual faculties, to communicate their exultant experience of that Kingdom of Reality which is neither "here" nor "there" but "everywhere."

Music and dancing, birds and flowers, the freshness of a living, growing world, all simple joyous things, all airy beauties, are used in the effort to tell us of that vision which Clement called the privilege of love. When we read these declarations we feel that it is always spring-time in those gardens of the soul of which they tell. St. John of the Cross, who described those spiritual gardens, said that fragrant roses brought from strange islands grew there -- those strange islands which are the romantic unexplored possibilities of God -- and that water-lilies shine like stars in that roaring torrent of supernal glory which pours without ceasing through the transfigured soul. This is high poetry; but sometimes the mystic imagination shows itself under simpler, more endearing forms, as when St. Mechthild of Hackeborn saw the prayers of her sisters flying up like larks into the presence of God; some soaring as high as His countenance and some falling down to rest upon His heart. An angel carried the little, fluttering prayers which were not strong enough to rise of themselves. Imagery less charming than this has gone to the making of many a successful poem.

Between the sublime intensity of St. John and the crystalline simplicity of St. Mechthild, mystical literature provides us with examples of almost every type of romantic and symbolic language; deliberate or involuntary translation of the heavenly fact into the earthly image. True, the earthly image is transfused by a new light, radiant with a new colour, has been lifted into a new atmosphere; and thus has often a

suggestive quality far in excess of its symbolic appropriate-ness. In their search for such images the mystics explore the resources of all the arts. In particular, music and dancing -- joyous harmony, unceasing measured movement -- have seemed to them specially significant media whereby to express their intuitions of Eternal Life. St. Francis, and after him Richard Rolle, heard celestial melodies; Kabir, the "Unstruck Music of the Infinite." Dante saw the saints dancing in the sphere of the sun; Suso heard the music of the angels, and was invited to join in their song and dance. It was not, he says, like the dancing of this world, but was like a celestial ebb and flow within that incomprehensible Abyss which is the secret being of the Deity. There is no need to dwell upon the remarkable way in which mystics of all countries and periods, from Plotinus to Jacob Boehme, resort to the dance as an image of the glad harmonious movements of liberated souls. I will take two characteristic examples, from the East and from the West. The first is a poem by Kabir:

"Dance, my heart ! dance to-day with joy.
The strains of love fill the days and the nights with music, and the world is listening to its melodies;
Mad with joy, life and death dance to the rhythm of this music. The hills and the sea and the earth dance. The world of man dances in laughter and tears. .
Behold ! my heart dances in the delight of a hundred arts, and the Creator is well pleased."

33

The next is the German mystic and poetess, Mechthild of Magdeburg, whose writings are amongst the finest products of mystical genius of the romantic and emotional type. This Mechthild's book, The Book of the Flowing Light of the Godhead, is a collection of visions, revelations, thoughts and letters, written in alternate prose and verse. The variety of its contents includes the most practical advice on daily conduct, the most sublime descriptions of high mystical experience. Mechthild was an artist, who was evidently familiar with the literary tradition and most of the literary expedients of her time. She uses many of them in the attempt to impartto others that vision of Life, Light and Love which she knew. I take, as an example of her genius, and a last specimen of the mystic's creative art, the celebrated letter addressed to a fellow-pilgrim on that spiritual "Love-path" which she trod herself with so great a fortitude. It represents not only the rich variety of Mechthild's literary resources, but also those several forms of artistic expression which the great mystics have employed. Here, concrete representation is perpetually reinforced by oblique suggestion; the imagery of the poet is double-edged, evoking moods as well as ideas. We observe that it opens with a spiritual love-scene, closely related in style to the secular and romantic literature of Mechthild's time; that this develops to a dramatic dialogue between soul and senses -- another common artifice of the mediaeval author -- and this again leads by a perfectly natural transition to the soul's great acclamation of its destiny, and the crowning announcement of the union of lover and beloved.

The movement of this mystical romance, then, like the movement of ascending consciousness, goes from the concrete image to the mysterious and sidelong apprehension of imageless facts. First we have picture, then dialectic, then intuitive certitude. Here, too, we find both those aspects of experience which dominate mystical literature : the personal and intimate encounter of love, and the self-loss of the soul in an utterly transcendent Absolute. Surely the union of these "completing opposites" in one work of art must rank as a great imaginative achievement.

Mechthild tells her story of the soul's adventure in snatches of freely-rhymed verse, linked together by prose narrative passages -- a form which is not uncommon in the secular literature of the Middle Ages.[1] We are further reminded of that secular literature by the imagery which she employs.

[1] For the verse-translations in the following extracts I am indebted to the great skill and kindness of Mrs. Theodore Beck, who, possessing a special talent for this difficult art, has most generously made for me these versions of Mechthild's poetry.The soul is described as a maiden, the Divine Lover is a fair youth whom she desires. The very setting of the story is just such a fairy landscape as we find in the lays and romances of chivalry; it has something of the spring-like charm that we feel in Aucassin and Nicolette -- the dewy morning, the bird- haunted forest, the song and dance. It is, in fact, a love story of the period adapted with extraordinary boldness to the purposes of mystical experience.

When the virgin soul, says Mechthild at the opening of her tale, has endured all the trials of mystical purification, she is very weary, and cries to her Love, saying, "Oh, beautiful youth! I long for thee. Where shall I find thee? "Then the Divine Youth answers :

"A gentle voice I hear,
Something of love sounds there :
I have wooed her long and long,
Yet not till now have I heard that song.
It moveth me so,
Towards her I must go.
She is the soul who with pain is torn,
And love, that is one with the pain.
In the early dew of the morn,
In the hidden depths, which are far below,
The life of the soul is born."

Then her vassals, which are the five senses, say to the soul, "Lady, adorn thyself."

"We have heard the whisper clear;
The Prince is coming towards thee here,
In the morning dew, in the bird's song.
Ah, fair Bride, tarry not long! "

So the soul adorns herself with the virtues, and goes out into the forest: and the forest, says Mechthild, is the company of the saints. Sweet nightingales sing there night and day of true union with God, and there in the thicket are heard the voices of the birds of holy wisdom. But the youth himself comes not to her. He sends messengers to the intent that she may dance : one by one he sends her the faith of Abraham, the aspirations of the Prophets, the pure humility of ourLady Saint Mary, all the virtues of Christ, and all the sanctity of His elect; and thus there is prepared a most noble dance. And then comes the youth and says to the soul, "Maiden, as gladly shouldst thou have danced, as mine elect have danced."But she replies:

"Unless thou lead me, Lord, I cannot dance;
Would'st thou have me leap and spring,
Thou thyself, dear Lord, must sing,
So shall I spring into thy love,
From thy love to understanding,
From understanding to delight.
Then, soaring human thought far, far above,
There circling will I dwell, and taste encircling love."

So sings the Bride; and so the youth must sing, that she may dance. Then says he:
"Maiden, thy dance of praise was well performed. Now thou shalt have thy will of the Virgin's Son, for thou art weary. Come at midday to the shady fountain, to the resting-place of love: and with him thou shalt find refreshment."
And the maiden replies:

"Oh Lord, it is too high, too great,
That she should be thy chosen mate,
Within whose heart no love can be
Till she is quickened, Lord, by thee."

By this romantic, story-telling method Mechthild has appealed to the fancy and emotion of the reader, and has enticed him into the heart of the spiritual situation. Next, she passes to her intellectual appeal; the argument between the soul and the senses. From this she proceeds, by a transition which seems to be free and natural, yet is the outcome of consummate art, to the supreme declarations of the deified spirit "at home with the Lord," as St. Paul said.

The dialogue moves by the process of reduction to a demonstration of God as the only satisfaction of the questing soul which has surrendered to the incantations of Reality. One after another, substitutes for the First and Only Fair areoffered and rejected. The soul says to the senses, which are her vassals: "Now I am for a while weary of the dance. Give place! for I would go where I may refresh myself." Then say the senses to the soul: "Lady, wilt thou refresh thyself in the tears of love of St. Mary Magdalene? This may well satisfy thee? "But the soul says: "Hush, sirs, you know not what I mean! Let me be, for I would drink a little of the unmingled wine."
Then say the senses:

"Oh Bride, in virgin chastity,
Is the Love of God made ready for thee."

And the soul says:

"Even so; yet though high and pure it be,
That path is not the highest for me."

And the senses:

"In the blood of the martyred saints
May'st thou refresh thy soul that faints."

And the soul:

"I have been martyred so many a day,
I cannot now tread in that way."

And the senses:

"By the wise Confessors' side,
The pure in heart love to abide."

And the soul:

"And their counsel will I obey,
Both when I go and when I stay;
And yet I cannot walk their way."

And the senses:

"In the Apostles' wisdom pure,
May'st thou find a refuge sure."

And the soul:

"I have their wisdom here in my heart,
And with it I choose the better part."And the senses
"O Bride, the angels are fair and bright,
Full of God's love, full of God's light;
Would'st thou refresh thee, mount to their height."

And the soul:

"The angel's joy is but heartache to me,
If their Lord and my Bridegroom I do not see."

And the senses:

"In holy penance refresh thee and save,
That God to St. John Baptist gave."

And the soul:

"I am ready for pain, ready for grief,
Yet the combat of love is first and chief."

And the senses:

"O Bride, would'st thou refreshed be,
So bend thee to the Virgin's knee,
To the little Babe, and taste and see
The milk of joy from the Maid's breast,
That the angels drink, in unearthly rest."

And the soul:

"It is but a childish love indeed,
Babes to cradle, babes to feed;
I am a fair, a full-grown bride,
I must haste to my Lover's side."

And the senses:

"O bride, if thou goest thou shalt find,
That we are utterly dazzled and blind.
Such fiery heat in God doth dwell --
Thou thyself knowest it well
That all the flame and all the glow
Which in Heaven above and the Saints below
Burneth and shineth -- all doth flow
From God Himself. His divine breath
Sighed by the Spirit's wisdom and power,
Through His human lips, born to death,
-- Who may abide it, e'en for an hour?"

And the soul says:

> *"The fish in the water cannot drown,*
> *The bird in the air cannot sink down,*
> *Gold in the fire cannot decay,*
> *But shineth fairer and clearer alway.*
> *To all creatures God doth give,*
> *After their own natures to live.*
> *How can I bind my nature's wings?*
> *I must haste to my God before all things.*
> *My God, by His nature my Father above,*
> *My Brother in His humanity,*
> *My Bridegroom in His ardent love,*
> *And I His from Eternity.*
> *Think ye, that Fire must utterly slay my soul?*
> *Nay -- fierce He can scorch -- then tenderly cool and console.*

"And so did the utterly loved go in to the utterly lovely; into the secret chamber of the Pure Divinity. And there she found the resting place of love, and the home of love, and the Divine Humanity that awaited her."

And the soul said:

> *"Lord, God, I am now a naked soul*
> *And Thou art arrayed all gloriously:*
> *We are Two in One, we have reached the goal,*
> *Immortal rapture that cannot die.*
> *Now, a blessed silence doth o'er us flow,*
> *Both wills together would have it so.*
> *He is given to her, she is given to Him,*
> *What now shall befall her, the soul doth know --*
> *And therefore am I consoled."*

This is the end of all mysticism. It is the term to which all the artistic efforts of the mystics have striven to lead the hearts of other men.

The Education of the Spirit

THE old mystics were fond of saying that "Man is a made trinity, like to the unmade Blessed Trinity." That particular form of words comes to us from Julian of Norwich; but it form of words comes to us from Julian of Norwich; but it expresses a thought which we often meet in the spiritual writers of the Middle Ages. Further, these writers were disposed to find in man's nature a reflection of the three special characters which theology attributes to the Christian Godhead. They thought that the power of the Father had Godhead. They thought that the power of the Father had its image in the physical nature of man: the wisdom of the Son in his reason: the creative vigour of the Holy Spirit in his soul. Some taught also that each of these three aspects of humanity corresponded with one aspect of the triune reality of the universe: the physical world of nature, the mental world of idea, the ultimate world of spirit. The sceptic of course would express this differently, and see in it but one more illustration of the fact that man always makes God in his own image. But without scepticism I think we may explain it thus: that those who have pondered most deeply on the Divine Nature have most easily found in its richness, and have best understood, just those attributes which are most clearly marked in human nature. Man has inevitably been for them a key to God.

These speculations seem at first sight to have little bearing upon the problems of education. But they are in reality intimately connected with it: for their consideration leads us back to the central fact out of which they have arisen -- namely, the abiding truth that man's deepest exploration of his own nature gives again and again this threefold result, that he feels that his real self-hood and real possibilities are not wholly exhausted by the terms "body " and "mind." He knows in his best moments another vivid aspect of his being, as strong as these, though often kept below the threshold of his consciousness: the spirit, which informs, yet is distinct from both his body and his mind.

Now the question which all serious educationalists are called upon to ask themselves is this: To what extent does that three-fold analysis of human personality influence our educational schemes? The object of education is to bring out the best and highest powers of the thing educated. Do we, in our education, even attempt to bring out the best and highest powers of the spirit, as we seek to develop those of the body and the mind?

The child as he comes to us is a bundle of physical, mental, and spiritual possibilities. He is related to three distinct yet interpenetrating worlds; all accessible to him, since he is human, and all offering endless opportunities of adventure to him.

> *" Heaven lies about us in our infancy,*
> *Shades of the prison-house begin to close*
> *About the growing boy. "*

Why should they close; whose fault is it that they do? Does not the fault lie with the poor and grovelling outlook of those to whom this sensitive, plastic thing is confided? Who so badly select and manipulate the bundle of possibilities offered to them, that they often contrive to manufacture a creature ruled by its own physical needs and appetites, its mental and emotional limitations; instead of a free, immortal being, master of its own body and mind. Here is this child, the germ of the future. To a great extent, we can control the way that germ develops; the special characters of the past which it shall transmit. We can have a hand in the shaping of the history that is to be when we have gone: for who candoubt that the controlling factor of history is the physical, mental, or spiritual character of those races that dominate the world? It is in the interplay, tension, and strife of these three universes that history in the last resort consists.

Now, on the eve of a new era, is it not worth while to remind ourselves of this terrific fact? To see whether our plans are so laid as to bring out all the balanced possibilities of the coming man; all his latent powers? We recognize the fact that body and mind must be trained whilst still in a plastic state. We are awake to the results of allowing them to atrophy. Where we find individuals with special powers in one of these directions, we aim at their perfect development; at the production of the athlete, scholar, man of action. But it cannot be said that we are equally on the look-out for special qualities of spirit; that when found, we train them with the same skill and care. Yet if we do not, can we expect to get the very best out of the race? To explore all its potentialities; some, perhaps, still unguessed? We know that the child's reactions to life will be determined by the mental furniture with which he is equipped. His perceptions, his choice from among the welter of possible impressions surrounding him, will depend on the character of his "apperceiving mass." Surely then it is our first duty so to equip him that he shall be able to lay hold on those intimations of spirit which are woven into the texture of our sensual universe: to lead him into that mood of receptivity in which the beautiful and the significant, the good and the true, stand out for him from the scene of life and hold his interest. A meadow which to one boy is merely a possible cricket field, to another is a place of romance and adventure, full of friendly life.

The mischief is that whatever our theoretic beliefs, we do not in practice really regard spirit as the chief element of our being; the chief object of our educational care. Our notions about it are shadowy, and have very little influence on our educational schemes. Were it present to us as a vivid reality, we shouldsurely provide our young people with a reasoned philosophy of life in which it is given its place: something which can provide honest answers to the questions of the awakening intelligence, and withstand the hostile criticism which wrecks so much adolescent faith. For ten parents who study the Montessori system of sense training, how many think of consulting those old specialists who taught how the powers of the spirit may be developed and disciplined, and given their true place in human life? How many educationalists realize that prayer, as taught to children, may and should be an exercise which gently develops a whole side of human consciousness that might otherwise be dormant; places it in communication with a real and valid universe awaiting the apprehension of man? How many give the subject the same close, skilled attention that they give, say, to Latin grammar on one hand or physical culture on the other? Those subjects, and many more, have emerged from vagueness into clarity because attention, the cutting point of the human will, has been concentrated upon them. Gradually in these departments an ordered world has been made, and the child or young person put in correspondence with that world. We cannot say that the same has been done for the world of spirit. The majority of the "well-educated" probably pass through life without any knowledge of the science of prayer, with at best the vaguest notions of the hygiene of the soul. Often our religious teachers are themselves no better instructed, and seem unable to offer the growing and hungry spirit any food more heavenly than practical ethics and dogmatic beliefs. Thus a complete world of experience is habitually ignored by us, and one great power of the human trinity allowed to atrophy.

We are just beginning as educators to pay ordered attention to that fringe-world in which sense, intellect, and spirit all have a part: I mean the world of aesthetic apprehension. It cannot be denied that the result has been, for many of theyoung people now growing up, an immense enlargement and enrichment of life. Look at one of the most striking intellectual characteristics of the last few years: the rapid growth of the taste and need for poetry, the amount of it that is written, the way in which it seems to supply a necessary outlet for young Englishmen in the present day. Look at the mass of verse which was composed, under conditions of utmost horror, on the battlefields; poetry the most pathetic in the world, in which we see the passionate effort of spirit to find adjustment, its assertion of unconquerable power, even in the teeth of this overwhelming manifestation of brute force. There is the power of the future: the spirit of beauty and truth seeking for utterance. There is that quickening spring, bubbling up afresh in every generation; and ready, if we will help it to find expression, to transfigure our human life.

There is a common idea that the spiritual life means something pious and mawkish: not very desirable in girls, and most objectionable in boys. It is strange that this notion, which both the Jewish and Christian Scriptures so emphatically contradict, should ever have grown up amongst us. The spirit, says St. Paul, is not a spirit of fearfulness; it is "a spirit of Power and Love and Discipline" -- qualities that make for vigour and manliness of the best type. It is the very source of our energies, both natural and supernatural. The mystics sometimes called it our "life-giving life," and modern psychologists are beginning to discover that it is, in the most literal sense, our "health's eternal spring." People say, "Come, Holy Spirit"; as if it were something foreign to us: yet it comes perpetually in every baby born into the world, for each new human life entering the temporal order implies a new influx or, least, a new manifestation of spirit. But, when spirit is thus wedded to mind and body to form human nature, it is submitted to the law governing human nature: the law of freedom. It is ours, to developor stunt as we please. Its mighty powers are not pressed on an unwilling race, but given us in germ to deal with as we will. Parents are responsible for giving it every opportunity of development, the food, the light, the nurture that all growing things require -- in fact, for its education: a great honour, and a great responsibility.

If we are asked wherein such education should consist, I think we must reply that its demands are not satisfied by teaching the child any series of religious doctrines divorced from practical experience. He is full of energies demanding expression. Our object is so to train those energies that they shall attain their full power and right balance; and enable him to set up relations with the spiritual world in which he truly lives. The first phase in this education will consist in a definite moral training, which is like the tilling and preparation of the earth in which the spiritual plant is to grow: and as regarding the special objects of this training I will take the definition of a great spiritual writer, a definition remarkable for its sanity and moderation: " If we would discover and know that Kingdom of God which is hidden in us, we must lead a life that is virtuous within, well ordered without, and fulfilled with true charity." What does that imply? It implies the cultivation of self-control, order, and disinterestedness. Order is a quality which all spiritual writers hold in great esteem; for they are far from being the ecstatic, unbalanced, and mood-ridden creatures of popular fancy. Now the untrained child has all the disorderly ways, the uncontrolled and self-interested instincts of the primitive man. He is a vigorous young animal, reacting promptly and completely to the stimulus of fear or of greed. The history of human society, the gradual exchange of license for law, self-interest for group-interest, spasmodic activity for orderly diligence must be repeated in him if he is to take his place in that human society. But if we would also prepare in him the way of spirit, the aim of this training must be something higher than that convenient social morality, that spirit of fair play, truth, justice, mutual tolerance, which public school discipline seeks to develop. That morality is relative and utilitarian. The morality in which alone the life of the spirit can flourish is absolute and ideal. It is sought, not because it makes life secure, or promotes the greatest happiness of the greatest number, but for its own sake. Yet in spite of this, the social order, in the form in which the child comes in contact with it, may be made one of the best instruments for producing those characters demanded by the spiritual life. For what, after all, is the exchanging of self-interest for group-interests but the beginning of love? And what is at the root of the spirit of give and take but humility? See how the approaches to the spiritual kingdom are found in the midst of the common life: what easy opportunity we have of initiating our children into these central virtues of the soul. The spiritual writers tell us that from love and humility all other virtues come; that on the moral side nothing else is required of us. And we, if we train wisely, may lead the young into them so gently and yet so deeply that their instinctive attitude to existence will be that of humbleness and love; and they will be spared the conflict and difficult reformation of those who wake to spiritual realities in later life.

Now humbleness and love, as understood by spiritual persons, are not passive virtues: they are energetic, and show themselves in mind, will, and heart. In the mind, by a constant desirous tendency to, and seeking after, that which is best; in the will by keenness, or, as the mystics would say, by diligence and zeal; in the heart, by an easy suppleness of relation with our fellow men -- patience, good temper, sympathy, generosity. Plainly the moral character which makes for spirituality is a moral character which also makes for happiness. Suppose, then, that our moral training has been directed towards this eager, supple state of humbleness and love: what special results may we expect as thepersonality develops? Spiritual writers tell us to expect certain qualities, which are traditionally called the "seven gifts of the spirit"; and if we study the special nature of these gifts, we see that they are the names of linked characters or powers, which together work an enhancement and clarification of the whole personality -- a tuning-up of human nature to fresh levels, a sublimation of its primitive instincts. The first pair of qualities which are to mark our spiritual humanity are called Godliness and Fear. By these are meant that solemn sense of direct relationship with an eternal order, that gravity and awe, which we ought to feel in the presence of the mysteries of the universe; the fear of the Lord, which is the beginning of wisdom. From these grow the gifts called Knowledge, that is, the power of discerning true from false values, of choosing a good path through the tangled world, and Strength, the steady central control of the diverse forces of the self: perhaps the gift most needed by our distracted generation. "Through the gift of spiritual strength," says Ruysbroeck, "a man transcends all creaturely things and possesses himself, powerful and free." This is surely a power which we should desire for the children of the future, and get for them if we can.

We see that the first four gifts of the spirit will govern the adjustment of man to his earthly life: that they will immensely increase the value of his personality in the social order, will clarify his mind and judgment, confer nobility on his aims. The last three gifts -- those called Counsel, Understanding and Wisdom -- will govern his intercourse with the spiritual order. By Counsel, the spiritual writers mean that inward voice which, as the soul matures, urges us to leave the transitory and seek the eternal: and this not as an act of duty, but as an act of love. When that voice is obeyed, the result is a new spiritual Understanding; which, says Ruysbroeck again, may be "likened to the sunshine, which fills the air with a simple brightness, and lights all forms and shows the dis-tinctions of all colours. "Even so does this spiritual gift irradiate the whole world with a new splendour, and shows us secrets that we never guessed before. Poets know flashes of it, and from it their power proceeds; for it enables its possessor to behold life truly, that is from the angle of God, not from the angle of man.

"Such an one," says Ruysbroeck, "walks in heaven, and beholds and apprehends the height, the length, the depth, and the breadth, the wisdom and truth, the bounty and unspeakable generosity, which are in God our Lover without number and without limit; for all this is Himself. Then that enlightened man looks down, and beholds himself and all other men and all creatures; and this gift, through the knowledge of truth which is given us in its light, establishes in us a wide-stretching love towards all in common."

" A wide-stretching love towards all in common." When we think of this as the ruling character of our future citizens, and so the ruling character of our future world, we begin to see that the education of the spirit may represent a political no less than a transcendental ideal. It alone can bring about that regeneration, working from the heart outwards, of which the prophets of every country have dreamed.

It seems hard to conceive anything beyond this. But there is something. To behold things as they are is not the end: beyond this is that Wisdom which comes not with observation, but is the fruit of intimate communion with Reality. Understanding is perception raised to its highest expression: Wisdom is intuition raised to its highest expression, and directed towards an absolute objective. It is, so far as we know here, the crown and goal of human development; the perfect fruition of love.

We have considered very shortly the chief possibilities of the human spirit, as they are described by those who have looked most deeply into its secrets. These seers tell us further that this spirit has its definite course to run, its definite con-summation: that it emerges within the physical order, grows, spreads, and at last enters into perfect union or communion with the real and spiritual world. How much attention do we pay to this statement, which, if true, is the transcendent fact of human history, the key to the nature of man? How much real influence does it have on our hopes and plans for our children? The so-called phenomenon of conversion -- the fact that so far nearly all the highest and best examples of the spiritual life have been twice-born types, that they have had to pass through a terrible crisis, in which their natural lives were thrown into confusion in order that their spiritual lives might emerge -- all this is really a confession of failure on the part of human nature: a proof that the plastic creature has been allowed to harden in the wrong shape. If our growth were rightly directed, the spirit would emerge and flower in all its strength and loveliness, as the physical and mental powers of normal children emerge and flower. What is wrong with education that it fails to achieve this? Partly, I think, that the values at which it aims are too often relative and self-interested; not absolute and disinterested. Its intelligent gaze is fixed too steadily on earthly society, earthly happiness. We encourage our young people to do the best things, but not always from the best motives. We forget the essential link between work and prayer: yet this alone lifts man from the position of a busy animal to that of the friend and helper of God. We forget that our duties ought to include the awakening of that clear consciousness of eternity which should be normal in every human being, and without which it is impossible for any man to grasp the true values and true proportion of life.

From the very beginning, then, we ought to raise the eyes of the young from the contemplation of the earth under their feet to that of the heavens above their heads: to give them absolute values, not utilitarian values, to aim at. There is nothing morbid or sickly in this: it is rather those who do not possess the broader consciousness who are the morbid, the sickly, and the maimed. The hope of the future is wide. We must train our children to a wide stretch of faith, of aim, of imagination, if they are to grasp it, and fully enter into the inheritance that awaits them.

How, then, should we begin this most delicate of all tasks; this education of the most sacred and subtle aspect of human nature? We must be careful; for difficulties and dangers crowd the path, cranks lie in wait at every corner. I have spoken of the moral preparation. That is always safe and sure. But there are two other safe ways of approach; the devotional and aesthetic. These two ways are not alternative, but complementary. Art, says Hegel, belongs to the highest sphere of spirit, and is to be placed in respect of its content on the same footing as religion and philosophy; and many others -- seers and philosophers -- have found in the revelation of beauty an authentic witness to God. But the love and realization of beauty, without reverence and devotion, soon degenerates into mere pleasure. So, too, devotion, unless informed with the spirit of beauty, becomes thin, hard and sterile. But where these two exist together, we find on one hand that the developed apprehension which discovers deep messages in nature, in music, in all the noble rhythms of art, makes the senses themselves into channels of Spirit: and this is an apprehension which we can foster and control. And on the other hand the devotional life, rightly understood as a vivid, joyful thing -- with that disciplining of the attention and will which is such an important part of it -- is the most direct way to an attainment of that simple and natural consciousness of our intangible spiritual environment which all ought to possess, and which the old mystics called by the beautiful name of the "practice of the Presence of God."

This linking up of the devotional life with the instinct for beauty and wonder, will check its concentration on the more sentimental and anthropomorphic aspects of religion; and so discourage that religious emotionalism which wise educationalists rightly condemn. Hence these two ways of approach, merged as they should be into one, can bring the self into that simple kind of contemplation which is a normal birthright of every soul, but of which our defective education deprives so many men and women; who cannot in later life quicken those faculties which have been left undeveloped in youth. As logic is a supreme exercise of the mind, so contemplation is a supreme exercise of the spirit: it represents the full activity of that intuitional faculty which is our medium of contact with absolute truth. Before the inevitable smile appears on the face of the reader, I say at once that I am not suggesting that we should teach young children contemplation; though I am sure that many brought up in a favouring atmosphere naturally practise it long before they know the meaning of the word. But I do suggest that we should bring them up in such a way that their developed spirits might in the end acquire this art, without any more sense of break with the normal than that which is felt by the developed mind when it acquires the art of logic.

The Essentials of Mysticism

'What is contemplation? It is attention to the things of the spirit: surely no outlandish or alarming practice, foreign to the general drift of human life. Were we true to our own beliefs, it should rather be our central and supremely natural activity; the way in which we turn to the spiritual world, and pick up the messages it sends to us. That world is always sending us messages of liberation, of hope, and of peace. Are we going to deprive our children of this unmeasured heritage, this extension of life -- perhaps the greatest of the rights of man -- or leave their enjoyment of it to some happy chance? We cannot read the wonderful records of the spiritually awakened without a sense of the duty that is laid on us, to develop if we can this spiritual consciousness in the generation that is to be.

All great spiritual literature is full of invitations to a new-ness of life, a great change of direction; which shall at last give our human faculties a worthy objective and redeem our consciousness from its present concentration upon unreal interests. It urges us perpetually, as a practical counsel, as something which is within human power and has already been achieved by the heroes of the race, to "put on the new man "; to "bring to birth the Son of God in the soul." But humanity as a whole has never responded to that invitation, and therefore its greatest possibilities are still latent. We, the guardians of the future, by furnishing to each emerging consciousness committed to our care such an apperceiving mass as shall enable it to discern the messages of reality, may do something to bring those possibilities into manifestation.

The Place of Will, Intellect and Feeling in Prayer

THE psychology of religious experience, as yet so little understood, has few more important problems proposed to it than that which concerns the true place and right use of will, intellect, and feeling in prayer. This question, which to some may appear merely academic, really involves the whole problem of the method and proportion in which the various powers and activities of our being may best be used, when they turn from the natural world of concrete things to attend to the so-called "supernatural" world of Spirit -- in fact, to God, Who is the source and sum of the reality of that world. That problem must be of practical interest to every Christian -- more, to every one who believes in the spiritual possibilities of man -- for it concerns itself with all those responses which are made by human personality to the impact of Infinite Life. It deals, in Maeterlinck's words, with " the harshest and most uninhabitable headlands of the Divine 'know thyself,'" and includes in its span the whole region "where the psychology of man mingles with the psychology of God."

In the first place, what do we mean by prayer? Surely just this: that part of our active and conscious life which is deliberately orientated towards, and exclusively responds to, spiritual reality. The Being of God, Who is that spiritual reality, we believe to be immanent in all things: "He is not far from each one of us: for in Him we live, and move, and have our being." In fact, as Christians we must believethis. Therefore in attending to those visible and concrete things, we are in a way attending to that immanent God; and in this sense all honest work is indeed, as the old proverb says, a sort of prayer. But when we speak of prayer as a separate act or activity of the self, we mean more than this. We mean, in fact, as a rule the other aspect of spiritual experience and communion; in the language of theology, attention to transcendent rather than to immanent Reality. Prayer, says Walter Hilton, in terms of which the origin goes back to the Neoplatonists, "is nothing else but an ascending or getting up of the desire of the heart into God, by withdrawing it from all earthly thoughts" -- an ascent, says Ruysbroeck, of the Ladder of Love. In the same spirit William Law defines it as "the rising of the soul out of the vanity of time into the riches of eternity." It entails, then, a going up or out from our ordinary circle of earthly interests; a cutting off, so far as we may, of the "torrent of use and wont," that we may attend to the changeless Reality which that flux too often hides. Prayer stretches out the tentacles of our consciousness not so much towards that Divine Life which is felt to be enshrined within the striving, changeful world of things; but rather to that "Eternal truth, true Love, and loved Eternity" wherein the world is felt to be enshrined; and in this act it brings to full circle the activities of the human soul -- that

> *"Swinging-wicket set between*
> *The Unseen and the Seen."*

The whole of man's life really consists in a series of balanced responses to this Transcendent-Immanent Reality; because man lives under two orders, is at once a citizen of Eternity and of Time. Like a pendulum, his consciousness moves perpetually -- or should move if it be healthy -- between God and his neighbour, between this world and that. The wholeness, sanity, and balance of his existence will entirely dependupon the perfection of his adjustment to this double situation; on the steady alternating beat of his outward swing of adoration, his homeward-turning swing of charity. Now, it is the outward swing which we are to consider: the powers that may be used in it, the best way in which these powers may be employed.

First, we observe that those three capacities or faculties which we have under consideration -- the thinking faculty, the feeling faculty, the willing or acting faculty -- practically cover all the ways in which the self can react to other selves and other things. From their combination come all the possibilities of self-expression which are open to man. In his natural life he needs and uses all of them. Shall he need and use all of them in his spiritual life too? Christians, I think, are bound to answer this question in the affirmative. According to Christianity, it is the whole self which is called to turn towards Divine Reality -- to enter the Kingdom -- not some supposed "spiritual" part thereof. "Thou hast made us for Thyself," said Augustine; not, as the Orphic initiate would have said, "Thou hast made one crumb out of our complex nature for Thyself, and the rest may go on to the rubbish heap." It is the whole man of intellect, of feeling, and of will, which finds its only true objective in the Christian God.

Surely, the real difference which marks out Christianity from all other religions lies just here; in this robust acceptance of humanity in its wholeness, and of life in its completeness, as something which is susceptible of the Divine. It demands, and deals with, the whole man, his Titanic energies and warring instincts; not, as did the antique mysteries, separating and cultivating some supposed transcendental principle in him, to the exclusion of all else. Christians believe in a God immanent and incarnate, Who transfuses the whole of the life which He has created, and calls that life in its wholeness to union with Him. If this be so, then Lex credendi, lex orandi; ourbelief should find its fullest expression in our prayer, and that prayer should take up, and turn towards the spiritual order all the powers of our mental, emotional, and volitional life. Prayer should be the highest exercise of these powers; for here they are directed to the only adequate object of thought, of love, and of desire. It should, as it were, lift us to the top of our condition, and represent the fullest flowering of our consciousness; for here we breathe the air of the supernal order, and attain according to our measure to that communion with Reality for which we were made.

Prayer so thought of will include, of course, many different kinds of spiritual work; and also -- what is too often forgotten -- the priceless gift of spiritual rest. It will include many kinds of intercourse with Reality -- adoration, petition, meditation, contemplation -- and all the shades and varieties of these which religious writers have named and classified. As in the natural order the living creature must feed and grow, must suffer and enjoy, must get energy from the external world and give it back again in creative acts, if he would live a whole and healthy life, so, too, in the spiritual order. All these things -- the giving and the receiving, the work and the rest -- should fall within the circle of prayer.

Now, when we do anything consciously and with purpose, the transition from inaction to action unfolds itself in a certain order. First we form a concept of that which we shall do; the idea of it looms up, dimly or distinctly, in the mind. Then, we feel that we want to do it, or must do it. Then we determine that we will do it. These phases may follow one another so swiftly that they seem to us to be fused into one; but when we analyze the process which lies behind each conscious act, we find that this is the normal sequence of development. First we think, then we feel, then we will. This little generalization must not be pressed too hard; but it is broadly true, and gives us a starting-point from which to trace out the way in which the three main powers of the self act in prayer. Itis practically important, as well as psychologically interesting, to know how they act or should act; as it is practically important to know, at least in outline, the normal operation of our bodily powers. Self-knowledge, said Richard of St. Victor, is the beginning of the spiritual life; and knowledge of one's self -- too often identified with knowledge of one's sins -- ought to include some slight acquaintance with the machinery we all have at our disposal. This machinery, as we see, falls into three divisions; and the perfection of the work which it does will depend upon the observing of an order in their operation, a due balance between them, without excessive development of one power at the expense of the others.

On the side of spiritual experience and activity, such an excessive and one-sided development often takes place. Where this exaggeration is in the direction of intellect, the theological or philosophical mood dominates all other aspects of religion. Where the purely emotional and instinctive side of the relation of the soul to God is released from the critical action of the intelligence, it often degenerates into an objectionable sentimentality, and may lead to forms of self-indulgence which are only superficially religious. Where the volitional element takes command, unchecked by humble love, an arrogant reliance upon our own powers, a restless determination to do certain hard things, to attain certain results -- a sort of supersensual ambition -- mars the harmony of the inner life. Any of these exaggerations must mean loss of balance, loss of wholeness; and their presence in the active life reflects back to their presence in the prayerful life, of which outward religion is but the visible sign. I think, therefore, that we ought to regard it as a part of our religious education to study the order in which our faculties should be employed when we turn towards our spiritual inheritance.

Prayer, as a rule -- save with those natural or highly trained contemplatives who live always in the prayerful state, tunedup to a perpetual consciousness of spiritual reality -- begins, or should begin, with something which we can only call an intellectual act; with thinking of what we arc going to do. In saying this, I am not expressing a merely personal opinion. All those great specialists of the spiritual life who have written on this subject are here in agreement. "When thou goest about to pray," says Walter Hilton, "first make and frame betwixt thee and God a full purpose and intention; then begin, and do as well as thou canst." "Prayer," says the writer of the Cloud of Unknowing, "may not goodly be gotten in beginners or proficients, without thinking coming before." All mediaeval writers on prayer take it as a matter of course that "meditation" comes before " orison"; and meditation is simply the art of thinking steadily and methodically about spiritual things. So, too, the most modern psychologists assure us that instinctive emotion does its best work when it acts in harmony with our reasoning powers.

St. Teresa, again, insists passionately on the primal need of thinking what we are doing when we begin to pray; on "recollecting the mind," calling in the scattered thoughts, and concentrating the intellect upon the business in hand. It is, in fact, obvious -- once we consider the matter in a practical light -- that we must form some conception of the supernal intercourse which we are going to attempt, and of the parties to it; though if our prayer be real, that conception will soon be transcended. The sword of the spirit is about to turn in a new direction; away from concrete actualities, towards eternal realities. This change -- the greatest of which our consciousness is capable -- must be realized as fully as possible by the self whose powers of will and love it will call into play. It seems necessary to insist on this point, because so much is said now, and no doubt rightly said, about the non-intellectual and supremely intuitional nature of the spiritual life; with the result that some people begin to think it their duty to cultivate a kind of pious imbecility. There is a notion in theair that when man turns to God he ought to leave his brains behind him. True, they will soon be left behind of necessity if man goes far on the road towards that Reality which is above all reason and all knowledge; for spirit in the swiftness of its flight to God quickly overpasses these imperfect instruments. But those whose feet are still firmly planted upon earth gain nothing by anticipating this moment; they will not attain to spiritual intuition by the mere annihilation of their intelligence. We cannot hope to imitate the crystalline simplicity of the saints; a simplicity which is the result, not of any deliberate neglect of reason, but of clearest vision, of intensest trust, of most ardent love -- that is, of Faith, Hope, and Charity in their most perfect expression, fused together to form a single state of enormous activity. But this is no reason why we should put imbecility, deliberate vagueness, or a silly want of logic in the place of their exquisite simpleness; any more than we should dare to put an unctuous familiarity in the place of their wonderful intimacy, or a cringing demeanour in the place of their matchless humility.

In saying this -- in insisting that the reason has a well-marked and necessary place in the mechanism of the soul's approach to God -- I am not advocating a religious intellectualism. It is true that our perception of all things, even the most divine, is conditioned by the previous content of our minds: the "apperceiving mass." Hence, the more worthy our thoughts about God, the more worthy our apprehensions of Him are likely to be. Yet I know that there is in the most apparently foolish prayer of feeling something warmly human, and therefore effective; something which in its value for life far transcends the consecrated sawdust offered up by devout intellectualism. "By love," said the old mystic, "He may be gotten and holden; by thought never." A whole world of experience separates the simple little church mouse saying her rosary, perhaps without much intelligence, yet with a humble and a loving faith, from the bishop whopreferred "Oh, Great First Cause" to "Our Father," because he thought that it was more in accordance with scientific truth; and few of us will feel much doubt as to the side on which the advantage lies. The advantage must always lie with those "full true sisters," humility and love; for these are the essential elements of all successful prayer. But surely it is a mistake to suppose that these qualities cannot exist side by side with an active and disciplined intelligence?

Prayer, then, begins by an intellectual adjustment. By thinking of God, or of Spiritual Reality, earnestly and humbly, and to the exclusion of other objects of thought; by deliberately surrendering the mind to spiritual things; by preparing the consciousness for the impact of a new order, the inflow of new life. But, having thought of God, the self, if it stop there, is no more in touch with Him than it was before. It may think as long as it likes, but nothing happens; thought unhelped by feeling ever remains exterior to its object. We are brought up short against the fact that the intellect is an essentially static thing: we cannot think our way along the royal road which leads to heaven.

Yet it is a commonplace of spiritual knowledge that, if the state of prayer be established, something does happen; consciousness does somehow travel along that road, the field of perception is shifted, new contacts are made. How is this done? A distinguished religious psychologist has answered, that it is done "by the synthesis of love and will" -- that is to say, by the craving in action which conditions all our essential deeds -- and I know no better answer to suggest.

Where the office of thought ends, there the office of will and feeling begins: "Where intellect must stay without," says Ruysbroeck, "these may enter in." Desire and intention are the most dynamic of our faculties; they do work. They are the true explorers of the Infinite, the instruments of our ascents to God. Reason comes to the foot of the mountain; it is the industrious will urged by the passionate heart whichclimbs the slope. It is the "blind intent stretching towards Him," says the Cloud of Unknowing, "the true lovely will of the heart," which succeeds at last; the tense determination, the effort, the hard work, the definite, eager, humble, outward thrust of the whole personality towards a Reality which is felt rather than known. "We are nothing else but wills," said St. Augustine. "The will," said William Law, "maketh the beginning, the middle, and the end of everything. It is the only workman in nature, and everything is its work." Experience endorses this emphasis on will and desire as the central facts of our personality, the part of us which is supremely our own. In turning that will and desire towards Spiritual Reality, we are doing all that we can of ourselves; are selecting one out of the sheaf-like tendencies of our complex nature, and deliberately concentrating upon it our passion and our power. Also, we are giving consciously, whole-heartedly, with intention, that with which we are free to deal; and self-donation is, we know, an essential part of prayer, as of all true intercourse.

Now, intellect and feeling are not wholly ours to give. A rich mental or emotional life is not possessed of all men; some are naturally stupid, some temperamentally cold. Even those who are greatly endowed with the powers of understanding or of love have not got these powers entirely under their own control. Both feeling and intellect often insist on taking their own line with us. Moreover, they fluctuate from day to day, from hour to hour; they arc dependent on many delicate adjustments. Sometimes we are mentally dull, sometimes we are emotionally flat: and this happens more often, perhaps, in regard to spiritual than in regard to merely human affairs. On such occasions it is notoriously useless to try to beat ourselves up to a froth: to make our-selves think more deeply or make ourselves care more intensely. Did the worth of man's prayerful life depend on the maintenance of a constant high level of feeling or understanding, hewere in a parlous case. But, though these often seem to fail him -- and with them all the joy of spiritual intercourse fails him too -- the regnant will remains. Even when his heart is cold and his mind is dim, the "blind intent stretching to God" is still possible to him. "Our wills are ours, to make them Thine."

The Kingdom of Heaven, says the Gospel, is taken by violence -- that is, by effort, by unfaltering courage -- not by cleverness, nor by ecstatic spiritual feelings. The freedom of the City of God is never earned by a mere limp acquiescence in those great currents of the transcendent order which bear life towards its home. The determined fixing of the will upon Spiritual Reality, and pressing towards that Reality steadily and without deflection; this is the very centre of the art of prayer. This is why those splendid psychologists, the mediaeval writers on prayer, told their pupils to "mean only God," and not to trouble about anything else; since "He who has Him has all." The most theological of thoughts soon becomes inadequate; the most spiritual of emotions is only a fair-weather breeze. Let the ship take advantage of it by all means, but not rely on it. She must be prepared to beat to windward if she would reach her goal. [EU was a competent sailor from her childhood. DCW]

In proportion to the strength and sincerity of the will, in fact, so shall be the measure of success in prayer. As the self pushes out towards Reality, so does Reality rush in on it. "Grace and the will," says one of the greatest of living writers on religion, "rise and fall together." "Grace" is, of course, the theological term for that inflow of spiritual vitality which is the response made by the divine order to the human motions of adoration, supplication, and love; and according to the energy and intensity with which our efforts are made -- the degree in which we concentrate our attention upon this high and difficult business of prayer -- will be the amount of new life that we receive. The efficacy of prayer, therefore, will be conditioned by the will of the praying self. "Thoughit be so, that prayer be not the cause of grace," says Hilton, "nevertheless it is a way or means by which grace freely given comes into the soul." Grace presses in upon life perpetually, and awaits our voluntary appropriation of it. It is accessible to sincere and loyal endeavour, to " the true lovely will of the heart," and to nothing else.

So much we have said of will. What place have we left for the operation of feeling in prayer? It is not easy to disentangle will and feeling; for in all intense will there is a strong element of emotion -- every volitional act has somewhere at the back of it a desire -- and in all great and energizing passions there is a pronounced volitional element. The "synthesis of love and will "is no mere fancy of the psychologist. It is a compound hard to break down in practice. But I think we can say generally that the business of feeling is to inflame the will, to give it intention, gladness, and vividness; to convert it from a dull determination into an eager, impassioned desire. It links up thought with action; effects, in psychological language, the movement of the prayerful self from a mere state of cognition to a state of conation; converts the soul from attention to the Transcendent to first-hand adventure within it. "All thy life now behoveth altogether to stand in desire," says the author of the Cloud of Unknowing to the disciple who has accepted the principle of prayer; and here he is declaring a psychological necessity rather than a religious platitude, for all successful action has its origin in emotion of some kind. Though we choose to imagine that "pure reason" directs our conduct, in the last resort we always do a thing because of the feeling that we have about it. Not necessarily because we like doing it; but because instinctive feeling of some sort -- selfish or unselfish, personal, social, conventional, sacrificial; the disturbing emotion called the sense of duty, or the glorious emotion called the passion of love -- is urging us to it. Instinctive emotions, more or less sublimated; Love, Hatred, Ambition, Fear, Anger, Hunger,Patriotism, Self-interest; these are the true names of our reasons for doing things.

If this be true of our reactions to the physical world, it is none the less true of our intercourse with the spiritual world. The will is moved to seek that intercourse by emotion, by feeling; never by a merely intellectual conviction. In the vigour and totality with which the heroes of religion give themselves to spiritual interests, and in the powers which they develop, we see the marks of instinctive feeling operating upon the highest levels. By "a leash of longing," says the Cloud of Unknowing again, man is led to be the servant of God; not by the faultless deductions of dialectic, but by the mysterious logic of the heart. He is moved most often, perhaps, by an innate unformulated craving for perfection, or by the complementary loathing of imperfection -- a love of God, or a hatred of self -- by the longing for peace, the miserable sensations of disillusion, of sin, and of unrest, the heart's deep conviction that it needs a changeless object for its love. Or, if by none of these, then by some other emotional stimulus.

A wide range of feeling states -- some, it is true, merely self-seeking, but others high and pure -- influence the prayerful consciousness; but those which are normal and healthy fall within two groups, one of subjective, the other of objective emotion. The dominant motive of the subjective group is the self's feeling of its own imperfection, helplessness, sinfulness, and need, over against the Perfect Reality towards which its prayer is set; a feeling which grows with the growth

of the soul's spiritual perceptions, and includes all the shaded emotions of penitence and of humility. "For meekness in itself is naught else but a true knowing and feeling of a man's self as he is." The objective group of feelings is complementary to this, and is centred on the goodness, beauty, and perfection of that Infinite Reality towards which the soul is stretching itself. Its dominant notes are adoration and love. Of these two fundamental emotions -- humility and love --the first lies at the back of all prayer of confession and petition, and is a necessary check upon the arrogant tendencies of the will. The second is the energizing cause of all adoration: adoration, the highest exercise of the spirit of man. Prayer, then, on its emotional side should begin in humble contrition and flower in loving adoration. Adoring love -- not mere emotional excitement, religious sentimentality or " spiritual feelings " -- but the strong, deep love, industrious, courageous and self-giving which fuses all the powers of the self into one single state of enormous intensity; this is the immortal element of prayer. Thought has done all that it may when it has set the scene, prepared the ground, adjusted the mind in the right direction. Will is wanted only whilst there are oppositions to be transcended, difficult things to be done. It represents the soul's effort and struggle to be where it ought to be. But there are levels of attainment in which the will does not seem to exist any more as a separate thing. It is caught in the mighty rhythms of the Divine will, merged in it and surrendered to it. Instead of its small personal activity, it forms a part of the great deep action of the Whole. In the higher degrees of prayer, in fact, will is transmuted into love. We are reminded of the old story of the phœnix: the active busy will seems to be burned up and utterly destroyed, but living love, strong and immortal, springs from the ashes and the flame. When the reasonable hope and the deliberate wilful faith in which man's prayer began are both fulfilled, this heavenly charity goes on to lose itself upon the heights.

Within the normal experience of the ordinary Christian, love should give two things to prayer; ardour and beauty. In his prayer, as it were, man swings a censer before the altar of the Universe. He may put into the thurible all his thoughts and dreams, all his will and energy. But unless the fire of love is communicated to that incense, nothing will happen; there will be no fragrance and no ascending smoke. These qualities -- ardour and beauty -- represent two distinct typesof feeling, which ought both to find a place in the complete spiritual life, balancing and completing one another. The first is in the highest degree intimate and personal; the second is disinterested and aesthetic.

The intimate and personal aspect of spiritual love has found supreme literary expression in the works of Richard of St. Victor, of St. Bernard, of Thomas a Kempis, of our own Richard Rolle, Hilton, and Julian of Norwich, and many others. We see it in our own day in its purest form in the living mystic who wrote The Golden Fountain. Those who discredit it as "mere religious emotionalism " do so because they utterly mistake its nature; regarding it, apparently, as the spiritual equivalent of the poorest and most foolish, rather than the noblest, most heroic, and least self-seeking, types of human love. "I find the lark the most wonderful of all birds," says the author of The Golden Fountain. "I cannot listen to his rhapsodies without being inspired (no matter what I may be in the midst of doing or saying) to throw up my own love to God. In the soaring insistence of his song and passion I find the only thing in Nature which so suggests the high soaring and rapturous flights of the soul. But I am glad that we surpass the lark in sustaining a far more lengthy and wonderful flight; and that we sing, not downwards to an earthly love, but upwards to a heavenly." Like real human love, this spiritual passion is poles asunder from every kind of sentimentality. It is profoundly creative, it is self-giving, it does not ask for anything in exchange. Although it is the source of the highest kind of joy -- though, as à Kempis says, the true lover "flies, runs, and rejoices; is free, and cannot be restrained" -- it has yet more kinship with suffering than with merely agreeable emotions. This is the feeling state, at once generous and desirous, which most of all enflames the will and makes it active; this it is which gives ardour and reality to man's prayers. " For love is born of God, and cannot rest save in God, above all created things."But there is another form of objective emotion besides this intimate and personal passion of love, which ought to play an important part in the life of prayer. I mean that exalted and essentially disinterested type of feeling which expresses itself in pure adoration, and is closely connected with the sense of the Beautiful. Surely this, since it represents the fullest expression of one power in our nature -- and that a power which is persistently stretched out in the direction of the Ideal -- should have a part in our communion with the spiritual, as well as with the natural world. The Beautiful, says Hegel, is the spiritual making itself known sensuously. It represents, then, a direct message to us from the heart of Reality; ministers to us of more abundant life. Therefore the widening of our horizon which takes place when we turn in prayer to a greater world than that which the senses reveal to us, should bring with it a more poignant vision of loveliness, a more eager passion for Beauty as well as for Goodness and Truth. When St. Augustine strove to express the intensity of his regret for wasted years, it was to his neglect of the Beauty of God that he went to show the poignancy of his feeling, the immensity of his loss. " Oh Beauty so old and so new! too late have I loved thee!"

It needs a special training, I think -- a special and deliberate use of our faculties -- if we are to avoid this deprivation; and learn, as an integral part of our communion with Reality, to lay hold of the loveliness of the First and Only Fair. " I was caught up to Thee by Thy beauty, but dragged back again by my own weight," says Augustine in another place; and the weight of the soul, he tells us, is its love -- the pull of a misplaced desire. All prayer which is primarily the expression of our wants rather than our worship, which places the demand for daily bread before instead of after the hallowing of the Ineffable Name, will have this dragging-back effect.

Now, as the artist's passion for sensuous beauty finds expression in his work, and urges him to create beauty as well ashe can, so too the soul's passion for spiritual beauty should find expression in its work; that is to say, in its prayer. A work of art, says Hegel again, is as much the work of the Spirit of God as is the beauty of Nature; but in art the Holy Spirit works through human consciousness. Therefore man's prayer ought to be as beautiful as he can make it; for thus it approaches more nearly to the mind of God. It should have dignity as well as intimacy, form as well as colour. More, all those little magic thoughts -- those delicate winged fancies, which seem like birds rejoicing in God's sight -- these, too, should have their place in it. We find many specimens of them, as it were stuffed and preserved under glass shades, in books of devotion. It is true that their charm and radiance cannot survive this process; the colour now seems crude, the sheen of the plumage is gone. But once these were the living, personal, spontaneous expressions of the love and faith -- the inborn poetry -- of those from whom they came. Many a liturgic prayer, which now seems to us impersonal and official -- foreign to us, perhaps, in its language and thought -- will show us, if we have but a little imaginative sympathy, the ardent mood, the exquisite tact, the unforced dignity, of the mind which first composed it; and form a standard by which we may measure our own efforts in this kind.

But the beauty which we seek to incorporate into our spiritual intercourse should not be the dead ceremonious beauty which comes of mere dependence on tradition. It should be the freely upspringing lyric beauty which is rooted in intense personal feeling; the living beauty of a living thing. Nor need we fear the reproach that here we confuse religion with poetry. Poetry ever goes like the royal banners before ascending life; therefore man may safely follow its leadership in his prayer, which is -- or should be -- life in its intensest form. Consider the lilies: those perfect examples of a measured, harmonious, natural and creative life, under a form of utmost loveliness. I cannot help thinking that it is theduty of all Christians to impart something of that flower-like beauty to their prayer; and only feeling of a special kind will do it -- that humble yet passionate love of the beautiful, which finds the perfect object of its adoration in God and something of His fairness in all created things. St. Francis had it strongly, and certain other of the mystics had it too. In one of his rapturous meditations, Suso, for whom faith and poetry were -- as they should be -- fused in one, calls the Eternal Wisdom a " sweet and beautiful wild flower." He recognized that flowery charm which makes the Gospels fragrant, and is included in that pattern which Christians are called to imitate if they can. Now, if this quality is to be manifested in human life, it must first be sought and actualized, consciously or unconsciously, in prayer; because it is in the pure, sharp air of the spiritual order that it lives. It must spring up from within outwards, must be the reflection of the soul's communion with "that Supreme Beauty which containeth in itself all goodness"; which was revealed to Angela of Foligno, but which "she could in no wise describe." The intellect may, and should, conceive of this Absolute Beauty as well as it can; the will may -- and must -- be set on the attaining of it. But only by intuitive feeling can man hope to know it, and only by love can he make it his own. The springs of the truest prayer and of the deepest poetry -- twin expressions of man's outward-going passion for that Eternity which is his home -- rise very near together in the heart.

The Mysticism of Plotinus

IN spite of his enormous importance for the history of Christian philosophy, Plotinus is still one of the least known and least understood among the great thinkers of the ancient world. The extreme difficulty of his style, which Porphyry well described as " dense with thought, and more lavish of ideas than words," together with the natural laziness of man, may perhaps account for this neglect. He was by choice a thinker, contemplative, and teacher, not a writer. Therefore the Enneads, which represent merely notes of lectures hastily and unwillingly written clown during the last fifteen years of his life, offer few inducements to hurried readers. The fact that he was a "mystic" has been held a further excuse for failure to understand the more cryptic passages of his works; though as a matter of fact these are the precipitations of a singularly clear and logical intellect, and will yield all their secrets to a sympathetic and industrious attention. His few translators have often been content to leave difficult phrases unelucidated, or surrounded by a haze of suggestive words; and though his splendid and poetic rhapsodies are quoted again and again, even those later mystics who are most indebted to him show few signs of first-hand study and comprehension of his system as a whole. Thanks to this same obscurity, and the richness, intricacy, and suggestive quality of his thought, most of his interpreters have tended to do for him that which he did for his master Plato: they have re-handled him in the interests of their own religion or philosophy. Of this, the Cambridge Platonists are the most notorious example; but the same inclination is seen in modernscholars. Thus Baron von Hügel seeks to introduce a dualism between his mysticism and his metaphysics. Even the brilliant exposition of his philosophy in the Dean of St. Paul's Gifford Lectures is not wholly exempt from this criticism. A comparison of his analysis with those of Baron von Hügel in Eternal Life, and of Mr. Whittaker in The Neoplalonists makes plain the part which temperament has played in each of these works.

Plotinus himself would probably have been astonished by this charge of obscurity. His teaching had by declaration two aims. The first was the definitely religious aim of bringing men to a knowledge of Divine reality; for he had the missionary ardour inseparable from the saintly type. The second was the faithful interpretation of Platonic philosophy, especially the doctrines of Plato, and of his own immediate master, the unknown Alexandrian Ammonius: for his academic teaching consisted wholly of a commentary on, and interpretation of, Plato's works. His system, therefore, is a synthesis of practical spirituality and formal philosophy, and will only be grasped by those who keep this twofold character in mind. There must always seem to be a conflict between any closed and self-consistent metaphysical system and the freedom and richness of the spiritual life: but since few metaphysicians are mystics, and few mystics are able to take metaphysics more seriously than the soldier takes the lectures of the armchair strategist, these two readings of reality are seldom brought into direct opposition. In Plotinus we have an almost unique example of the philosopher who is also a practical mystic; and consequently of a mind that cannot be satisfied with anything less than an intellectual system which finds room for the most profound experiences of the spiritual life. In this peculiarity some scholars have found his principal merit; others a source of weakness. The position of his critics has been excellently stated by Baron von Hugel in Eternal Life. He finds in the Enneads a "ceaseless conflict"between "the formal principles of the philosopher" and "the experiences of a profoundly religious soul." The philosophy issues in an utterly transcendent Godhead without qualities, activity, or being: the mysticism issues in ecstatic union, actual contact, with a God, "the atmosphere and home of souls" whose richness is the sum of all affirmations. Yet, as a matter of fact, this disharmony is only apparent; and is resolved when we understand the formal character of the Plotinian dialectic as a "way," a stepping-stone, the reduction to terms of reason of some aspects of a reality beyond reason's grasp. The discrepancy is like that which exists between map and landscape. Plotinus, constantly passing over from argument to vision, speaks sometimes the language of geography, sometimes that of adventure: yet both, within their spheres, are true. The Neoplatonic via negativa always implies an unexpressed because ineffable affirmation. Therefore its Absolute, of which reason can predicate no qualities, may yet be the "flower of all beauty" as apprehended by the contemplative soul.

Since the doctrine of Ammonius is unknown to us, we have no means of gauging the extent to which Plotinus depends on him: but probably we shall not be far wrong if we attribute to his influence the peculiar sense of reality, the deep spiritual inwardness, colour and life, with which his great pupil invests the dogmas of Platonism. The main elements of the Plotinian philosophy, however, are undoubtedly Platonic. The Divine Triad, the precession of spirit and its return to its origin, the unreal world of sense, the universal soul, the " real " or intelligible world of the Ideas -- these and other ingredients of his system are a part of the common stock of Platonism. His originality and his attraction consist in the use which he makes of them, the colour and atmosphere with which they are endowed. That which is truly his own is the living vision which creates from these formulae a vivid world both actual and poetic, answering with fresh revelations of reality the widening demands and apprehensions of the human soul. This spiritual world is not merely arrived at by a dialectic process. It is the world of his own intense experience from which he speaks to us; using his texts, as Christian mystics have often used the Bible, to support doctrines inspired by his personal vision of truth. In spite of his passion for exactitude, the sharpness and detail of his universe, he is thrown back, again and again, on the methods of symbol and poetry. We must always be ready to look past his formal words to the felt reality which he is struggling to impart; a reality which is beyond the grasp of reason, and can only be apprehended by the faculty which he calls spiritual intuition. To this we owe the richness and suppleness of his system, the absence of watertight compartments, the intimate relation with life. Whilst many philosophers have spent their powers on proving the necessary existence of an unglimpsed universe which shall satisfy the cravings of the mind, Plotinus spent his in making a map, based on his own adventures in "that country which is no mere vision, but a home;" and his apparently rigid contours and gradients are attempts to tell at least the characteristics of a living land.

Though the Enneads are a storehouse of profound and subtle thought, the main principles on which their philosophy is based are simple, and can be expressed briefly. All things, according to Plotinus, have come forth from the Absolute Godhead or One, and only fulfil their destiny when they return to their origin. The real life of the universe consists in this flux and reflux: the outflow and self-expression of spirit in matter, the "conversion" or return of spirit to the One. With the rest of the Neoplatonists, he conceives of the Universe as an emanation, eternally poured forth from this One, and diminishing in reality and splendour the further it is removed from its source. The general position is somewhat like that given by Dante in the opening of the Paradiso:

> *"La gloria di colui the tutto move*
> *Per l'universo penetra, e resplende*

In una parte pia, e meno altrove,"though Plotinus would have rejected the spatial implications of the last line, for to him the One was present everywhere. The Divine nature is a trinity; but not, as in Christian theology, of co-equal persons. Its three descending degrees, or hypostases, are the unconditioned One or the Good -- a term which implies perfection but carries no ethical implications -- the Divine Mind, Spirit, or Nous, and the Soul or Life of the World. Nothing is real which does not participate in one or other of these principles. Though the first two hypostases are roughly parallel to the Eternal Father and Logos-Christ of Christian Platonism, and some have found in the Plotinian Psyche a likeness to the immanent Holy Spirit, this superficial resemblance must not be pressed. Fatherhood cannot be ascribed to the One save in so far as it is the first cause of life, for it transcends all our notions of personality. Its real parallel in Christian theology is that conception of the "Superessential Godhead, beyond and above the Trinity of Persons," which Eckhart and a few other daring mystics took through Dionysius the Areopagite from the Neoplatonists. The One is, in fact, the Absolute as apprehended by a religious soul. Nor is the Plotinian Nous a person, in any sense in which orthodox Christianity has understood that term, though it is called by Plotinus our Father and Companion. Further, the triadic series does not involve a succession either in time, or order of generation; but only in value. The worlds of spirit and of soul are co-eternal with the Absolute, the inevitable and unceasing expressions of its creative activity. The utterly transcendent Perfect manifests as Mind or Spirit (Nous); and this is the world of being. Mind or Spirit manifests as Life or Soul (Psyche); and this is the reality of the world of becoming. The lower orders are contained in the higher, which are everywhere present, though each "remains in its own place." "Of all things the governance and existence are in these three." Whilst every image of the universe is deceptive, since itstrue nature is beyond our apprehension, Plotinus invites us to picture the Triad, as Dante did, by concentric circles through which radiate the energy and splendour of the "flower of all beauty," the Transcendent One." The first act is the act of the Good, at rest within itself, and the first existence is the self-contained existence of the Good. But there is also an act upon it, that of the Nous; which, as it were, lives about it. And the Soul, outside, circles about the Nous, and by gazing upon it, seeing into the depths of it, through it sees God" (I. 8. 2). Again, "The One is not a Being, but the Source of being, which is its first offspring. The One is perfect, that is, it has nothing, seeks nothing, needs nothing; but as we may say it overflows, and this overflowing is creative " (V. 1. 2). Yet this eternal creative action " beyond spirit, sense, and life," involves no self-loss. It is the welling forth of an unquenchable spring, the eternal fountain of life.

As Christian Platonists described the Son as the self-expression of the Father, so Plotinus describes his second Divine Principle as the eternal irradiation of the Absolute -- il ciel the piis della sua

Luce prende. This principle he calls Nous; a word carrying many shades of meaning, which the older commentators generally rendered as Divine Mind, or Intelligible Principle. Dean Inge has shown good reason for translating it as " Spirit," thus bringing the language of Plotinus into line with the many later mystics who derive from him. As a matter of fact, Nous contains both meanings. It is more spiritual than mind, more intellectual than spirit, in the sense in which that word is commonly employed. Those mediæval theologians who made a mystical identification between the Hebrew conception of the Eternal Wisdom as we find it described in Proverbs and Ecclesiasticus, and the Second Person of the Trinity, came very near the Plotinian concept of Nous, which is at once Intelligence and the intelligible sphere, Spirit and the spiritual universe; the home of reality, and object of religious and poetic intuition. It is,in one aspect, the "Father and Companion " of the soul (V. I. 3), in another "the Intellectual Universe, that sphere constituted by a Principle wholly unlike what is known as intelligence in us " (I. 8. 2). This is the " Yonder" to which he so often refers; the "middle heaven" of Indian philosophy, Ruysbroeck's "clear-shining world between ourselves and God.

> ". . . e questo cielo non ha altro dov
> Che la mente divina,"

says Dante; once more condensing the whole Neoplatonic vision in one vivid phrase.

This rich and suggestive conception of the Second Principle, as at once King and Creator of the world of life, and also itself the archetypal world of true values, is the central fact of the Plotinian philosophy. Its apprehension, he says, is beyond ordinary human reason, which is fitted for correspondence with the world of life or soul. It is the function of spiritual intuition; "a faculty which all possess, though few use." Such communion with the world of supernal reality is possible, because man is potentially an inhabitant of it. "The Fatherland to us is there, whence we have come: and there is the Father" (I. 6. 8). The "apex" or celestial aspect of our soul is domiciled there. It "never leaves the Divine Mind; but, while it clings yonder, allows the lower soul, as it were, to hang down" (VI. 7. 5). Man is, in fact, intermediary between the two Plotinian worlds of Spirit and Soul, and participates in both. Eucken, in describing him as the meeting-place of two orders of reality, is merely restating the doctrine of the Neoplatonists.

As Spirit is the outbirth and manifestation of the One, so Soul, or Life -- the third member of the Triad -- is the manifestation or matter of Spirit; and forms the link between the physical and the supersensual worlds. Spirit is "at once its Father and ever-present Companion" (V. 1. 3). Soul is a term covering the whole vital essence (a) of the world,and (b) of the individual. It has two aspects. The celestial soul aspires toward, and is in communion with, the spiritual order; the natural soul hangs down and inspires the physical order, thereby conferring on it a measure of reality. We are not, however, to understand by Soul merely the aggregate of individuals. Psyche is the divine and eternal life of the created universe, comprehending its infinite variety in a unity which embraces every object in the sense-known scheme, and makes it "like one animal" (IV. 4. 32). It is:

> "A motion and a spirit, that impels
> All thinking things, all objects of all thought,
> And rolls through all things."

The whole creation, says Plotinus, in one of his great poetic passages, is "awake and alive at every point." Each thing has its own peculiar life in the all; though we, because our senses cannot discern the life within wood and stone, deny that life. "Their living is in secret, but they live " (IV. 4. 36). Here we are reminded of the Logos-Christ of the "Sayings" -- "Raise the stone and thou shalt find me: cleave the wood, and there am I." By this conception, which is elaborated from the doctrine of the world-soul in the Timaeus, Neoplatonism bridges the gap between appearance and reality, and also solves the paradox of multitude in unity. "We do not declare the Soul to be one in the sense of entirely excluding multiplicity. This absolute oneness belongs only to the higher nature. We make it both one and manifold; it has part in the nature which is divided among bodies, but it has part also in the indivisible, and so again we find it to be one" (IV. 9. 2).

Soul, which has in its highest manifestations many of the characters of Spirit, is the eternal upholder of the world of change. "Things have a beginning, and perish when the soul that leads the chorus-dance of life departs; but the soul itself is eternal and cannot suffer change . . . what the soulis, and what its power, will be more manifestly, more splendidly evident, if we think how its counsel comprehends and conducts the heavens; how it communicates itself to all this vast bulk and ensouls it through all its extension, so that every fragment lives by the soul entire, which is present everywhere like the Father which begat it" (V. 1. 2). Soul, then, which is in one sense the reality of the world of becoming and immanent therein, is also a denizen of eternity, in virtue of its continuity with and direct dependence on Nous. An unbroken series of ascending values unites the world of living effort with the

One. It is this which makes the system of Plotinus a philosophy of infinite adventure and infinite hope.

Soul is the lowest of the Divine hypostases. Below it in the scale of values is the material universe to which its lower activities give form, slumbering in the rocks and dreaming in the plants. In plants, says Plotinus, "the more rebellious and self-willed phase of soul is expressed": a doctrine which will find an echo in many a gardener's heart. The sensible beauty of the world is the signature of soul, and points to something "Yonder"; for through loveliness it participates in the world of spiritual values, and we in apprehending beauty turn away from matter to Nous (I. 8. 4). Matter, as such, has no reality except as the stuff from which soul weaves up its outward vesture. Deprived of soul, it is in itself, he says, "not-being" and "no-thing": "its very nature is one long want " (I. 8. 5). As a picture is the crude and partial condensation of an artist's dream -- all that he can force his recalcitrant material to express -- so the physical world is but a fragmentary manifestation of the great and vivid universe of soul, and the body is the smallest part of the real man. When we grasp this, we see how great is the sum of possibilities opened to us by the Cosmos; how easily the country "Yonder" can find room for all the visions and intuitions of artists, poets, and saints.

The Plotinian doctrine of man, which became in due coursethe classical doctrine of Christian mysticism, is the logical outcome of this cosmology. Man, like the rest of Creation, has come forth from God and will only find happiness and full life when his true being is re-united, first with the Divine Mind, and ultimately with the One. "When the phantasm has returned to the Original, the journey is achieved" (VI. 9. II). Hence "our quest is of an End, and not of Ends. That only can be chosen which is ultimate and noblest, that which calls to the tenderest longings of the soul" (I. 4. 6). As the descending stages of reality are three, so the stages of the ascent are three. They are called in the Enneads purification, the work of reason, which marks the transference of interest from sense to soul; enlightenment -- the work of spiritual intuition -- which lifts life into communion with the eternal world of spirit; and ecstasy, that profound transfiguration of consciousness whereby the " spirit in love " achieves union with the One. These stages are familiar to all students of Christian asceticism, as the codified "mystic way" of purgation, illumination, and union: a formula which Dionysius the Areopagite took from the Neoplatonists. But it is important to remember that in Plotinus this "way" is not -- as it sometimes becomes in medieval writers -- a rigid series of mutually exclusive psychological states, separated by water-tight bulkheads. It is rather a diagram by which he seeks to describe one undivided movement of life; a prolonged effort and adventure, which has for its object a deeper and deeper penetration into Reality, the achievement of a true scale of values, in order that the real proportions of existence may be grasped. In this movement nothing is left behind; but everything is carried up into a higher synthesis, as the latent possibilities of humanity are gradually realized, and man grows up into eternal life.

"Since your soul is so exalted a power, so divine, be confident that in virtue of its possession you are close to God. Begin therefore with the help of this principle to make your way to Him. You have not far to go: there is not muchbetween. Lay hold of that which is more divine than this god-like thing; lay hold of that apex of the soul which borders on the Supreme (Nous), from which the soul immediately derives" (V. 1. 3).

All practical mysticism is at bottom a process of transcendence, "passing on the upward way all that is other than God" (I. 6. 7): and this process, in different temperaments, assumes different forms. Since Plotinus united in his own person the characteristics of the metaphysician, the poet and the saint, he tends to present it under three aspects; as the logical outcome of a reasoned philosophy, as a moral purification which strips us of all unreality, and as a progressive initiation into beauty. "Beholding this Being, the Conductor of all existence, the self-intent that ever gives and never takes, resting rapt in the vision and possession of so lofty a loveliness, what beauty can the soul then lack? For this, the beauty supreme, the absolute and the primal, fashions its lovers to beauty and makes them also worthy of love. And for this the sternest and uttermost combat is set before these souls; all our labour is for this, lest we be left without part in this noblest vision, which to attain is to be blessed in the blissful sight, which to fail of is to fail utterly " (I. 6. 7). In the high place which he gives to the category of beauty, which is to him one of the three final attributes of God, the strongly poetic character of his vision of Reality becomes evident. He anticipates Hegel in regarding natural beauty as the sensuous manifestation of spirit and signature of the world-soul "fragment as it were of the Primal Beauty, making beautiful to the fullness of their capacity whatsoever it grasps and moulds " (I. 6. 6): and those lovers, artists, and musicians who can apprehend it have already made the first step towards the inner vision of the One. Therefore the harsh other-worldliness which made some mediæval ascetics turn from visible loveliness as a snare, would have seemed blasphemy to Plotinus, who would certainly have argued with St. Augustine that "there is no healthin those who find fault with any part of Thy creation " (Conf. vii. 14). On the contrary, his doctrine gives a religious sanction and a philosophic explanation to those special experiences and apprehensions of artists, poets, and so-called "nature-mystics" -- known to many normal persons in moments of exaltation -- when

"The world is so charged with the grandeur of God
It must shine out, like shining from shook foil."

In such hours, he would say, we perceive through matter the inhabiting Psyche, and by it reach out to communion with Nous, for "this is how the material becomes beautiful; by participating in the thought which flows from the Divine" (I. 6. 2). He would have understood Blake's claim to see the universe as "a world of imagination and vision," and accepted Erigena's great saying, "every visible and invisible creature is a theophany or appearance of God."

Thus the whole mystic ascent can be conceived as a movement through visible beauty to its invisible source, and thence to "the inaccessible Beauty, dwelling as if in consecrated precincts apart from the common ways" (I. 6. 8). Yet this progress is not so much a change in our consciousness of the world and of ourselves, as a shifting of the centre of our being from sense to soul, from soul to spirit, whereby we come actually to live at new levels of existence. "For all there are two stages of the path, according to whether they are ascending or have already gained the upper sphere. The first stage is conversion from the lower life: the second -- taken by those who have already reached the Spiritual sphere, as it were set a footprint there, but must still advance within that realm -- lasts till they reach its extreme summit, the term attained when the topmost peak of the Spiritual realm is won" (I. 3. I).

The process is both intellectual and moral, since its goal is the absolute Truth and Beauty no less than the absoluteGood. "Each must become God-like and beautiful who cares to see God and Beauty" (I. 6. 9). It involves deliberate effort and drastic purification of mind and heart, "cutting away all that is excessive, straightening all that is crooked, bringing light to all that is in shadow, labouring to make all one glow of beauty" (I. 6. 9). As "all knowing comes by likeness" (I. 8. 1), we must ourselves have moral beauty if we would see the "Beauty There." But whether this way be conceived under aesthetic or ascetic symbols, Plotinus is at one with all the mystics in declaring that the driving force which urges the soul along the pathway to reality is love. This inspires its labour, supports its stern purifications, "detaches it from the body and lifts it to the Intelligible World" (III. 6. 5), and gives it at last "the only eye that sees the mighty Beauty" (I. 6. 9). Love means for him active desire; "the longing for conjunction and rest." All shades of spiritual and poetic passion, the graded meanings of admiration, enthusiasm, and worship, are included in it. It is "the true magic of the universe"; an attribute of Nous, and an earnest of real life. "The fullest life is the fullest love, and the love comes from the celestial light which streams forth from the Absolute One" (VI. 7. 23). It is true that the impersonal nature of the Neoplatonic One gives no apparent scope to the intimate feeling which plays so large a part in Christian devotion. But the reality and warmth of the true mystical passion for the Absolute -- its complete independence of anthropomorphic conceptions -- is strikingly demonstrated by those glowing passages in which Plotinus allows his overpowering emotion, "that veritable love, that sharp desire," to speak; and appeals to the experience of those fellow-mystics who have attained the vision of "the splendour yonder, and felt the burning of the flame of love for that which is there to know; the passion of the lover resting on the bosom of his love" (VI. 9. 4). This passion is the instrument of that ecstasy inwhich he taught that those men who have "wrought themselves into harmony with the Supreme "may briefly experience the vision of the ineffable One. In it the spirit is burned to a white heat, which fuses in one single state the highest activities of feeling, thought, and will. Though the doctrine of ecstasy appears in Philo, and could reasonably be deduced from Plato himself, its treatment by Plotinus, the intense actuality and poetic fervour of its presentation, are the obvious results of such personal experiences as Porphyry describes to us. This ecstasy, according to him -- and here he is supported by the majority of later mystics -- is not a merely passive state, nor does it result in a barren satisfaction. When, withdrawing from all lesser interests, the soul passes beyond all contingency "through virtue to the Divine Mind, through wisdom to the Supreme," and poises itself upon God in a simple state of rapt attention, it receives as a reward of its effort not only the beatific vision of the Perfect, but also an accession of vitality. At this moment, says Plotinus, it "has another life" and "knows that the Supplier of true life is present." The mystic, or "sage," is not a spiritual freak; but the man who has grown up to the full stature of humanity and united himself with that Source of life which is "present everywhere, yet absent except only to those prepared to receive it" (VI. 9. 4). Therefore he alone can be trusted to be fully active; since his action is not a mere restless striving after the discordant objects of a scattered attention, but an ordered movement based on the contemplation of Reality."

We always move round the One. If we did not, we should be dissolved and no longer exist. But we do not always look at the One. When we do, we attain the end of our existence, and our rest; and no longer sing out of tune, but form a divine chorus round the One" (VI. 9. 7).

Yet in spite of the majesty and purity of his vision, the devil's advocate is not without material for an attack uponPlotinus. The charge brought by St. Augustine against "the books of the Platonists" as a whole -- and by these he meant chiefly the Enneads -- is well known. He found in their philosophy no response to the needs of the struggling and the imperfect. In its complete escape from the standing religious snare of anthropomorphism, Neoplatonism also escaped from the grasp of humanity. It left man everything to do for himself. For the Christian philosophy of divine incarnation, dramatized in history, and expressed in the phrase "God so loved the world," the Neoplatonist substitutes "So the world loves God." "No one there," says Augustine of their school, "hearkens to Him who calleth, Come unto Me all ye that labour." The One is the transcendent Source and the Magnet of the Universe, the object and satisfaction of spiritual passion; but not the lover, helper, or saviour of the soul. It "needs nothing, desires nothing." The quality of mercy cannot be ascribed to it. As a term, it is as attractive and impersonal as a mountain peak; and the mystic attaining it has something of the aristocratic self-satisfaction of the successful mountaineer. The Christian and Sufi mystics, even when most deeply influenced by Neoplatonism, have always felt the incompleteness of this conception. They see the soul's achievement of reality as the result of two movements, one human and one divine: a "mutual attraction." "God needs me as much as I need Him," said Meister Eckhart. "Our natural will," said Julian of Norwich, " is to have God, and the goodwill of God is to have us."

"I was given," says Angela of Foligno, "a deep insight into the humility of God, towards man and all other things." "The love of God," says Ruysbroeck, "is an outpouring and an indrawing tide." These statements undoubtedly represent a normal element in spiritual experience; that sense of a response, a self-giving on the part of its transcendent object which -- whatever explanation we may choose to give of it -- is integral to a developed mysticism. Neoplatonism, considered as a religious philosophy, is impoverished by its failure to recognize and find a place for this.

Moreover, the so-called social side of religion, so grossly exaggerated by the amateur theologians of the present day, certainly receives less than justice from Plotinus; for whom the "political virtues" are merely preparatory to the spiritual life, and that spiritual life an exclusive system of self-culture, having as its final stage a "flight of the alone to the Alone." Moral goodness is a form of beauty, and therefore "real"; but there is no suggestion that goodness as such is dearer to the Absolute than beauty or truth. The problem of evil is looked at, but left unsolved: a weakness which Plotinus shares with most mystical philosophers. Evil, he says, has no place in the "untroubled blissful life" of the three Divine Principles. Therefore it is not real, but "a form of non-being" (I. 8. 3): a doctrine which makes an unexpected reappearance eleven hundred years later in the Revelations of Julian of Norwich. Since the aim of the "wise man" is the transcendence of the sense world, there is, moreover, no adequate recognition of those sins, wrongs, and sufferings with which that " half-real" world is charged. Though effort and self-denial have their part in the Plotinian scheme, that transfiguration of pain which was the greatest achievement of the Gospel is beyond the scope of his philosophy. Its remedy for failure and grief is not humble consecration, but lofty withdrawal to that spiritual sphere where the divine element of the soul is at home, untroubled by the conflicts, evils, and chances of life. Even the selfless sorrow of a father or a patriot is to be transcended. Though in this his practice was doubtless better than his doctrine -- for we know that he was a good citizen, a beloved teacher, and a loyal friend -- he speaks in a tone of icy contempt of those who allow themselves to be disturbed by the world's woe.

" If the man that has attained felicity meets some turn of fortune that he would not have chosen, there is not the slightest lessening of his happiness for that. If there were, his felicity would be veering or falling from day to day; the death of a child would bring him down, or the loss of some trivial possession. . . . How can he take any great account of the vacillations of power, or the ruin of his fatherland? Verily, if he thought any such event a great disaster, or any disaster at all, he must be of a strange way of thinking" (I. 4. 7).

Such a sentence, however we look at it, goes far to justify the description of the Neoplatonic saint as "a self-sufficient sage"; and explains the question with which Augustine turned from the Enneads -- "When would those books have taught me charity?"

In spite, however, of this fundamental difference in tone, the wider our reading the more clearly we must realize the extent to which the Christian mystics are conscious or unconscious disciples of Plotinus. That unity of witness which is one of the most impressive facts in the history of mysticism, may reasonably be regarded as evidence of the reality of that world of spiritual values which contemplatives persistently describe. But on its literary side, this same unity of witness depends closely upon the fact that these contemplatives, however widely separated by time and formal creed, were able to make plain their adventures to other men by means of conceptions drawn from the Plotinian scheme; which has proved itself able to rationalize and find room for the deepest spiritual intuitions of man. It could do this because a great mystic made it. Hence we find it implied, even where unexpressed, in many of the masterpieces of later mysticism-- both Christian and Mahomedan -- and some knowledge of it is a necessary clue to the full understanding of these writings. The Sufi 'Attar, describing the soul's arrival in the Valley of Unity where it contemplates the naked Godhead," is equally its debtor with the Protestant mystic William Law, declaring that "everything in temporal nature is descended out of that which is eternal, and stands as a palpable visible outbirth of it; so that when we know how to separate the grossness, death, and darkness of time from it, we find what it is in its eternal state." Yet few of the theologians and contemplatives who owe most to Plotinus had any first-hand acquaintance with the Enneads. Their influence reached the mediaeval world by two main channels. The first line of descent is through the works of Victorinus and St. Augustine; the second through the philosopher Proclus and his mysterious disciple Dionysius the Areopagite. These lines meet in the Divina Commedia, which may be regarded in one aspect as the supreme poetic flower of Neoplatonism.

The dramatic life-history and exuberant self-revelations of St. Augustine have obscured the debt which Christian philosophy owes to that less assertive convert and theologian, Victorinus. Yet since Augustinian Neoplatonism is derived from his writings and translations, he is the real link between Plotinus and the mystics of the Latin Church. A celebrated man of letters and a professor of rhetoric, he had been formed by Neoplatonic philosophy; and is said to have been the author of that Latin translation of the Enneads, which was chief among those "books of the Platonists" that provided St. Augustine's stepping-stones to faith. The stir, not to say scandal, caused by his conversion -- so vividly described in the "Confessions" -- was justified: for the event was crucial in the history of western Christianity. After his conversion, which took the form of a re-interpretation, not an abandonment, of his old beliefs, he set himself to the creation of a Neoplatonic theology; in which the Plotinian triad, and doctrine of the soul's precession and return to the One, appear almost undisguised. The One he tries to identify with the transcendent and immutable Father. "Son" and "Spirit" are to him twoaspects of Nous; the fount of all substantial existence, and containing from eternity all things in their archetypal reality. The Son or Logos is "the Logos of all that is, "ever gushing forth from the "living fountain" of the Father. It was from Victorinus that Catholicism obtained the characteristic Plotinian notions of Deity as "ever active and ever at rest," and of the life of reality as consisting in immanence, progress, and return, which meet us again and again in the writings of the mystics.

It is plain that St. Augustine, in his first Christian period, was deeply indebted to Plotinus, whom he knew through Victorinus and frequently quotes by name; calling him "one of those more excellent philosophers" whose doctrine of the soul is in harmony with the Prologue of the Fourth Gospel. When he came to write the "Confessions," the glamour of the Platonic vision had begun to fade, and he was able to deal in a critical spirit with his own brief Plotinian experience of "that which Is" (VII. 17). Nevertheless, none can understand that book without some knowledge of the Enneads, from which all its finest passages are derived, and in more than one instance -- especially Book VII and the celebrated tenth chapter of Book IX -- closely imitated. In Augustine's invocation of "the Beauty so old and so new," in his description of the "Country which is no vision but a Fatherland," or of "the Light which never changes, above the soul, above the intelligence," we see how closely he had studied them, the extent to which their language had permeated his thought. It is, however, in the tracts composed soon after his conversion -- e.g. De Quantitate Anima, written about A.D. 388 -- that their influence is most strongly marked; and the ecstatic vision of the One is definitely put forward as the summit of Christian experience. From this time onwards, the main outlines of mystical theology were more or less fixed: and since St. Augustine was one of the most widely read and deeply reverenced of the Fathers, with anauthority hardly inferior to that of Scripture itself, its Neoplatonic colour was never lost. Wherever Christian mysticism passes from the emotional and empirical to the philosophic, this colour is clearly seen, and the concepts of Plotinus, more or less disguised, reappear: even in those medieval writers who had no direct acquaintance with Greek philosophy. The immense popularity of the so-called Dionysian writings, which derive much of their doctrine through Proclus from the Enneads, helped to establish yet more firmly the Neoplatonic character of Christian and also of Sufi mysticism. Through these writings the conceptions of the Super-essential Godhead; of successive spiritual spheres or emanations of descending splendour, intervening between the Absolute and the physical world; and of ecstatic union with the transcendent and unconditioned One as the term of religious experience, passed over from the ancient to the mediaval world. Translated from Greek into Syriac in the fifth century, they deeply affected Sufi philosophy. They entered Western thought in the ninth century, through Erigena's Latin translation. It is said that by A.D. 850 Dionysius was known from the Tigris to the Atlantic: and from this time onwards his influence, and through him that of Plotinus, can be traced in the spiritual literature of Christianity and Islam.

Erigena, whose original works are strongly coloured by Neoplatonism, is the first medieval writer in whom this influence appears. He follows Plotinus and Dionysius closely in teaching that the Absolute Godhead is "beyond being" and therefore transcendent to the trinity of Persons; a doctrine of doubtful orthodoxy, which was of great importance in the later development of mysticism. But a still closer approximation to the thought, and especially to the psychology of Plotinus, is found in Richard of St. Victor; perhaps the greatest mystical theologian, certainly one of the most influential writers, of the early Middle Ages. Inthe thirteenth and fourteenth centuries his works, which are now hardly read, circulated through western Europe, and shaped the developing mysticism of England, Germany, and Flanders. Dante, who calls him one "who in contemplation was more than man," places his radiant soul among those of the great teachers in the Heaven of the Sun (Par. X. 131). Abandoning alike the many worlds of Dionysius and the crude dualism of popular religion, Richard taught that three spheres are open to human contemplation: sensibilia, intelligibilia, and intellectibilia -- a series closely analogous to the three worlds of Plotinus. He said that three kinds of contemplation on man's part corresponded with these worlds. These are mentis dilatalio, a widening of the soul's vision, which yet remains within the natural order: mentis sublevatio, an uplifting of the illuminated mind to the apprehension of "things above itself" (or, as Neoplatonists would say, intelligibles); and finally mentis alienatio or ecstasy, in which the soul gazes on Truth in its naked simplicity. Then "elevated above itself and rapt in ecstasy, it beholds things in the Divine Light at which all human reason succumbs." This divine light is the lumen glories, the radiance of the spiritual or intelligible world, which transforms the soul and makes it capable of beholding God; a conception which became a commonplace of medieval theology, was adopted by nearly all the mystics, and plays an important part in the Paradiso.

> *"Lume a lassu, the visibile face*
> *to Creatore a quella creatura*
> *che solo in lui vedere ha la sua pace "* (xxx. 100).

Ruysbroeck -- a student of Dionysius and of Richard -- says of it in The Twelve Beguines: "From the Face of the Father there shines a clear light on those souls whose thought is bare and stripped of images, uplifted above the senses and above similitudes, beyond and without reason, in high purity of spirit. This Light is not God, but it is the mediator between the seeing thought and God." These passages and many like them can be shown to derive directly through St. Augustine from the Enneads. Thus Plotinus says: "Light is visible by Light. The Nous sees itself, and this light, shining on the soul, enlightens it and makes it a member of the spiritual world" (V. 3. 8). Augustine, apparently referring to this passage among others, says: "Often and in many places does Plotinus declare, expounding the meaning of Plato, that what they believe to be the Soul of the World has its bliss from the same source as ours, namely, a Light which it is not, but by which it was created, and from whose spiritual illumination it shines spiritually "(De Civ. Del. X. 2). And, of his own ecstatic experience, "I entered and beheld with the mysterious eye of my soul the Light that never changes, above the eye of my soul, above my intelligence. . . . He who knows the truth knows that Light, and he who knows that Light knows Eternity" (Cont. VII. 10).

From the thirteenth century onwards, the majority of the mediæval mystics show knowledge and appreciation of those Plotinian ideas which reached them -- though in an attenuated form -- through St. Augustine, Dionysius, and Richard of St. Victor. Even the Franciscan and Christo-centric enthusiasm of such contemplatives as Jacopone da Todi and Angela of Foligno was affected by these lofty conceptions. Thus Jacopone takes from the Neoplatonists the three stages of spiritual experience, and describes in unequivocal language his successive achievements of that Logos-Christ -- so near the Plotinian Nous -- "che de omne bellezze se' fattore," and of the "Imageless Good" who cannot be named. So too, Angela's successive visions of the divine fullness and beauty, and of "the ineffable Thing of which nought may be said" depend for their expression on the same philosophy.Nor was its penetrative influence confined to the mystical schools. St. Thomas Aquinas, who accepts and expounds in the Summa (I. q.12. a.5) the doctrine of the lumen glorice, is considerably indebted to Plotinus in several other particulars; though he cites him inaccurately, and does not seem to have known him at first hand. In a remarkable passage, which afterwards influenced one of the finest rhapsodies of Ruysbroeck, he has actually "lifted" the most celebrated phrase in the Sixth Ennead, and adapted it to the distinctively Christian and non-Platonic view of divine union, as a "mutual act" of God and the soul. "In a wonderful and unspeakable manner," says St. Thomas of the soul in this place, "she both seizes and is seized upon, devours and is herself devoured, embraces and is violently embraced; and by the knot of love she unites herself with God, and is with Him as the Alone with the Alone."

It is in a later and less orthodox son of St. Dominic, the formidable and adventurous thinker Eckhart, that the influence of Plotinus on the mediæval mind is best seen: passing through him to Suso, Tauler, Ruysbroeck, and other mystics of the fourteenth century. Eckhart's philosophy still provides one of the most suggestive glosses upon the Enneads. He made that distinction between the absolute and suprapersonal Godhead and the God of devotion, which was almost inevitable for a Christian thinker trying to find a place in theology for the Neoplatonic One. The Godhead, he says, is "a non-God, a non-Spirit, a non-person, a non-image: a sheer pure One." The Son, in whom "the Father becomes conscious of Himself," combines the attributes of the Logos-Christ with those of the Nous. In Him are the archetypes of all created things. There is thus an emanation from the Godhead, through the Son, into creation. The soul's destiny is exactly that conceived by Plotinus: it must ascend to the spiritual world, and through it to its origin, the One, "flowing back into the bottom of the bottomless fountain from whichit flowed forth." In Tauler and Suso, and especially in the great Flemish contemplative Ruysbroeck, these ideas-- though modified by their inferior speculative ability and more ardent spirit of Christian devotion -- are still strongly felt: and since their works and those of their disciples nourished many succeeding generations of contemplatives, through them the mystical side of the Neoplatonic tradition was handed down. In Ruysbroeck, with his threefold division of spiritual experience into "the moral life, the contemplative life, and the super-essential life," and his astonishing and detailed descriptions of the soul's achievement of the Essential Unity, the "death into the One through love," the vision of Plotinus is fully baptized into the Catholic Church. In Jacob Boehme, who drew through Schwenkenfeld and Weigel from Eckhart and his school, the doctrine of the three worlds which forms the basis of his cosmology contains distinct reminiscences of the Plotinian Triad. "These three," he says, "are nought else than the One God in His wonderful works . . . and we are thus to understand a threefold Being, or three worlds in one another." His conception of the Light-world, source of all spiritual beauty and home of "the true human essence," is very near to the Nous. Yet the very closeness with which all these mystics follow those parts of the Neoplatonic doctrine which appeal to them, makes it possible for us to measure the distance which separates their minds, their tone and temper, from that of Plotinus and his school. The calm, the austerity of thought, the emphasis on beauty, the clear cool light of the Intelligible World have departed. These men see philosophy through the haze of Christian feeling. Their work is full of passionate effort; is centred on the ideas of sacrifice and of pain. Their religion is coloured by the sharp Christian consciousness of sin, and by the difficulty -- never squarely faced -- of reconciling devotion to a personal redeemer with the mystical passion for the Absolute. That the philosophyof the Enneads was able to enter a world so remote from its spirit, and come to terms with an attitude of mind in many respects opposed to that of its creator, is an oblique proof of the authenticity of its claim to interpret the spiritual experiences of man.

Three Mediæval Mystics

1: The Mirror of Simple Souls

The Mirror of Simple Souls -- a rare work on the spiritual life, of which manuscripts exist in the British Museum, the Bodleian, and one or two other public libraries -- has so far received little or no attention from students of religious literature. Yet it may turn out to possess great importance, as one of the missing links in the history of English mysticism: for it is a middle-English translation, made at the close of the fourteenth century or beginning of the fifteenth, of the lost work of a French thirteenth-century mystic. It shows, therefore, that the common view of French mediaeval religion as unmystical needs qualification; and further indicates a path by which the contemplative tradition of western Europe reached England and affected the development of our native mystical school.

The Mirror of Simple Souls, as we now have it, is a work of nearly 60,000 words in length. So far from being simple, it deals almost exclusively with the rarest and most sublime aspects of spiritual experience. Its theme is the theme of all mysticism: the soul's adventures on its way towards union with God. It is not, like the Melum of Richard Rolle, or Revelations of Julian of Norwich, a subjective book; the record of personal experiences and actual "conversations inheaven." Rather it is objective and didactic, a work of geography, not a history of travel; an advanced text-book of the contemplative life. Only from the ardour and exactitude of its descriptions, its strange air of authority, its defiance of pious convention, can we gather that it is the fruit of first-hand experience, not merely of theological study: though its writer was clearly a trained theologian, familiar with the works of St. Augustine and Dionysius the Areopagite, whom no mystic of the Middle Ages wholly escaped, and apparently with those of St. Bernard, Hugh and Richard of St. Victor, and other mediæval authorities on the inner life.

I have said that the Mirror, as we have it, purports to be the translation of an unknown French treatise. This translation, so far as we can judge from its language, was probably made in the early years of the fifteenth century, perhaps at the end of the fourteenth. Its author, then, lived at the close of the golden age of English mysticism: he was the contemporary of Julian of Norwich, who was still living in 1413, and of Walter Hilton, who died in 1395. Himself a mystic, he was no servile translator; rather the eager interpreter of the book which he wished to make accessible to his countrymen. Our manuscripts begin with his prologue: an ingenuous confession of the difficulties of the undertaking, his own temerity in daring to touch these "high divine matters," his fear lest the book should fall into unsuitable hands and its more extreme teachings be misunderstood. It appears from this prologue that our version of the Mirror is a second, or revised edition; the first having failed to be comprehensible to its readers.

The character of the translator, as disclosed for us in his prologue, is itself interesting. Clearly he was a contemplative; and the "high ghostly feelings" of which he treats are to him the strictly practical objects of supreme desire, though he modestly disclaims their possession. He appearsbefore us as a gentle, humble, rather timid soul: often frankly terrified by the daring flights of his "French book," which he is at pains to explain in a safe sense. One would judge him, from the peeps which he gives us into his mind, a disciple of the devout and homely school of Walter Hilton, rather than a descendant of the group of advanced mystics which produced in the mid-fourteenth century The Cloud of Unknowing, The Pistle of Private Counsel, and other profound studies of the inner life. These books were written under the strong influence of Dionysius the Areopagite; whose Mystical Theology, under the title of Dionise Hid Divinite, was first translated into English by some member of the school. But to the translator of the Mirror his author's drastic applications of the Dionysian paradoxes of indifference, passivity, and nescience as the path to knowledge teem with "hard sayings." His attitude towards them is that of reverential alarm: he fears their probable effect on the mind of the hasty reader. They seem, as he says in one place, "fable or error or hard to understand" until one has read them several times. He is sure that their real meaning is unexceptionable; but terribly afraid that they will be misunderstood.

Here, then, is the prologue which sets forth his point of view.

"To the worship and laud of the Trinity be this work begun and ended ! Amen.

"This book, the which is called The Mirror of Simple Souls, I, most unworthy creature and outcast of all other, many years gone wrote it out of French into English after my lewd [=lay, unlearned DCW] cunning; in hope that by the grace of God it should profit the devout souls that shall read it. This was forsooth mine intent. But now I am stirred to labour it again new, for because I am informed that some words thereof have been mistaken. Therefore, if God will, I shall declare these words more openly. For though Love declare the pointsin the same book, it is but shortly spoken, and may be taken otherwise than it is meant of them that read it suddenly and take no further heed. Therefore such words to be twice opened it would be more of audience [understanding]: and so by grace of our Lord good God it shall the more profit to the auditors. But both the first time and now, I have great dread to do it. For the book is of high divine matters and high ghostly feelings, and cunningly and full mystically it is spoken; and I am a creature right wretched and unable to do any such work: poor and naked of ghostly fruits, darkened with sins and defaults, environed and wrapped therein oft times, the which taketh away my taste and my clear sight; so that little I have of ghostly understanding and less of the feeling of divine love. Therefore I may say the words of the prophet: 'My teeth be nought white to bite of this bread.' But Almighty Jesu, God that feedeth the worm and gives sight to the blind and wit to the unwitty; give me grace of wit and wisdom in all times wisely to govern myself, following alway His will, and send me clear sight and true understanding well to do this work to His worship and pleasaunce: profit also and increase of grace to ghostly lovers that be disposed and called to this high election of the freedom of soul."

He goes on to the difficulty which dogs all writers on mysticism; the impossibility of making mystic truth seem real to those who have no experience of the mystic life. It has been said that only mystics can write about mysticism. It were truer to say that only mystics can read about it.

"Oh ye that shall read this book! do ye as David says in the Psalter, Gustate et videte: that is to say, "Taste and see.' But why trow ye he said, taste first, e'er than he said see? For first a soul must taste, e'er it have very understanding and true sight; sight of ghostly workings of divine love. Oh full naked and dark, dry and unsavoury be the speakings and writings of these high ghostly feelings of thelove of God to them that have not tasted the sweetness thereof. But when a soul is touched with grace, by which she has tasted somewhat of the sweetness of this divine fruition, and begins to wade, and draweth the draughts to her-ward, then it savours the soul so sweetly that she desires greatly to have of it more and more, and pursueth thereafter. And then the soul is glad and joyful to hear and to read of all thing that pertains to this high feeling of the workings of divine love, in nourishing and increasing her love and devotion to the will and pleasing of Him that she loves, God Christ Jesu. Thus she enters and walks in the way of illumination, that she might be taught into the ghostly influences of the divine work of God, there to be drowned in the high flood, and oned to God by ravishing of love, by which she is all one spirit with her Spouse. Therefore to these souls that be disposed to these high feelings Love has made of him this book in fulfilling of their desire."

But even for those who have been initiated into this way of illumination, the translator acknowledges that many things in the Mirror are difficult and obscure: "often he leaveth the nut and the kernel within the shell unbroken, that is to say, that Love in this book leaves to souls the touches of his divine works privily hid under dark speech, for they should taste the deeper the draughts of his love and drink; and also to make them have the more clear insight in divine understandings to divine love, and declare himself." Therefore he has added his own explanations to the more difficult passages. "Where meseems most need I will write more words thereto in manner of gloss after my simple cunning as meseems best. And in these few places that I put in more than I find written I will begin with the first letter of my name M. and end with this letter N. the first of my surname."

He ends with a gentle complaint of the badness of the text from which he worked, and the confession that he has allowed himself a certain amount of editorial liberty. "The Frenchbook that I shall write after is evil written, and in some places for default of words and syllables the reason is away. Also in translating of French some words need to be changed, or it will fare ungoodly, not according to the sentence. Wherefore I will follow the sentence according to the matter, as near as God will give me grace; obeying me ever to the correction of Holy Kirk, praying ghostly livers and clerks that they will vouchsafe to correct and amend there that I do amiss."

So much for M.N., the English mystic. The prologue of the author, which comes next, tells us all that we know about the anonymous French writer of the book. This person was of a very different temper from M.N. As a Catholic scholar has observed of St. Teresa, " L'auteur ne se faisait pas illusion sur le merite de son oeuvre." Like Teresa, he believed himself to have written underder immediate divine inspiration; a fact which somewhat excuses his complacency in regard to the result. This is a common claim with the mystics, in whom subconscious cerebration is always exceptionally active, and whose writings often exhibit an automatic and involuntary character, seeming to them the work of another mind. Jacob Boehme, Madame Guyon, and Blake are obvious cases in point. The author of the Mirror, however, was anxious that his claim to inspiration should be endorsed. He therefore -- most fortunately for us -- sent his work to various "learned clerks," persons of importance in the theological world, and chronicles their appreciatory remarks in the prologue; which becomes in his hands a form of mediaeval "advance-notice." It will be observed that his critics share the opinion of M.N., that though full of "ghostly cunning" this is a dangerous work to put into the hands of the plain man.

Of these critics " The first was a Friar Minor of great name, of life of perfection. Men called him Friar John of Querayne. . . . He said soothly that this book is made by the HolyGhost. And though all the clerks of the world heard it, but if they understand it, that is to say, but if they have high ghostly feelings and this same working, they shall nought wit what it means. And he prayed for the love of God that it be wisely kept: and that but few should see it. And he said thus, that it was so high that himself might not understand it. And after him a monk of Cisetyns [Citeaux] read it, that hight Dan Frank, Chantor of the Abbey of Viliers: and he said that it proved well by the Scripture that it is all truth that this book says. And after him read it a Master of Divinity, that hight Master Godfrey of Fountaynes: and he blamed it nought, no more than did the other. But he said thus, that he counselled nought [sic] that few should see it; and for this cause, for they might leave their own working and follow this calling, to the which they should never come, and so they might deceive themselves, for it is made of a spirit so strong and so cutting, that there be but few such or none. . . . For the peace of auditors was this proved, and for your peace we say it to you. For this seed should bear holy fruit to them that hear it and worthy be."

Of the three persons here mentioned, Friar John and Dan Frank still remain unidentified: but Godfrey of Fountaynes is almost certainly the Master of Divinity, called Doctor Venerandus, who was a prominent member of the University of Paris at the end of the thirteenth century. He was at the height of his fame about 1280-1290, and died about 1306. "Grande lumen sludii magister Godefridum de Fontanis," he is called in a letter of 1301. In the great war between Friars and Seculars which divided the University at the end of the thirteenth century, this Godfrey was one of the bitterest opponents of the Mendicant Orders. He wrote against them, and attacked them in the Synod of Paris in 1283. We see therefore that the author of the Mirror, in placing Godfrey's testimonial beside that of Friar John, secured with a cunning other than ghostly a friend in each of the opposing camps.

There is, however, one obvious and significant omission in this list of patrons. There is no name which emanates directly from the great school of St. Thomas Aquinas; supreme at that moment in the University, and the custodian of orthodox philosophy. There is, indeed, little trace of scholastic influence in the Mirror, which is far more in harmony with the mystical theology favoured by St. Bonaventura, and continued during the following century in the Franciscan schools: a fact which explains at once the guarded approbation of Friar John, and the absence of Dominican patronage. In the thirteenth and fourteenth centuries the Franciscans were eager students of and commentators on Dionysius the Areopagite: and the order which produced and upheld the hardy speculations of Duns Scotus might well look with indulgence on the most extravagant statements of The Mirror of Simple Souls.

The original version of this book, then, was. probably written in the last quarter of the thirteenth century, and certainly before 1306. Its writer was therefore the contemporary of Eckhart and Jacopone da Todi, the great mystical lights of the Preaching and the Minor Friars. He was no provincial recluse, but a person in touch with the intellectual life of his time. He had connections with the University of Paris, but the names of his patrons prove him to have been neither a member nor an enemy of the Mendicant Orders. It is probable that he was a monk, possible that he was a Carthusian; a strictly contemplative order celebrated for its mystical leanings, which produced in the later Middle Ages many students of the Dionysian writings, and many works upon contemplation. He was widely read, and many parallels could be established between his doctrines and the classics of Christian mysticism. His lost book is so far our only evidence that abstruse prose treatises of this kind were already written in the vernacular; and this alone gives it great interest from the literary point of view. He was, sofar as we know, the first French mystic to write in French; the forerunner of St. Francis de Sales, of Madame Guyon, of Malaval. If we except the semi-mystical writings of Gerson, we must wait till the seventeenth century to provide him with a worthy successor.

II

We come next to the manner and content of the book. The manner is that of a dramatic dialogue: an unusual if not unique form for works of this kind. It consists of a debate -- often a lively debate -- between Love, the Soul, Reason, and a few intervening characters, of whom Pure Courtesy and Discretion are the chief. The student will at once be reminded of the Romaunt de la Rose: but he will have difficulty in matching this form within the confines of ascetic literature. Duologues, such as those in the Third Book of the Imitatio, or Suso's conversations with Eternal Wisdom, are not uncommon: but I know of no other instance of an elaborate mystical doctrine presented through the mouths of a group of symbolic personages.

The Soul is naturally that of the author. Lady Love is his instructress, and all the most beautiful passages are given to her. Reason's role is interrogatory. He catechises Love sharply though respectfully, and represents the invariable attitude of common sense confronted by the claims of

mysticism. Sometimes he goes too far; Love or the Soul is driven
to put him in his place. "Oh, understanding of Reason!" says this soul noughted, "what thou hast of rudeness! Thou takest the shell or the chaff and leavest the kernel or the grain. Thine understanding is so low, that thou mayst not so highly reach as them behoves that well would have understanding of the Being that we speak of." In general, howeverever, the figure of Reason is used with great art to elucidate the hard sayings of Love. The alert intelligence of the writer notes all possible objections to his doctrine, and states and refutes them out of the mouths of his characters. " Lady Love, what is this that you say?" says the shocked voice of Reason whenever the argument becomes paradoxical or abstruse. "Reason," says Love to this, "I will answer for the profit of them for whom thou makest to us this piteous request. Reason," says Love, " where be these double words that thou prayest me to discuss . . . it is well asked, and I will," says Love, "answer thee to all thy asking."

What, then, is the doctrine which these discussions put before us? It is the doctrine of the soul's possible ascent from illusion to reality, from separateness to union with the Divine: the primal creed of all mysticism, here stated in its most extreme form, and pressed to its logical conclusion. It offers, not a chart of the way to a distant heaven of beatitude and recompense, but initiation into that state of being wherein we find our heaven here and now. "I took Jesus for my heaven," said Julian of Norwich. So the writer of the Mirror: "Paradise is no other thing than God Himself . . . why was the thief in Paradise anon as the soul was departed from his body? . . . He saw God, that is Paradise; for other thing is not Paradise than to see God. And this doth she [the soul] in sooth at all times that she is uncumbered of herself." The super-essential and unknowable Godhead, whose nature is but partially revealed in the Blessed Trinity, is the only substance of reality, and the only satisfaction of the soul's desire. " Though this soul had all the knowledge, love and learning that ever was given, or shall be given, of the Divine Trinity, it should be naught as in regard of that that she loves and shall love . . . for there is no other God but He that none may know, which may not be known." The history of human transcendence is the history of the soul's transmutation to that condition of love in which it is, as the author is not afraid to say, deified; and so merged in the Reality from which it came forth, that it is no longer aware of its own separate experience but is "all one spirit with its Spouse."

"I am God," says Love, "for Love is God and God is Love. And this soul is God by condition of love, and I am God by nature divine. And this is hers by right-wiseness of love. So that this Precious, loved of me, is learned and led by me out of herself, for she is turned to me, in me."

This process is set forth by the writer of the Mirror under three chief heads: those of Liberty as the aim, the Will as the agent, and Surrender as the method of the spiritual quest.

In the conception of Liberty as the supreme aim of the spiritual life we have what is perhaps the most original feature of his work: though it is a conception which of course implicit in the New Testament. Where most contemplatives lay emphasis on the glad servitude of love, and use the symbols of wedlock to express the willing subjugation of the soul to its Divine Bridegroom, the key of this book is the idea of spiritual freedom; and that freedom as consisting in the liberation of man's will from finite desires that it may rejoin and lose itself within the Will of the Infinite. We are to learn, it says in the first chapter, something of "the pure love, of the noble love, and of the high love of the free soul; and how the Holy Ghost has His sail in his ship." With our "inward subtle understanding" -- that spiritual intuition which is the instrument of all real knowledge -- we are to follow its progress from the bondage of desire to the point at which, purged of self-will, perfected in meekness and love, " noughted and abased," it reaches the "Seventh Estate of Grace," and participates in the perfect liberty of Pure Being, wherein "the soul has fulhead of perception by divine fruition in life of peace." "Not-willing" is the secret of liberation, and lord of our true life. "And this not-willing sows in souls the Divine Seed, fulfilled of the divine will of God. This seed may never fail, but few souls dispose them to receive this seed." Though this emancipation is only attained by the utter surrender of all personal desire and achievement, yet throughout the book the dominant note is of glad liberation, of flying, of a rapturous ascent. As we read, we seem to hear from every page "the thunder of new wings." The free soul is "six-winged like the seraphim." She is "the eagle that flies high: so right high and yet more high than does any other bird; for she is feathered with fine love, and she beholds above other the beauty of the sun, and the beams and the brightness of the sun. Dame Nature," says she, "I take leave of you: Love is me nigh, that holds me free of him against all without dread. Then," says Love," she afraies her nought for tribulation, nor stints for consolation."

It is clear to the writer that only certain persons are capable of this complete freedom in love: and is to them -- the natural mystics, the people with a genius for reality -- that his book is addressed. They are "of that lineage that be folks royal," "called without fail of the Divine goodness," and it is on their spiritual intuition, their transcendent knowledge, that "all Holy Church is founded"; a suspicious statement in the eyes of orthodox theology. They possess, or are able to possess, the incommunicable gift of spiritual vision.

"This gift is given," says Love, "sometimes in a moment of time. Who that has it, keep it: for it is the most perfect gift that God gives to creature." So removed is the resulting perception of reality from human wisdom that no one can teach the illuminated soul anything. "Now for God," says Reason, "Lady Love, say what is this to say? This is to say," says Love, "that this soul is of so great knowing that though she had all the knowing of all creatures that ever were, be or shall be, she would think it naught in regard of that that she loves." Yet, true to Neoplatonic principles, she is aware that her highest perceptions are nothing, and her "right great and high words" but "gabbynge" or idle talk, compared with the ineffable reality. She wots all and wots naught," and is content it should be so. "He only is my God that none can one word of say, nor all they of Paradise one only point attain nor understand, for all the knowing that they have of Him."

But though the Transcendent God is unknowable, the free soul, in singular contradiction to contemporary asceticism, finds Him everywhere immanent in the world. " And for this, that He is all in all, this soul, says Love, finds Him over all. So that for this all things are to this soul covetable, for she nor finds anything but she finds God." So Meister Eckhart: "To it all creatures are pure to enjoy; for it enjoyeth all creatures in God and God in all creatures."

The preliminary discipline of the mystic, the hard acquirement of that "very charity" which is "the perfection of virtues" and "dwelleth always in God's sight . . . obeying to nothing that is made but to love " is little dwelt on by the author of the Mirror; who did not write for beginners in the contemplative life, but for the mature soul whose love has made him free, and who therefore needs "nor masses nor sermons nor fasting nor orisons, and gives to nature all that he asks, without grudging of conscience" -- a practical application of St. Augustine's dangerous saying, " Love, and do what you like." M.N., however, interpolates a prudent reminder that "by this way and by sharp contricion souls must go, or than they come to these divine usages."

The author's own instructions are really reducible to one point: the complete and loving surrender of the individual will to the Primal Will -- detachment, or, as he calls it, the" noughting " of the soul. This is that "peace of charity in life noughted," which constitutes the higher life of love; in contrast to the active life of virtue, struggling to keep unbroken its attitude of charity to God and man. In itthe soul dwells, as do the Seraphim, within the divine atmosphere, and has direct access to the sources of its life." This is the proper being of Seraphim: there is nought mediate between their love and the Divine Love; they have always its tidings without means. So hath this soul, that seeks not the divine science amongst the masters of the world, but the world and herself inwardly despises. Ah, God! what great difference it is between a gift given by means, of the Loved to the Lover, and the gift given without means of the Loved to the Lover. This book says sooth of this soul. It says she hath six wings as have the Seraphim. With two she covers the face of our Lord: that is to say, the more knowledge this soul hath of the Divine Goodness the more she knows that she knows not the amount of a mote as in regard to His Goodness, the which is not comprehended but of Himself. And with two she covers His feet: this is to say, the more that this soul hath knowledge of the sufferance that Jesu Christ suffered for us, the more perfectly she knows that she knows naught, as in regard of it that He suffered for us, the which is not known but of Him. And with two she flies, and so dwells in standing and sitting: this is to say, that all she covets and loves and prizes, it is the Divine Goodness. These be the wings that she flies with, and so dwells in standing, for she is alway in the sight of God: and sitting, for she dwells alway in the Divine Will. Whereof should this soul have dread, though she be in the world? An the world, the flesh, and our Enemy the Fiend, and the four elements, the birds of the air and the beasts of the field, tormented her and despised her and devoured her if it might so be, what might she lose if God dwelled with her? Oh, is he not Almightiful? Yea, without doubt: He is all might, all wisdom and all goodness, our Father and Brother and our true Friend."

"This soul," says Love, "can no more speak of God; for she is noughted to all outward desires, and of all theaffections of the spirit. So that what this soul does, she does it by usage of good custom, and by commandment of Holy Church, without any desire: for will is dead, that gave her desire. . . . Who that asks these free souls, sure and peaceful, if they would be in purgatory, they say nay. If they would living be certified of their salvation, they say nay. Eh, what would they? They have nothing of will, this for to will; and if they willed, they should descend from Love: for He it is that hath their will. . . . Thus departs the soul from her will and the will departs from this soul, so she again puts it and gives and yields it in God where it was first." Such a doctrine easily slides into the complete passivity or "holy indifference" which was the ideal of the seventeenth century Quietists: and the Mirror certainly does contain passages which, if taken alone, would convict their author of a fondness for this heresy. " I certify thee that these souls that fine love leads, they have as lief shame as worship, and worship as shame; and poverty as riches and riches as poverty; and torments of God and of His creatures as comforts of God and of His creatures; and to be hated as loved, and loved as hated; and hell as paradise and paradise as hell . . . the free soul has no will to will or unwill, but only to will the will of God and suffer in peace His divine ordinance."

Nevertheless, other passages make it clear that active surrender, not mere passivity is the aim, and that the "noughting" of the self within the All is a loving sacrifice, consistent with its achievement of completest happiness. " True love has but only one intent; and that is, that she might alway love truly, for of the love of her Lover has she no doubt, that He does what best is. And she follows this: that she does that that she ought to do. And she wills nought but one thing; and that is, that the Will of God be alway in her done. . . . This soul," says Love, "swims in the sea of joy, that is, in the sea of delights, streaming of divine influences. She feels no joy, for she herself is joy. She swims and drenchesin joy, for she lives in joy without feeling any joy. So is joy in her, that she herself is joy, by the virtue of joy that has merged her in Him. And so is the will of the Loved and the will of this soul turned into one as fire and flame."

The teaching of the writer seems to be, that so long as the will is consciously active and desirous -- however good its actions or desires -- its owner cannot be liberated from the illusions and anxieties of the personal life. What he needs, if he did but know it, is reunion with that fontal life from which he came, to which he is perpetually drawn by love. Here his separate will finds its meaning, and is not annihilated but absorbed. "The understanding, that gives light, shows to the soul the thing that she loves. And the soul that receives by light of understanding the nighing and the knitting by accord of union in plenteous love, sees the Being, where that she holds to have her seat; receiving gladly the light of knowing that brings her tidings of love. And then she would become so, that she had but one will and love; and that is, the only will of Him that she loves."

The detached soul who is thus "noughted in God" enjoys a freedom from stress, an immunity from disappointment incredible to those who still live the individual life. "Now shall I say to you what they be that sit in the mountain above the wind and the rain? These be they that have in earth neither shame nor worship, nor dread of anything that befalls." She has, moreover, passed beyond that moral conflict which arises from the discord between conscience and desire, and is the essential character of the active life; for she has within her "the Master of Virtues, that is called Divine Love, that has her merged in them all and to Him united." Thus she is able to say, "Virtues, I take leave of you for evermore. Now shall my heart be more free and more in peace than it has been. Forsooth, I wot well your service is too travaillous. Sometime I laid my heart in you without any dissevering: ye wot well this. I was in all thing to youobedient. , I was then your servant: but now I am delivered out of your thralldom."

M.N. is quick to gloss this dangerous declaration: "I am stirred here to say more to the matter . . . when a soul gives her to perfection, she labours busily day and night to get virtues by counsel of reason, and strives with vices at every point, at every word and deed . . . thus the virtues be mistresses and every virtue makes her to war with her contrary. . . . But so long one may bite on the bitter bark of the nut that at last he shall come to the sweet kernel. Right so, ghostly to understand, it fares with these souls that be come to peacefulness. They have so long striven with vices and wrought by virtues that they be come to the nut's kernel, that is to say, to the love of God, which is sweetness. And when the soul has deeply tasted this love . . . then is she mistress and lady over the virtues, for she has them all within herself . . . and then this soul takes leave of virtues, as of thralldom and painful travail . . . and now she is lady and sovereign and they be subjects."

In the technical language of mysticism she has passed from the active to the contemplative life, the crucial phase in the evolution of man's transcendental consciousness. This evolution is described for us with great psychological exactness in the Mirror, under the traditional formula of the "States" of the soul's ascent. Since few mystics have escaped the mania for significant numbers, one is not surprised to find seven steps on this " steep stairway of love." "I am called," says this soul, "of the touchings of Love, something to say of the Seven Estates that we call beings: for so it is. And these be the degrees by which man climbs from the valley, to the top of the mountain that is so several [apart] that it sees but God."

"The First Estate is, That a soul is touched of God by grace and dissevered from sin: and, as to her power, in intention to keep the commandments of God." This is, of course,equivalent to the conversion or change of heart which begins the spiritual life. "The Second is, that a soul hold what God counsels to His special lovers, passing that what he commands. And he is no good lover that demenes him not to fulfill all that the which he wist might best please to his Beloved.

"The Third is, that a soul holds the affection of love of works of perfection, by which her spirit is ripened by desires: taking the love of these works to multiply in her. And what does the subtlety of her thought, but makes it seem to the understanding of her humble affection, that she cannot make offering to her Love that might comfort her, but of thing that He loves: for other gift is not prized in love.

"The Fourth is that a soul is drawn by highness of love into delight of thought by meditation, and relinquishes all labours outward, and obedience to others, by highness of love in contemplation. Then the soul is dangerous, noble and delicious: in which she may not suffer that anything her touch but the touchings of pure delight of love, in the which she is singularly gladsome and jolly. What marvel is it if this soul be upheld and updrawn thus graciously? Love makes her all drunken, that suffers her not to attend but to Him." These four stages have brought the self to the complete practice of the contemplative life, and prepared the way for that second great phase in the achievement of reality which consists in the surrender of the separate will.

"The Fifth is, that a soul beholds what God is, and His Goodness, by Divine Light. She sees the

Will, by the spreading illumination of Divine Light, the which light gives her the will again to put in God this will; which she may not without this light yield, that may not her profit unless she departs from her own will. Thus departs the soul from her will, and the will departs from this soul, so she again puts it and gives and yields it in God, where it was first."Now is this soul fallen of love into nought, without the which nought, she may not all be. The which falling is so perfectly fallen, if she be fallen aright, that the soul may not arise out of this deepness, nor she ought not to do it. Within she ought to dwell. And then leaves the soul pride and play, for the spirit has become bitter, that suffers her no more to be playing nor jolly; for the spirit is departed from her that made her oft love in the highness of contemplation, and in the fourth estate fierce and dangerous." Here the spirit of the mystic experiences that terrible and characteristic reaction from the exalted joys of contemplation which is sometimes called the "mystic death" or "dark night of the soul," and destroys in it the last roots of selfhood. In this stage she completes the abandonment or "self-noughting" which initiate her into that which the German mystics called" the Upper School of the Holy Spirit." Thence she passes to the Sixth Estate, of union with the Divine life, in so far as it can be achieved by those still in the flesh. The Seventh is that indescribable state of "glory" or super-essential life, which constitutes the beatific vision of the Saints, known only of those that "be fallen of love into this being."

"The Sixth is, that a soul sees neither her nought by deepness of meekness, nor God by highful bounty. But God sees it in her of His Divine Majesty that illuminated her of Him. So that she sees that none is, but God Himself. And then is a soul in the Sixth Estate of all things made free, pure and illuminated. Not glorified, for gloryfying [sic] is in the Seventh Estate, that we shall have in glory that none can speak of. But, pure and clarified, she sees nor God nor herself: but God sees this of Him, in her, for her, withouten her, that shows her that there is none but He. Nay, she knows but Him, nor she loves but Him, nor she praises but Him, for there is but He. And the Seventh keeps He within Him, for to give us in everlasting glory. If we wit it not now, we shall wit it when the body our soul leaves."

2: *The Blessed Angela of Foligno*

IT is a curious fact that in the modern revival of interest in the Franciscan movement, little attention has been paid to the life and works of Angela of Foligno. Yet, excepting only St. Bonaventura, this woman has probably exerted a more enduring, more far-reaching influence than any other Franciscan of the century which followed the Founder's death. In saying this, I do not forget the claims of such great Franciscans as John of Parma or Jacopone da Todi, nor yet of St. Clare, the Founder of the Second Order. But the influence of John of Parma was comparatively shortlived; and that of Jacopone's superb poetry, though great in Italy, did not go beyond it. His ecstasies could not be translated into other tongues. As to St. Clare, with whom the feminine aspect of the Franciscan ideal first showed itself, her vocation was to the foundation of a contemplative order, which should support by its heavenly correspondences the active and missionary life of the Franciscan friars. The business of the Second Order is the essential woman's business, of keeping the fire of love alight upon the hearth. Its influence, therefore, was and is almost entirely confined within the boundaries of the spiritual family. The deepest wells of Franciscan mysticism are there hidden, and must always be hidden, from the outer world.

But the vocation of Angela of Foligno was, in a sense, more thoroughly Franciscan than this, more broadly human, more complete. Like that of St. Catherine of Genoa, a mysticwhom she resembles in certain respects, it was a twofold vocation: to the eternal and to the temporal, to the divine and to the human. She was a great contemplative, but she was also an exceedingly successful teacher of the secrets of the spiritual life: one of the great line of artist-mediators between the infinite and the human mind.

We know nothing of St. Clare's mystical experience. We know of Angela's all that she was able to express; and she tried hard, though for want of language she confesses that she often failed. This passionate, faulty, very human woman, who came to the Mystic Way from a discorderly life, and was hampered by a natural egotism which she transmuted, it is true, but never perhaps really killed, has earned the great title of "Mistress of Theologians." She penetrated to that world of realities which the diagrams of theology, like the temple built with hands, foreshadow upon earth. Her book of visions and revelations, now so little read, profoundly affected the religious life of Europe. During the sixteenth and the seventeenth century we often come upon its traces in England and in France, as well as in Italy itself; for in this period it was one of the most widely circulated religious works. It exerted great influence on St. Francis de Sales, and also upon the French Quietists. It is quoted as an authority by Madame Guyon, Poiret, and Malaval; and through the great English Benedictine, Augustine Baker, and his pupil, Gertrude More, it has left its mark on the English Catholic mysticism of the seventeenth century.

This book is practically our only trustworthy source for the facts of Angela's inner and outer life. It was written in Latin, at her dictation, by her Franciscan confessor Fra Arnaldo; at some date subsequent to 1294, since it dates a past event by the pontificate of Celestine V. It was not printed till the sixteenth century, when first an Italian translation, and then the Latin text appeared. Both soon became popular; the translation being one of the first Italian books of devotion to appear in the vulgar tongue. It is divided into three parts, which must be read in relation with one another. First we have the history of Angela's conversion, penitence, and slow, difficult education in the mystic way: a detailed psychological document of much interest. Secondly we have, grouped together, all the visions and revelations which she received in that way. Unfortunately Fra Arnaldo has seen fit to arrange these according to their subjects, and not according to the order in which they were experienced; thereby increasing their edifying character at the expense of their scientific worth. Last comes "the evangelical doctrine of the Blessed Angela "; a treatise largely made up of letters addressed to her disciples, but, like the writings of St. Teresa, full of illuminating autobiographical touches.

Here, then, we have in one volume three aspects of human life as seen within the limits of one personality: the biographical facts, the supernal vision, and the ordered conclusions drawn from those facts and that vision, for the instruction of other men. All are of value to us in our study of her personality; for we shall never understand her as a mystic unless we try first to understand her as a human creature.

First as to her outward life. Angela was born of a prosperous Umbrian family in 1248; twenty-two years after the death of St. Francis, seventeen years before the birth of Dante. She was one year younger than St. Margaret of Cortona, the other great Franciscan penitent and contemplative. Her life, covering the second half of the thirteenth century, was roughly contemporary with that of Jacopone da Todi, who was twenty years her senior; and with those " spiritual" friars, such as Conrad of Offida and John of La Verna, who are commemorated in the "Little Flowers." The period, in Italy, was one of contrasted worldly luxury and spiritual enthusiasm, and Angela's life-history appears to have included experience of both extremes. She married when very young and had children, but lived a thoroughly worldly if not an actually immoral life: posing before society as an excellent Christian, but actually denying herself few indulgences. We learn from the list of sins of which she afterwards accused herself, that these "infirmities and diseases" had included the washing of her face, the curling, braiding, washing, combing, and anointing of her hair, wearing of "needless vain and curious clothes," and laced shoes adorned with cut leather. She had also incurred the risk of hell by "vain running and dancing and walking about for pleasure," and even by enjoying the scent of flowers: a crime which St. Francis could hardly have condemned. Remembering the intensely ascetic tone of Franciscan penitence and the puritan ideals of the Spiritual zealots, we need not take these confessions too seriously, or interpret in the worst sense the "embraces, touches, and other evil deeds" which she deplores. Nevertheless, the unregenerate Angela in early womanhood was not the kind of person whom one would pick out as likely to develop into a saint. She makes it quite clear to us that she was a vain, self-important, and hypocritical little egotist, "painted in false colours, a dissembler within and without." Probably, like many women of the world, a nominal Tertiary, she loved to make a pious impression, but loved comfort even more. " I diligently made an outward show of being poor, but caused many sheets and coverings to be put down where I slept, and taken up in the morning so that none might see them." There was an offensive sanctimoniousness about her too. "During the whole of my life," she says frankly, "I have studied how that I might obtain the fame of sanctity."

We do not know the date of Angela's conversion, or the circumstances which brought it about; save that it took place under Franciscan influence, which was of course paramount in that part of Umbria in her day. It seems to have taken the form of a gradual awakening of conscience to the sinfulness and hypocrisy of her life. In her mental distress she prayed to St. Francis, and he appeared to her in a dream, the earliest of her visionary experiences; the confessor to whom she then went for advice was a Friar Minor, and after her husband's death she adopted the plain habit worn by the more fervent Tertiaries, and remained faithful to the Order till her death. The fixed dates in her life are few and confusing. Her own book only gives two: the date of her final purification and the date of her death. We gather from this and other sources, however, that after her widowhood she lived at first with one companion in great retirement; but by about 1290, had formed a small sisterhood in Foligno. Its members, who observed Franciscan poverty in its full rigour, took the rule of the Third Order and the three vows of religion, but they were not cloistered. They devoted themselves to the care of the sick, and other works of charity.

In this community Angela spent the rest of her life; gradually becoming known as a teacher of "Seraphic wisdom " amongst those Spiritual Franciscans who were struggling to keep the ideals of St. Francis alive. She seems to have been the centre of a group of Franciscan Tertiaries of both sexes, for whom she was at once friend and prophetess, like St. Catherine of Siena in the next century. Several of her letters to these "sons" of hers are embedded in her book of "Evangelical Doctrine." One of them, the turbulent and ardent friar Ubertino da Casale, owed to her his true initiation into the spiritual life: and his account of the impression which she made on him helps us understand the nature of her influence. He came to her from Paris in 1298, when he was twenty-five years old; a successful preacher, but already conscious of the inward call to a life of greater perfection. "She restored," he says, " a thousandfold all those spiritual gifts I had lost through my own sins; so that from that time I have not been the same man that I was before. When I had experienced the splendour of her radiant virtue, she changed the whole face of my mind, and so drove out the weakness and languor from my soul and body and healed my mind that was torn with distraction,that no one who knew me before could doubt that the Spirit Christ was newly begotten in me through her." This is almost our only glimpse of Angela as she was seen by contemporary eyes: but it indicates the position she came to occupy among the more devout Franciscan zelanti.

She died, surrounded by her spiritual children, in the octave of the Feast of the Holy Innocents, 1309, aged sixty-one; and was buried in the Church of the Franciscans at Foligno, where her body still lies. An Office in her honour was approved by Gregory XIV in 1701, and her Feast is kept throughout the Franciscan Order on March 30.

So much for the scanty outer history. Of greater interest is our knowledge of her inner life; the real life of mystics and contemplatives. The history of this inner life assures us that Angela was of the stuff of which great mystics are made though not at all of the stuff of which many amateurs of mysticism expect them to be made. First great necessity, she possessed a strongly romantic temperament; like St. Francis, Suso, St. Ignatius, Mechthild, St. Teresa, her companions on the highway of the soul. Like these, she had also an innate simplicity and ardour, a character at once childlike and heroic; that "all-or-none" reaction, the power of total self-giving to the matter in hand, which distinguishes the hero, whether as man of action, as artist, or as saint. Indeed, heroism may properly be ascribed to a comfortable and self-indulgent married woman, who leaves all for the lonely adventure of Sinai, however many tumbles she may have upon the road. With this courage she combined an extreme sensibility to impressions, great power of endurance, a strong will ; all the potentialities of a great sinner or a great saint. Further, she evidently possessed that peculiar, unstable psychic makeup, which the mystic shares with other types of genius; and which is seen in its full development in the two greatest of Italian saints, Francis of Assisi and Catherine of Siena She experienced all the normal episodes of complete mysticaldevelopment: the phases of penitence and self-discipline, illumination and dereliction, and at last that ecstatic union with the Divine Nature which is the goal of the Way. Her mysticism was deeply coloured by the Franciscan atmosphere in which it was nurtured; it exhibited the highly emotional and enthusiastic character, the tendency to eccentric penances, the concentration upon the Cross and Passion of Christ, which are found in her contemporary Jacopone da Todi, and are typical of the Franciscan mystics at their best. Indeed, the many parallels between Angela and Jacopone suggest to us that the favourite subjects of their contemplations were those in vogue in "Spiritual" circles at this time; and that we have in their works the surviving examples of a complete school of mysticism, which taught, as Ubertino da Casale says that Cecilia of Florence did, "the whole art of the higher contemplation."

"As I walked," said the Blessed Angela, "by the way of penitence, I took eighteen spiritual steps before I came to know the imperfections of my life." This is the first sentence of the book of Conversion and Penitence, which analyses in detail the changes through which she passed on her way to complete self-knowledge and self-adjustment. Those "eighteen steps" extended over many years. When they began, Angela was living luxuriously, as a married woman, in her husband's house. When they ended, she was a poor widow vowed to the religious life; stripped of every superfluity, everything that would entangle her in the web of appearance, apt in contemplation, companioned by visions, esteemed as a teacher and an ecstatic, and the centre of a group of disciples. Her inner life, during these years of ascent, of hard and difficult growth, seems to have been a life of bitter and almost continuous struggle. Even after the preliminary steps of repentance were over, and her visionary powers had developed, the new spiritual ideals demanded of her ever more difficult renunciations. We see her, as we read thewonderful memoirs of her years of penitence, perpetually flung to and fro between adoration and contrition; as first one element and then the other of her complex personality took the upper hand. In her long and slow ascent towards the stars, she alternately experienced the sunshine and the shade.

From the turmoil which surrounded the hard re-making of Angela's character, there emerged two great principles round which her subsequent life and teaching were to be grouped. The first was poverty, the second was self-knowledge. Naturally her instinct for poverty would be fostered by her Franciscan environment; but it is an instinct implicit in the mystical temperament, and not peculiar to the Poor Man of Assisi. Mystics know that possessions dissipate the energy which they need for other and more real things; that they must give up ownership, the verb " to have," if they are to attain the freedom which they seek, and all the fullness of the verb "to be." Thus Jacopone in his great ode expressed a universal spiritual law:

"Povertate è nulla avere
e nulla cosa poi volere;
ed omne coca possedere
en spirito de libertate."

It cost Angela many struggles before she fully accepted and acted upon this truth, and attained that which she calls the "liberty of poverty." Self-knowledge, that hard essential of the soul's re-education which Richard of St. Victor, and afterwards St. Catherine of Siena, made the starting-point of all mysticism, she recognized from the first as the true objective towards which her hard penances and long meditations must tend.

The eighteen "steps," then, exhibit with extraordinary honesty her gradual progress in these two arts of self-knowledge and renunciation. At the first step, as we have seen, she was by something -- we know not what -- startled intoattention to the real, and terrified by the vision of her own naked reality stripped of its pleasant veils and self-deceits. Her first reaction to this vision was avoidance. She was ashamed to look her sins in the face, or confess them. But having prayed to St. Francis, she was led by a dream -- the form under which her unconscious mind most frequently controlled her -- to seek a Franciscan friar and make a general confession of her sins. She performed his penance loyally, and became increasingly contrite for her faults: the sense of Divine Mercy touching her, and evoking an ever more humble and repentant grief. By the eighth step this contrition had become love, the passion for perfection triumphing over the hatred of imperfection. By that contemplation of the Cross which was specially dear to Franciscan devotion, and is the subject of one of Jacopone's most splendid poems, she was led into an ever deeper understanding of the mystery of redemption by pain. Angela was now definitely committed to the mystic way. "In this beholding of the Cross," she says, "I burned with the fire of love and remorse: so that standing before that Cross I divested myself of everything and offered myself to Him. . . and the aforesaid fire compelled me, and I had no power to resist." The special form which her renunciation took -- that of a vow of chastity in deed and thought -- suggests the direction in which her chief temptations lay; and this deduction is made more probable by the emotional quality of her visionary experience, in which the repressed ardours of her temperament found relief.

At the ninth step, this instinct for renunciation achieved more complete expression. "Enlightened and instructed" -- doubtless by some member of the spiritual group -- she learned that nothing less than a total sacrifice of friends, kindred, possessions, her very self, would serve her if she wished to tread the Way of Holy Cross. But in her acceptance of this bitter truth we still see something of the vanity, self-importance and narrow egotism of the old Angela. Thisis the one passage in all her writings which every one knows, and by which she is generally, and most unfairly, judged.

"I elected to walk on the thorny path which is the path of tribulation. So I began to put aside the fine clothing and adornments which I had, and the most delicate food, and also the covering of my head. But as yet, to do all these things was hard, and shamed me, because I did not feel much love for God, and was living with my husband. So that it was a bitter thing to me when anything offensive was said or done to me; but I bore it as patiently as I could. In that time, and by God's will, there died my mother, who was a great hindrance to me in following the way of God; my husband died likewise; and in a short time there also died all my children. And because I had begun to follow the aforesaid way, and had prayed God to rid me of them, I had great consolation of their deaths, although I also felt some grief; wherefore, because God had shown me this grace, I imagined that my heart was in the heart of God and His will and His heart in my heart."

This unfortunate paragraph outweighs for many minds the whole of Angela's subsequent life and achievements. I do not deny that, taken alone, it appears to be a monument of spiritual egotism. But we must remember that it represents, not Angela the peaceful mystic, but Angela the worried and storm-tossed penitent at the most difficult moment of her career. The emotional centre of her life had shifted. An inexorable inner voice now urged her to a total concentration on God, and she knew that the way of penance and renunciation was her only hope. Yet living in a thoroughly discordant, thoroughly unspiritual environment, hemmed in on all sides by conventional existence and unsympathetic surroundings, this way seemed impossible to follow in its completeness; for she was not one of those who are able to harmonize the demands of both worlds. Moreover, these words were written by one who had long outlived the human sorrow which, as she sayshere and in another place, she felt at these accumulated bereavements. Now, looking back and seeing her past existence spread out before her, she recognized even this awful and drastic series of deprivations as a necessary factor in the life to which she was called.

After all, it is fair to acknowledge that family affection is not the strongest point in the character of the mystical saints. In the interests of their vocation, they are always ready to leave father, mother, brothers, and sisters; and moreover there is evangelical authority for this attitude. They are specialists, and are therefore bound, in the interests of the race, to give up many things which other men must develop and preserve. Artists are under much the same necessity. The vitality which we diffuse amongst many interests and loves, these must concentrate on the one object of their quest. Hence St. Francis himself flung his family aside without scruple when it came to the parting of the ways. Hence Jacopone da Todi was warned that even spiritual friendships must be held lightly by the pilgrim on the way of the Cross. Angela was only following in their footsteps, though she doubtless expressed herself with unnecessary and ill-regulated vigour, when she recognized human ties and human affections as possible impediments of the spiritual life. An easy capitulation to love and friendship in their most engrossing aspects seems always to have been her standing danger. It caused her in later life to say that she "feared love more than all other things"; even regarding with suspicion the deep affection which unites teacher and disciples, or two fellow-initiates of the contemplative life.

It was after her release from the duties of family life, and her more complete concentration on the ascetic life, that her visionary powers began to develop. At first they were little more than waking dreams of a commonplace kind; imaginary pictures of the Passion, the Crucifix, the Sacred Heart, such as have been experienced by innumerable Catholicsaints. These vivid symbolic presentations of Divine love moved Angela to greater and more heroic heights of penitential love; and the passion for complete evangelical poverty came on her with renewed force. Her possessions enchained her, and she knew it. She made many efforts to screw herself up bit by bit to those heights of renunciation which St. Francis seems to have reached almost without effort." For this cause -- namely, to have the liberty of poverty I journeyed to Rome, to pray the Blessed Peter that he would obtain for me the grace of true poverty. It seemed to me at last that I could not sufficiently do penance whilst I was possessed of worldly things . . . so I determined to forsake everything. In my imagination I had a great desire to become poor, and such was my zeal, that I often feared to die before I attained this state of poverty. On the other hand, I was assailed by temptations, which whispered to me that I was still young, that begging for alms might lead me into shame and danger; that if I did this, I should die of hunger, cold, and nakedness. Moreover, all my friends dissuaded me from it. But at last Divine mercy sent a great illumination into my heart, which, as I believed then and do now, I shall never lose even in eternity. . . . So then I did resolve in good earnest."

Here is the final, deliberate act of will: the turning once for all from the unreal to the real -- under whatever form the charms of unreality appear to the growing self -- which all mystics have to make. It was Angela's eleventh step. Her mystical powers were now developing rapidly. They showed themselves in visions, dreams, and ecstasies. Not all of these, it is true, can be accepted as marks of spiritual growth: for some clearly represent the re-emergence under religious symbols of old emotions and desires. But the deep and vivid intuitions of spiritual realities which came to her more and more frequently, show that a steady sublimation of those emotions and desires was in progress, and that they tended more and more towards supersensual ends.At the fifteenth step, with truly Franciscan thoroughness -- though, oddly enough, the Friars Minor whom she consulted forbade her to do it -- she distributed the whole of her possessions amongst the poor. "Because methought I could not keep anything for myself without greatly offending Him who did thus enlighten me." With this crucial act she seems to have attained at last the true and full state of illumination. "Then," she says, "I began to feel the sweetness of God in my heart": that which other mystics have called the "sense of the Presence." Also, "I began to have understanding of the visions and the words"; a new spiritual lucidity running side by side with the symbolic pictures and imaginary voices that she saw and heard with the inner eye and ear. This, too, is normal and characteristic. From this point, then, we must read the book of Visions and Consolations side by side with the book of Penances if we would understand Angela's inner life; for these two forms of experience, which she has unfortunately chosen to treat separately, alternated with one another.

In the time of her total acceptance of holy poverty, Angela seems to have been living in a state of almost hermit-like simplicity with one companion, the Blessed Paschalina of Foligno; whom at first she found a "weariness," but afterwards discovered to be a fellow traveller on the Mystic Way. Some years had now passed since her conversion; and she was already accepted -- perhaps indeed celebrated -- as a religious teacher among the members of the Spiritual group. Definitely vowed to the service of the Franciscan Order, she seems soon to have become like St. Catherine of Siena, St. Catherine of Genoa, and many other women mystics, the centre of a group of adoring disciples or "spiritual sons." Yet her inner life was still in a state of confusion, the remaking of her character was still in progress. She was flung perpetually to the extremes of joy and anguish. She would rise to great heights of mystical passion " filled with the fire and fervourof Divine love," only to fall back to her old temptations. The repressed instinctive life began to take its revenge, and tortured her by vicious suggestions which she had never known before. "I would have chosen rather to be roasted than to endure such pains." Also the great strain put upon her nervous system by the growing spiritual faculties resulted in absolute physical illness, as has been the case with many of the mystical saints. "The torments of my body," she says, "were veritably numberless. There remained not one of my members that was not grievously tormented, nor was I ever free from pain, infirmity, or weariness."

We need not be afraid to recognize in this struggle a reflection of the stresses and difficulties -- some physical -- which attend on the complete sublimation of man's psychic life; especially in persons of a strongly emotional temperament. In Angela's case the visions and dreams that accompanied it assure us of the character of the crisis through which she was passing. Many of her symptoms at this time were undoubtedly hysterical. She cried aloud when she heard the name of God, and fell into a fever on seeing a picture of the Passion of Christ. Her tears were perpetual, and often she longed to tear herself in pieces. Unfortunately Franciscan piety of the more extreme sort encouraged emotional extravagances of this kind, as we may see by the account of Angela's contemporaries given in the "Little Flowers," and failed to appreciate Jacopone's profound distinction between ordered and disordered love. It also gave unqualified approval to those public and grotesque acts of self-abasement which play so large a part in the legend of his penitence; and here again, Angela was true to type. Still grieved by the memory of her old hypocrisies, made more poignant by the reverence she received from her disciples, she went through the city and open places with meat and fishes hanging from her neck, and crying, "I am that woman full of evil and dissembling, slave of all vices and iniquities, who did good deeds that she might obtain honour among men; and especially when I caused those bidden to my house to be told that I ate neither fish nor meat, and -- being the while greedy, gluttonous, and drunken -- feigned to desire nought but what was needful."

Those familiar with the lives of the mystics will remember many parallels to this state of conflict: the ups and downs of Suso, his alternate illumination and despair, his great self-denials balanced by foolish little sins: the thirty years during which Teresa -- already, like Angela, regarded as a great example -- swayed between her mystical vocation and the claims of a more normal life. In Angela this inward battle culminated, she says, "some little while before the time of the pontificate of Celestino" -- that is to say about 1294, when she was forty-six -- and endured for more than two years. In it, in addition to bodily and mental agony, she was humiliated by recurrent temptations to sensual indulgence. Her depression was extreme, and her intellect often so clouded that she could not even recall the idea of God to her mind. It was her last lesson in humility and self-knowledge -- an excellent antidote to the dangers of professional sanctity -- and answered to that terrible period of final purification which other mystics have called the "Dark Night of the Soul."

From this last purgation, in which all the elements of her character seemed flung back into the melting-pot, she emerged into that condition of spiritual equilibrium, of perfect harmony with transcendent reality, which is known to mystic writers as the Unitive Way. "A divine change," she says, "took place in my soul, which neither saint nor angel could describe or explain. Wherefore I say again that it seems to me evil speaking or blasphemy if I try and tell of it." Again, "I came not to this state of my own self, but was led and drawn thereto by God; so that though of my own self I should not have known how to desire or ask for it, I am now in that state continually." Though the capacity for pain never left her, and is implied in many of her greatest revelations -- for, like all the great Catholic mystics, she found the Christian paradox of joyous suffering at the very centre of truth -- yet the last twelve years of her life seem to have been years of profound inward peace. " He hath placed within my soul," she said, "a state which changes little, and I possess God in such fullness that I am no longer in the state in which I used to be; but I walk in such perfect peace of heart and mind that I am content in all things."

It was that state of which Jacopone has written:

"La guerra a terminata
de le virtú battaglia,
de la mente travaglia
cosa nulla contende.
La mente è renovata
vestita a tal entaglia,
de tal ferro a la maglia
feruta no l'offerende."

Angela has two claims to the title of a great mystic: that of her life, which we have briefly considered, and that of the revelations and experiences which she reports; our chief evidence of the unique nature of her consciousness. What then was the nature of these visions and revelations? There are signs in her book that she ran through the whole gamut of mystical experience. She practised, and described, all those degrees of contemplative prayer which are analyzed by St. Teresa and St. John of the Cross. She heard interior voices. She saw visions. She was an ecstatic. Moreover, at least after her achievement of spiritual equilibrium -- for it would be unfair to take into account the morbid states from which she suffered during the period of readjustment -- her ecstasies were of that rare and supernal kind which, far from being signs of mental or nervous disease, actually renew and invigorate the physical life of those who experience them. There is a beautiful passage in the life of St. Catherine of Genoa in which she is described as coming joyous and rosy-faced from the ecstatic encounter with God's love. So Angela says: "Because of the change in my body, therefore I was not able to conceal my state from my companion, or from other people with whom I consorted; because at times my face was all resplendent and rosy, and my eyes shone like candles. When the soul is assured of God and refreshed by His presence, the body also receives health, satisfaction, and nobility."

Her revelations were of two kinds. First we have a long series of "imaginary visions": pictures, no doubt representing deep and imageless intuitions, resulting as it were from some communion with reality, but taking their form -- as distinct from their content -- from the memory and imagination of the visionary. Though many of these must be classed as dreams, and some indeed were received in sleep, others were definite experiences; seen, as she says, with the eyes of the mind, far more clearly than anything can be seen with the eyes of the body. Nevertheless we are bound to consider them less as objective revelations than as vivid artistic reconstructions; symbols of something that she has felt and known. Angela's religious beliefs and romantic leanings are both clearly reflected in them. Some deal with the physical accidents of the Passion -- always a favourite subject of the mediæval visionary -- and these closely resemble the series of Passion-pictures seen by Julian of Norwich. Others are inspired by her devotion to the Eucharist. One or two seem, like the visions of St. Gertrude, to anticipate the later cult of the Sacred Heart. In virtue of these visions Angela belongs to the great family of women Catholic mystics; women possessing a rich emotional life, and, largely by means of that emotional life, actualizing and expressing their communion with the spiritual world.

We see this emotional character clearly in one of Angela's most celebrated experiences; the one of all others which seems to have set the seal on her career as a religious teacher, andwhich is placed at the beginning of her book of visions and revelations, though there was no vision involved in it. I mean the beautiful scene in which she talked with the Holy Ghost, walking on "the narrow road which leads upward to Assisi, and is beyond Spello." That sense of heavenly intimacy, of divine communion, of a destiny pressed upon her from the spiritual sphere, which then took possession of her consciousness, was translated by the surface-mind of the natural Angela -- whose nearest parallels to such an experience were found amongst the emotional incidents of human love -- into the wonderful imaginary conversation in which, as she climbs the path between the vineyards, she is wooed by the Holy Spirit, and assured of His peculiar interest and affection. " I will bear thee company and speak with thee all the way," He says to her. " I will make no end to My speaking, and thou wilt not be able to attend to anything save Me." "Then did He begin to speak the following words to me, which persuaded me to love after this manner, 'My daughter, who art sweet to Me, My daughter who art My temple, My beloved daughter, do thou love Me, for I love thee greatly, and much more than thou lovest Me.' And very often He said to me, ' Bride and daughter! sweet art thou to Me; I love thee better than any other in the valley of Spoleto.' These and other similar things did He say to me. Then when I heard these words, I counted my sins, and I considered my faults; how that I was unworthy of so great a love. And I began to doubt these words; for which cause, my soul said to him who had spoken to it, 'If thou wert indeed the Holy Spirit, thou wouldest not speak thus; for it is not right or proper, because I am weak and frail and might grow vainglorious thereat.' He answered, 'Think and see if thou couldst become vainglorious because of the things for which thou art now made glad. . . Then I tried to grow vainglorious, that I might prove if He spoke truth; and I began to look at the vineyards, that I might learn the folly of my words. And wherever I looked, He saidto me, 'Behold and see! this is My creation': and at this I felt ineffable delight."

This is the poetry of mysticism, an artistic reduction of supernal intuitions, and is to be interpreted in poetic terms. But there is another, and rarer, form of spiritual perception: that imageless intuition of pure truth, which St. Teresa and other mystics call intellectual, but which would be better named metaphysical vision. Angela's real importance amongst the mystics comes from the fact that she possessed this power in a high degree of development. In virtue of her immediate apprehensions of transcendent reality, she belongs to the rarest and highest type of mystic seer: a class in which Plotinus holds perhaps the first place, and of which Ruysbroeck is the most conspicuous mediaeval example. The poetry of Jacopone da Todi shows us that he too knew the secret of those strange astounding regions, "beyond the polar circle of the mind," where Angela tasted of unconditioned reality, and the language in which he describes them often reminds us of her. It is an interesting question, whether these two great Franciscan contemplatives directly influenced one another, or must be regarded as the twin stars of a school of "Seraphic wisdom" which taught the deepest mysteries of the spiritual life.

There are eight of these great visionary experiences recorded in Angela's book. In them she says that she apprehended God successively under the attributes of Goodness, Beauty, Power, Wisdom, Love, Justice; and that after this she beheld the totality of the Godhead "darkly " -- a way of describing her perceptions which is of course traceable to the "Divine darkness" of Dionysius the Areopagite. Finally she beheld it, " as clearly as is possible in this life." All these visions seem to have come to her when she was in a state of ecstasy or trance. She speaks of being " exalted in spirit,""rapt to the first elevation"; lifted to wholly new levels of consciousness. She describes them as well as she can, yetplainly she is only able to tell us a fraction of her experience. Over and over again she declares the hopeless inadequacy of human speech, the impossibility of "speaking as she saw." Her state is like that of Dante at the end of the Paradiso, save that her wings were fitted for these flights.

"I beheld the ineffable fullness of God; but I can relate nothing of it, save that I have seen the fullness of Divine Wisdom, wherein is all goodness." Again, "inasmuch as this was a supernatural thing, I cannot express it in words." " Many other things were clearly set forth to one; but I neither can nor will relate them." " All that I say of this, seems to me to be nothing. I feel as though I offended in speaking of it, for so greatly does the Good exceed all my words that my speech seems to be but blasphemy."

Those things, however, which she does contrive to relate, have an astonishing suggestive quality, a great philosophic sweep, combined with an intimate appeal to our own deepest intuitions, which place them, so far as mystical history is concerned, on a level with some of the greatest passages in Jacopone da Todi and in Ruysbroeck; and in my opinion far beyond the more celebrated intellectual visions of St. Teresa.

Thus she says, " the eyes of my soul were opened and I beheld the plenitude of God, by which I understood the whole world both here and beyond the sea, the abyss, and all other things. And in this I beheld nothing save the Divine Power, in a way that is utterly indescribable, so that through the greatness of its wonder the soul cried with a loud voice, saying, 'The whole world is full of God.' Wherefore I understood that the world is but a little thing; and I saw that the power of God was above all things, and the whole world was filled with it."

Here we are reminded of Julian of Norwich -- " He showed me a little thing, the quantity of an hazel nut. I looked thereon with the eye of my understanding and thought; Whatmay this be? and it was answered generally thus: It is all that is made."

"After I had seen the power of God, His will and His justice," says Angela, again, "I was lifted higher still; and then I no longer beheld the power and will as before. But I beheld a Thing, as fixed and stable as it was indescribable; and more than this I cannot say, save that I have often said already, namely, that it was all good. And although my soul beheld not love, yet when it saw that indescribable Thing, it was itself filled with indescribable joy, so that it was taken out of the state it was in before, and placed in this great and ineffable state. I know not whether I was then in the body or out of the body. It is enough to say that all the other visions seemed to me less great than this."

Again, " One time in Lent . . . the eyes of my soul were opened, and I saw Love advancing gently towards me, and I saw the beginning but not the end. There seemed to me only a continuation and an eternity thereof, so that I cannot tell its likeness nor colour; but directly this Love reached me I beheld all these things more clearly with the eyes of the soul than I could do with the eyes of the body. This Love came towards me after the manner of a sickle. Not that there was any actual and measureable likeness; but when first it appeared to me it did not give itself to me in such abundance as I expected, but a part was withdrawn, Therefore I say, after the manner of a sickle. Then I was filled with love and a great satisfaction, but although it satisfied me, it generated within me so great a hunger that all my members were loosened; and my soul fainted with longing to attain to the All."

I give one more, particularly interesting to English students because of its parallels with our own great mystical work, The Cloud of Unknowing: "There was a time when my soul was exalted to behold God with so much clearness that never before had I beheld Him so distinctly. But I did not here see Love sofully; rather I lost that which I had before, and was left without love. Afterwards I saw Him darkly, and this darkness was the greatest blessing that could be imagined, and thought can conceive nothing equal to this. . . . Here likewise I see all Good. . . . The soul delights unspeakably therein, yet it beholds nothing that can be spoken by the tongue or conceived by the heart. It sees nothing yet sees all, because it beholds the Good darkly; and the more darkly and secretly the Good is seen, the more certain it is, and excellent above all things. Wherefore all other good that can be seen or imagined is doubtless less than this, and even when the soul sees the Divine wisdom, power and will of God (which I have seen marvellously at other times), it is all less than this most certain Good. Because this is the whole, and those other things are but part of the whole. . . . But seen thus darkly, the Good brings no smile to the lips, no fervour of love to the heart; for the body does not tremble or become moved and distressed as at other times; because the soul sees, and not the body, which rests and sleeps, and the tongue is dumb and speechless. All the many ineffable kindnesses which God has shown me, all the sweet words and divine sayings and doings, are so much less than this that I saw in the darkness, that I put no hope in them. . . . But to this most high power of beholding God ineffably through great darkness, my spirit was uplifted three times only and no more."

"This cloud," says The Cloud of Unknowing, of that same Divine Dark, "is evermore between thee and thy God . . . therefore shape thyself to abide in this darkness so long as thou mayest, evermore crying after Him whom thou lovest, for if ever thou shalt feel Him or see Him (in such sort as He may be seen or felt in this life) it behoveth always to be in this cloud or darkness." So Angela: " When I behold and am in that Good, although I seem to see nothing yet I see all things." In this achievement she reaches the goal of the mystic experience, the ecstatic communion with the Absolute One.I have called her a Franciscan mystic. If by Franciscan mysticism we mean that exquisite sense of the Divine immanence in nature, that poetic temperament, that peculiar and elusive charm, which we associate with St. Francis himself; then, perhaps, there seems little that is characteristically Franciscan in Angela. But if, looking past the special character of the Founder, we try to seize the essence of that secret he was seeking to impart, then, allowing for the inevitable development which any idea undergoes when it enters the world of change, we may regard her as a typical Franciscan of the second generation. She was indeed conditioned at all points by the Franciscan environment in which her religious life developed;

that ardent society of " Spirituals," mostly recruited from the devout laity, which sprang up in her time in the Italian cities. This society, with its advanced contemplative tradition, its demand for a close imitation of Christ, was a forcing-house of the mystical life. Angela shows her close connection with it in the character of her penitence, in her passionate devotion to the Cross and Passion, and also in the metaphysical quality of her greatest mystical apprehensions. These three outstanding characteristics, corresponding in a general sense to the three great phases of the mystical life, are again seen in the poetry in which her contemporary Jacopone discloses to us the stages of anguished contrition and of uncontrolled fervour through which he moved to the heights of union with God. These two great converts and initiates of love illuminate and explain one another: for in them we see an identical tradition of the spiritual life interpreted by different temperaments. For each the Way is an education in love, and Jacopone speaks for both of them when he says of it:

> *"Distinguese l'amore en terzo stato:*
> *bono, meglio, sommo, sublimato;*
> *to sommo si vole essere amato*
> *senza compagnia."*

3: *Julian of Norwich*

ALL that we know directly of Julian of Norwich -- the most attractive, if not the greatest of the English mystics -- comes to us from her book, The Revelations of Divine Love, in which she has set down her spiritual experiences and meditations. Like her contemporaries, Walter Hilton and the author of The Cloud of Unknowing, she lives only in her vision and her thought. Her external circumstances are almost unknown to us, but some of these can be recovered, or at least deduced, from the study of contemporary history and art; a source of information too often neglected by those who specialize in religious literature, yet without which that literature can never wholly be understood.

Julian, who was born about 1342, in the reign of Edward III, grew up among the surroundings and influences natural to a deeply religious East Anglian gentlewoman at the close of the Middle Ages. Though she speaks of herself as " unlettered," which perhaps means unable to write, she certainly received considerable education, including some Latin, before her Revelations were composed. Her known connection with the Benedictine convent of Carrow, near Norwich, in whose gift was the anchorage to which she retired, suggests that she may have been educated by the nuns; and perhaps made her first religious profession at this house, which was in her time the principal "young ladies' school" of the Norwich diocese, and a favourite retreat of those adopting the religious life. During her most impressionable years she must have seen in

their freshness some of the greatest creations of Gothic art, for in Norfolk both architecture and painting had been carried to the highest pitch of excellence by the beginning of the fourteenth century. The great East Anglian school of miniature painting had already produced its masterpieces and was in its decadence. But if we look at these masterpieces -- the wonderful manuscripts illuminated at Gorleston near Yarmouth, and other religious houses of the district -- and remember that these are merely the surviving examples of an art which decorated the walls of the churches as richly as the pages of its service-books, we begin to realize the sort of iconography, the view of the Christian landscape, from which Julian's mental furniture was derived. Some of the best of these manuscripts are in the British Museum; and those who wish to understand the atmosphere in which the mediæval mystics flourished would do well to study Julian's Revelations in their light. There they will find expressed in design that mixture of gaiety and awe, that balanced understanding of the natural and the divine, which is one of her strong characteristics. She, like these artists, can afford to wreathe her images of supernatural mysteries in homely details drawn from the common life. Moreover, the more pictorial her revelations become, the more closely they approximate to the pictures in the psalters and Books of Hours of her time. From this source came her detailed visions of incidents in the Passion -- the blood that she saw running down under the garland of thorns, the dried, discoloured body, the gaping wounds, and "rueful and wasted" face of Christ -- and those of the Blessed Virgin as a "little maiden," as "Mater Dolorosa," and as the crowned Queen of Heaven. All these were common subjects with the miniature artists and wall painters of the time, and the form which they took in Julian's revelations must be attributed to a large extent to unconscious memory of those artists' works.

Another more inward aspect of contemporary religion has also affected her; the cult of the Holy Name of Jesus. This beautiful devotion was specially characteristic of English personal religion in the late Middle Ages, and is strongly marked in the writings of the mystics; especially Hilton and Rolle. The great popularity in England of the hymn Jesu Dulcis Memoria, and the many vernacular imitations of it current in Julian's day, helped in the spread of this cult; with which was associated that intense and highly emotional preoccupation with the physical accidents of the Passion so constantly reflected in her visionary experience. " good Jesu!" cried Rolle, "my heart thou hast bound in love of Thy Name and now I cannot but sing it"; and he spoke not for himself only but for all the best religious lyrists of the early fourteenth century, whose characteristic mood was that of personal, intimate, and sorrowing love of Jesus.

> *"Sweet Jesu, now will I sing*
> *To thee, a song of love longing.*
> *Teach me, Lord, thy love song*
> *With sweet tears ever among."*
> Thus, one of these Middle English poets could write:
> *"Jesu, well owe I to love thee*
> *For that me showed the roode tree,*
> *The crown of thorns, the nailes three,*
> *The sharp spear that through-stong thee,*
> *Jesu of love is sooth tokening*
> *Thy head down-bowed to love-kissing,*
> *Thine arms spread to love-clipping,*
> *Thy side all open to love-showing."*

Of such poetry as this -- with which she was probably familiar -- Julian often reminds us; and sometimes her parallels with it are close. Thus she says in her tenth Revelation: "Then with a glad cheer our Lord looked into his side, and beheld rejoicing. With his sweet looking he led forth the understanding of his creature by the same wound into his side within. And then he showed a fair delectable place and large enough for all mankind that shall be saved to rest in peace and in love. . . . And with this our good Lord said fullblissfully; Lo! how that I loved thee." In such passages as this, in her highly visualized meditations on the Crown of Thorns and the Precious Blood, and in such phrases as "I liked none other heaven than Jesus, who shall be my bliss when I am there," and other ardent expressions of religious love, she is speaking the common devotional language and using the common devotional imagery of her own day. Hence those merely visionary experiences with which her book opens and which form by far the least important part of it, can be accounted for as the result of unconscious memory, weaving new vivid pictures from the current religious and artistic conceptions in which she had been reared. A correspondence has indeed been detected between the order of these fifteen "showings," and the fifteen prayers on the Passion known as the "XV Os," which occur in the Sarum Horse. They are, in fact, dreams of which any devout and imaginative person of that time was capable; and need not be taken too seriously when estimating the character of Julian's mysticism.

This, then, was the religious, artistic, and emotional environment in which she grew up; an environment to which new sombre colour and new realization of pain had been given by the Black Death which swept through Norfolk when she was a child. More important, however, than any external influence, was the part her own temperament played in her special apprehension of God. It is plain that she was from the first of an intensely religious, meditative disposition. As a girl, she says, she asked of God three things. The first was, that she might have a keen realization of Christ's Passion; because although she had great feeling of it, she desired more, and specially a bodily sight of His pains. The second was bodily sickness, much esteemed in the Middle Ages as a means of grace; and this she wished to suffer at thirty years of age. The third was, that as Saint Cecilia was pierced by three wounds, so she might be pierced with the three wounds of contrition, compassion, and eager longing towards God. The first two desires she forgot for a while; but the three wounds she prayed for continually. When she was thirty years old, the gift of sickness was granted her, and it was exactly such a sickness, "so hard as unto death," as she had asked; a fact which tells us a good deal about Julian's mental make-up, revealing her as the possessor of an extremely active "psychic background." By the law of association we may be sure that her illness brought back to mind the other forgotten prayer, for a deeper insight into, and vision of, the Passion. It is supposed that she was at this time already an anchoress, shut in that tiny room against the south wall of St. Julian's church at Norwich, of which the foundations can still be traced. But nothing in her own account suggests this, and the presence of her mother and "other persons" round her sick bed is rather against it. At the same time, a single woman of strong religious bent is hardly likely in that period to have remained in the world till she was thirty. Julian was perhaps a Benedictine nun at Carrow, and after her vision sought a life of greater seclusion and austerity at St. Julian's, which was the property of the Carrow convent. The anchoress was often, but not always, a professed nun; and though no reminiscences of cloister life can be traced in Julian's writings, such a life would account in part for the theological knowledge and familiarity with dogmatic language which those writings display.

Julian's account of what happened in her illness is extremely precise, and makes this part of her revelation an interesting psychological document. She fell ill early in May 1373 and on the fourth night was thought to be dying and given the last sacraments. For two days more she lingered, quite conscious and expecting death; and early in the morning of the third day, lost all feeling in her lower limbs. When the priest came to help her agony she was already speechless; but made her nurses prop her upright in bed, so that she could fix her failing eyes on the crucifix he held towards her. Thisshe could see, though everything else grew dim to her sight. Then her head fell on one side, breath failed, and she was sure that the end had come.

With this conviction and acceptance of death, the stress of the involuntary struggle for life seems suddenly to have ended. She had passed into a new state of consciousness, in which her mind was clear and her body free of pain, "as whole as ever before or after." In this condition her old and forgotten desires came back into her mind. The first, for sickness, had been granted. Now, she was impelled to ask the other, for a keener realization of the Passion; and this buried wish, surging back abruptly into consciousness, became the starting point of her mystical experiences. We cannot deny that these experiences had their pathological side. Her physical and psychic state were abnormal. With the perfect candour and common sense which add so much to our delight in her, she confesses that she at first mistook her revelations for delirium, and said to the monk who afterwards visited her that she had raved. There are, however, in these revelations, as in all visionary experience of any value, two distinct sides. One is the visual or auditory hallucination -- the vision seen, the voice heard -- the materials for which clearly come from the unconscious mind of the visionary, and can generally be traced to their source. The other is the intuitive spiritual teaching that accompanies it, and often far exceeds the visionary's own knowledge or power. Julian, in her account of what happened to her, keeps these two elements perfectly distinct. "All the blessed teaching of our Lord God," she says, "was shown to me by three parts -- that is to say, by the bodily sight, by words formed in mine understanding, and by ghostly sight."

The bodily vision, as she expressly affirms, she did not ask for; and here she agrees with all true mystics, who invariably distrust these quasi-physical experiences. Yet it was in such visionary hallucination that her revelations began. With hereyes still fixed on the crucifix, and apparently at the point of death, she suddenly saw red blood running down from the Crown of Thorns, as if in answer to her prayer for more feeling of the Passion of Christ. The Cross had become for her, as the shining pewter dish did for Jacob Boehme, or the running stream for St. Ignatius, a focal point on which to concentrate; and so a door to a deeper state of consciousness. Spiritual insight went side by side with the bodily vision, which was accepted without question by Julian as a direct message from Christ to strengthen her, "lest she be tempted of fiends before she died"; for in spite of her intuitive philosophic sense, we must remember that she lived in imagination in that Gothic world of concrete devils and angels which the cathedral sculptors reproduced. The double experience -- outward pictures of the Passion, and inward teachings of the nature of God -- continued for five hours, whilst she lay in a state of trance which her mother mistook for death. "The first began early in the morn, about the hour of four; and they lasted, showing by process full fair and steadily, each following other, till it was nine of the day overpassed." In those five hours Julian received the whole substance of her teaching, afterwards divided by her into sixteen "revelations of love." When they had passed, normal consciousness returned, or, as she says, she "fell to herself," and knew that she must live. She lay for some time in weakness and depression, tormented by evil dreams; but she recovered from her sickness, and lived to a great age. Her careful account of that illness, and of the psychic experiences accompanying it, helps us to understand those experiences from the psychological as well as the mystical point of view. Seen thus, they are not unique; but classic examples of a type which turns up from time to time in medical history. Thus Dr. Edwin Ash, in Faith and Suggestion, has described a case which strikingly resembles that of Julian. Here, too, at the crisis of an apparently hopeless illness, the patient fell into a death-like trance, had visionsof a religious type, and emerged cured. Her mind was far inferior to that of Julian, hence her experience had less beauty and significance and was of little value for other souls. Nevertheless, its general outline forces us to acknowledge that it belongs to the same class, and helps us to interpret the facts which lie behind Julian's words.

Julian's revelations have come down to us in two distinct versions, which have both been edited for modern readers. The best known is the long version, reproduced in Miss Warrack's delightful edition; but our earliest manuscript of this only goes back to the sixteenth century, at least a hundred years after Julian's death. Another, much shorter, is found in one fifteenth-century manuscript in the British Museum, and this has been edited by Mr. Dundas Herford, who claims -- I think with good reason -- that it represents ,Julian's first account of her visions, written or told while they were still fresh in her mind, and before her memory of them had been coloured by long meditation, or by the theological learning which she certainly acquired in later life. It briefly sets forth her chain of visions, and the " ghostly words" and inward teachings that accompanied them. These, she says, she has set down for the help of her fellow-Christians and because she saw it to be God's will. "But," she adds, "God forbid that ye should say or take it so, that I am a teacher; for I mean not so! No! I never meant so! For I am a woman, unlearned, feeble and frail; but I know well that this that I say, I have it of the showing of Him that is Sovereign Teacher." In the long version these deprecatory words are omitted. Julian no longer fears to be regarded as a teacher. On the contrary, she speaks with a gentle authority as one whose position is assured. She is now, without doubt, the established anchoress; the devout woman whose special vocation is known, and to whom people come for spiritual teaching. Moreover, she tells us in this book that only twenty years, less three months, after her vision was she inwardly taught the importance of all its details, however "misty and indifferent" they seemed. She was therefore past fifty when she wrote or dictated it; and it contains the fruit, not only of her first vivid experience, but of all the ponderings by which the last atom of significance was extracted from it, the "enlightenings and touchings of the same Spirit," which kept the revelation fresh in after life.

As she says herself -- for her introspective powers were remarkable -- the "first beginnings" and subsequent " ghostly teachings" at last became so merged in her understanding that she could not separate them. There is a parallel to this in the life of Boehme. He says that in the abnormal state which was induced by gazing at the polished pewter dish he "understood the Being of all Beings" -- even as Julian " saw God in a Point" -- but this stupendous revelation only left him dazed and inarticulate. Only after twelve years of meditation, during which he felt the seed of truth "unfolding within him like a young plant," was he able to describe it.

When we compare the two versions of Julian's work, we find many differences which remind us of this confession. Although the whole doctrine of the long book is really implied in the short book -- for it is, in Boehme's phrase, an unfolding of the plant from that one seed -- we see that the most beautiful and poetical passages are found in the long version only. They are the fruit of meditation upon vision. The workings of Julian's unconscious mind in her trance have only provided the raw material, as the inspiration of the poet gives only the crude beginnings of the poem. Moreover, with age her character deepened and grew richer. She used her talent to help other souls, and it increased. She studied, too, and found language of great subtlety and beauty in which to express her vision of truth. Though even the first version of her book shows theological knowledge which would put to shame most present-day Christians, in the later work this knowledge is much increased. Reading was part of the duty of an anchoress,being regarded as an essential element in the life of prayer; and intelligent reading has clearly nourished Julian's deep meditations on the character of God. In her there was an almost perfect balance between the intellectual and the emotional life, and there are few women mystics of whom we can say this.

The question of her literary sources is an interesting one. A careful examination of her revelations makes it plain that even when the short version was written, she was already acquainted with many theological conceptions; whilst the meditations with which the long version is enriched, and its fuller descriptions of her spiritual "Showings," reveal her as possessing at least by middle life a considerable knowledge of the language of Augustinian theology and of the root-ideas of Christian mysticism. As used by her, many of these ideas have the special colour which was given to them by Meister Eckhart and his school; and suggest that Julian at one time or another had come into contact with the characteristically Dominican type of mysticism which is best known to us in the works of Suso and Tauler. In her teaching on sin -- " I saw not sin, for I believe it hath no substance nor any part of being" -- she is following, indeed almost quoting, Eckhart's saying that "evil is nothing but a privation of being; not an effect, but a defect." So, too, Eckhart's daring assertion that sin has its place in the scheme -- " Since God, in a way, also wills that I should have committed sins, I do not wish not to have committed them" -- appears to be echoed in gentler form in Julian's view of sin as a purifying scourge, and of the scars which it leaves on the redeemed soul as being " not wounds but worships." Her beautiful saying that we are God's bliss," for in us He enjoyeth without end," seems like a deduction from the Eckhartian paradox, "God needs me as much as I need Him." She has received, perhaps from the same source, the antique mystical notion of the soul's precession from and return to God." The soul," said Eckhart, "is created that itmay flow back into the bottom of the bottomless fountain whence it came forth." "Thus I understood," says Julian," that all His blessed children which be come out of Him by nature shall be brought again into Him by grace"; and again, "all kinds that He hath made to flow out of Him to work His will shall be restored and brought again into Him." Here, again, the naked Eckhartian monism seems to be transmitted through a more human and more spiritual temperament. She agrees, too, with the German mystics in her doctrine of God as the "ground of the soul." "Our soul is so deep-grounded in God and so endlessly treasured that we may not come to the knowing thereof till we have first knowing of God. . . . God is nearer to us than our own soul, for He is the ground in whom our soul standeth, and He is the mean that keepeth the substance and the sensuality together so that they shall never depart." So Tauler says, " A man who verily desires to enter in will surely find God here, for God never separates Himself from this ground. God will be present with him and he will find and enjoy eternity here."

Julian's revelation was received in 1373, and the long text as we have it was written at some date after 1393. Eckhart had died in 1329, Tauler in 1361; and the great Ruysbroeck, whose mysticism owes much on its speculative side to Eckhart's philosophy, in 1381. The influence of their teaching spread rapidly, and few preaching friars of an inward disposition can have escaped it. To these preaching friars was committed in the fourteenth century the special duty of giving solid theological teaching to nuns. This was commonly done by way of vernacular sermons and instructions, of which Tauler's surviving sermons are types; and it was possibly through such instructions given in the Carrow convent that Julian obtained that peculiar knowledge of Dominican mysticism, those contacts with Augustinian and Victorine thought, on which the more philosophic side of her revelation seems to depend. The parallels with her great contemporary St.Catherine of Siena, which Professor Edmund Gardner has noted, are probably due to the fact that both women drew their ideas from some earlier source. Her likenesses to Ruysbroeck can also be accounted for. His Seven Cloisters, Kingdom of God's Lovers, and Ornaments of the Spiritual Marriage were all completed before 1350, and knowledge of them would reach East Anglia quickly, through the Flemish colony established at Norwich. Several close correspondences with him can be traced in Julian's work; especially her conception of God's eternal thirst and love-longing, so similar to Ruysbroeck's "hungry yet generous love of God," and the opening phrase of her Third Revelation, "After this I saw God in a Point," which reminds us of the great definition in the Seven Cloisters, "That Point in which all our lives find their end." Julian thus represents the first emergence in English literature of a stream of tradition which is not represented in the classic school of English mysticism descended from Rolle. By this school she does not appear to have been greatly influenced; there is little in her that reminds us of it, or of that group of contemplatives who produced the Cloud of Unknowing and its companion works. Her true affinities are with the Christian Platonism which St. Augustine introduced into theology, and its developments in the works of Erigena and Eckhart. But when we have given full weight to the effects upon her work of oral teaching and of reading, the true originality of that work only becomes more manifest. Reading and teaching fed her speculative mind, and helped her to understand and express her own experience; but this experience in its essence was independent of intellectual knowledge. It was the fruit of a deeply mystical and poetic nature, brooding on the conception of God common to mediaeval Christianity. Julian had in a high degree constructive religious genius; and for such a nature an evocative phrase is enough to waken the " ghostly sight."

It is impossible in a short essay to give any full account ofher teaching. That teaching is centred on her own ardent consciousness of God, as an all-transcending yet all-enclosing reality; a conception at once philosophic and practical. For Julian, as for the Platonists, God is the sum of the highest spiritual values -- "He is all-thing that is good to my seeming, and all-thing that is good, it is He." Her perception of the Divine Immanence is peculiarly intense, and expressed in the strongest terms. " God is kind (nature) in His being; that is to say, that goodness that is in kind, that is God. He is the ground, He is the substance, He is the same thing that is kind-head," and again, "I saw full assuredly that our substance is in God, and also I saw that in our sensuality God is . . . for it is His good pleasure to reign in our understanding blissfully, and sit in our soul restfully, and to dwell in our soul endlessly, us all working into Him." But this vivid sense of Divine reality, as the very ground of being, is closely bound up with her devotion to the person of Christ. Her theological path, like her mystical experience, lay through the human to the Divine, through emotional realization of the Passion to intellectual vision of the Godhead. In the first revelation of all we get these two aspects of truth sharply contrasted; for there her vision of the bloodstained Crown of Thorns, with its intimate appeal to the heart, is balanced by her other interior sight of "the Godhead seen in mine understanding." The long version of her book elaborates this simple intuition of the Deity into a very beautiful description of the Holy Trinity -- always one of Julian's favourite subjects -- but the whole is really implied in the first brief statement, which strikes at once her characteristic chord of intimacy and awe, or, as she puts it, "the dread and the homeliness of God." In the Catholic doctrine of the Trinity, which was never far from her thoughts, she found the link between these personal and impersonal apprehensions. That half-Platonic notion of Christ the Eternal Wisdom as "Mother" of the soul, which is one of her most original conceptions, heretakes its place side by side with the other, more metaphysical intuition of that unconditioned Deity in whom "All-thing hath the Being." "For all our life is in three; in the first we have our being, in the second we have our increasing, and in the third we have our fulfilling; the first is nature, the second is mercy, and the third is grace. For the first I understood that the high might of the Trinity is our Father, and the deep wisdom of the Trinity is our Mother, and the great love of the Trinity is our Lord; and all this we have in nature and in our substantial making. . . . All the fair working, and all the sweet kindly office of dearworthy motherhood is impropriated to the Second Person . . . and all is one Love."

This blend of personal and metaphysical vision is not unique. We find it again in the Franciscan contemplative, Angela of Foligno. But Julian's nature is richer and more mellow, and the doctrine of love which she deduced from her experience is more profound. Here, in this harmonized consciousness of the most human and most philosophic aspects of religious experience, she is typical of Christian mysticism at its best. She avoids on the one hand the excessive intellectualism of the Neoplatonist, and on the other the unpleasant exuberance of the religious emotionalist, yet draws from the apprehensions of both the heart and the head all the elements needed to feed a full spiritual life. The human element brought in by Christianity, with all the emotional values belonging to it -- however symbolic this side of contemplation must necessarily be -- redeems philosophic mysticism from the clear coldness, the lofty superiority, that St. Augustine condemned in the Platonists. But, equally, it is the philosophic background, the austere worship of that trinity of Light, Life, and Love, in whom, as Julian says, we are clad more closely than a body in its clothes, which saves mystical fervour from its worst extravagances. Here she is and will ever be one of the safest guides to the contemplative life.

Another special quality of Julian's teaching is its healthy, vigorous, affirmative character. The only two sins she sternly condemns -- and she calls them not sins, but sickness -- are sloth or lack of zest, and doubtful dread or lack of hope. Zest and hope she regards as essential factors in the life of the soul. The Light, Life, and Love which form her ultimate definition of triune Reality -- the Mother, Brother, and Saviour, which are her nearest images for Christ's relation with man -- these are

conceptions which kill the sort of pious moods that R. L. Stevenson called "dim, dem, and dowie." God's attitude to man is "courteous, glad, and merry," and we do Him less honour by solemnity than by " cheer of mirth and joy." To her, only the good is the true, and evil is a void, a lack of the only reality; a Platonic notion which has always been dear to the mystics. "In this naked word Sin," says Julian, "our

Lord brought to my mind generally all that is not good . . . but I saw not sin, for I believe it hath no manner of substance nor no part of being, nor could it be known but by the pain it is cause of." It follows that our attention should not be given to the avoidance or consideration of sin, but to the understanding and enjoyment of the good and the real. "The beholding of other men's sins, it maketh as it were a thick mist before the eyes of the soul," says Julian. Her strongest condemnation is given to morbid pondering of past sins and mistakes. "Right as by the courtesy of God He forgets our sins when we repent, right so will He that we forget our sin, and all our heaviness and all our doubtful dreads." This world, after all, is only a nursery for heaven, and its inhabitants mostly spiritual babies who need not be taken too seriously. "I understood no higher stature in this life than childhood; "and the attitude of God to our infant souls is that of "the kindly loving Mother that witteth and knoweth the need of her child and keepeth it full tenderly as the kind and condition of Motherhood will."

No modern psychologist could be more emphatic than this fourteenth-century recluse on the foolishness of worry, the duty of confidence, gaiety, and hope. "Notwithstanding our simple living and our blindness here, yet endlessly our courteous Lord beholdeth us in this working rejoicing; and of all things we may please him best, wisely and truly to believe, and to enjoy with Him and in Him." She brings back the primitive Christian insistence on joy -- confident happiness -- as the one sure sign of the spiritual life. If we have not got this, it is because we lack the faith and common sense which sees life in a universal and disinterested light. Once, Julian says, she was inclined to worry about God's work in the soul of a friend whom she loved, and she was answered in her reason "as it were by a friendly man," " Take it generally! and behold the courtesy of thy Lord God as He shows it to thee, for it is more worship to God to behold Him in all than in any special thing." In those words we have a complete prescription for happiness and inward peace. All that is made, as Julian saw in her vision, is but "a little thing the quantity of an hazel nut" in comparison with the Divine life that creates, keeps, and loves it, and may be known in those sudden glimpses of perfection which we call the Good, the Beautiful, and the True. These, in her language, are "God's courteous showings of Himself," and we are most likely to encounter them when we take the worlds of nature and grace "generally," and refrain from partial or egoistic criticisms and demands. Failure in this simple rule, she thinks, is the true cause of human misery and unrest. "This is the cause why we be not all in ease of heart and soul; that we seek here rest in those things that are so little, wherein is no rest, and know not our God that is All-mighty, All-wise, and All-good."

Mysticism in Modern France

1. Soeur Thérèse de l'Enfant Jésus

THAT Christian tradition of the spiritual life which has been specially developed within the religious orders -- with its definite objective, its methodical training in self-conquest and the art of prayer -- is often regarded as a mere survival of medievalism, lingering in odd corners but having no points of contact with our modern world. Yet this tradition lives now, as surely as in the days of St. Gertrude or St. Teresa. It continues to exercise its mysterious attraction; transmuting those who give themselves to its influence, and producing that special type of character and experience which is so clearly marked in the histories of the Catholic saints. In a world of change, this has hardly altered. Within the contemplative convents there obtains that same scale of values, that same contempt for the body and undivided attention to the interests of the soul, that same avoidance of all comfort or pleasure and eager acceptance of pain, which is revealed in the standard writings of Christian asceticism. In these houses, mysticism is still a practical art: the education there given represents the classic spiritual discipline of the west, and still retains its transforming power. Through it, souls obtain access to a veritable world of spirit; and apprehend under symbols eternal values, which are unperceived by their fellow men. By it they are supported throughthe difficult adjustments of consciousness and sublimation of instinct, which are needed when the centre of life's interest is shifted from physical to supernal levels. This is a fact which students of psychology, and especially of religious experience in its intensive form, should not ignore. They need not go to the Middle Ages for their examples of the effect of ascetic training and contemplative practice, or for characteristic specimens of the "saintly type"; for these may be found within our own period, and studied in their relation to our modern world.

Those who regard this saintly type as a hot-house plant, raised under conditions which appear to defend it from the temptations and distractions of ordinary existence, can have little acquaintance either with cloister ideals or with cloistered lives. A thoroughgoing monastic discipline is the most searching school of virtue ever invented. It withers easygoing piety and "other-worldliness" at the root. It confers a robust humility which is proof against all mortifications and disappointments. It leaves no room for individual tastes and preferences, religious or secular. Its pupils must learn to resent nothing, to demand nothing; to thrive on humiliations, to love and serve all without distinction, without personal choice; even to renounce the special consolations of religion. The common idea of the cloister, as providing a career of impressive religious ceremonial varied by plain sewing, pious gossip, and "devotionettes" is far from the truth. On its external side, a well-ordered convent provides a busy, practical, family life of the most austere kind, with many duties, both religious and domestic, countless demands upon patience, good-temper and unselfishness, and few relaxations. On its hidden side, it is a device to train and toughen the spirit, develop its highest powers, and help it to concentrate its attention more and more completely on eternal realities. That training is still given in its completeness; and the classic, saintly character is still being produced,with its special cultivation of love, meekness, and self-sacrifice, balanced by energy, courage, and strength of will.

Sanctity is the orientation of the spirit towards supreme Reality. To the believer in any theistic religion, no attitude of the soul could be simpler, more natural than this. There is nothing about it which deserves to be called abnormal, archaic, or fantastic. The complications with which it is surrounded, the unnatural aspect which it wears for practical men, all come from its collision with the entangled interests and perverse ideals of the world. Thus, retreat from this tangle of sham interests, the building up of a consistent universe within which the self can develop its highest powers and purest loves, is felt to be imperative for those selves in whom this innate aptitude for God reaches the conscious level. In these spirits, the "vocation" for the special life of correspondence with the supersensual reproduces on a higher plane the vocation of the artist or the poet. All the self's best energies and desires tend in this direction, and it will achieve harmonious development only by unifying itself about this centre of interest, and submitting to the nurture and discipline which shall assure its dominance. The symbols with which the universe of religion is furnished, the moral law which there obtains, are all contributory to the one end; and find their justification in its achievement.

Within the Christian Church, and especially in that which is technically called the "religious life," these symbols and this law have not varied for many centuries; nor has the type of personality which they develop changed much since it first appeared in monastic history. The sharp sense of close communion with, and immediate responsibility to, a personal God possessing human attributes; the complete abandonment of desire, combined with astonishing tenacity of purpose; contempt for the merely comfortable either in spiritual or physical affairs; a glad and eager acceptance of pain -- these are the qualities of the Christian saint, and these are stillfostered in appropriate subjects by the cloistered life. These facts have been abundantly demonstrated during the last thirty years in a group of French Carmelite mystics, of whom the best known is Thérèse Martin, already the object of a widespread cultus under the name of Soeur Thérèse de l' Enfant Jésus. Others who will repay study are Elizabeth Catez, or Soeur Elizabeth de la Trinité (18801906) and Mère Marie-Ange de l' Enfant- Jésus (1881-1909). It is clear that we have in these young women -- for they all died before they were thirty years of age -- a genuine renaissance of traditional Catholic mysticism. Their experience exhibits many close correspondences with that of the great mystics of the past; the same development of the interior life can be traced in them, and they knew at first hand some at least among those forms of spiritual consciousness which are described by Ruysbroeck, Angela of Foligno, St. Teresa, and St. John of the Cross.

The first in time and in importance -- for the others depended to a greater or less degree on her influence and example -- was Thérèse Martin, who was born at Alençon in 1873 and died in 1897. The last nine years of her life were spent in the Carmelite Convent of Lisieux in Normandy; and she there wrote the spiritual autobiography, L'histoire d'une âme, which has since been translated into every European language. In her life -- which shows with exceptional clearness the reality and driving power of that instinct which is known as religious vocation -- and in the incidents connected with her death and cultus, we find many suggestive parallels with the histories of the historical saints. These parallels often help us to determine the true meaning of statements in those histories; indicating the possible origin of much that now appears extravagant and abnormal, and restoring to their real position in the human race men and women who dropped their living characteristics in ascending to the altars of the Church.We notice first in Thérèse the extent to which heredity and environment contributed to the formation in her of an exclusively religious temperament. She inherited from both parents an ascetic tendency. Her father, as a young man, had sought without success to become a novice at the Great St. Bernard; her mother had wished to be a Sister of Charity. Their marriage had the character of a religious dedication; and their one wish was for children who might be consecrated to the service of God. Nine were born, of whom four died in infancy. The five girls who survived all entered the cloister, for which indeed their whole life had been a perfect preparation. The idea of marriage seems never to have occurred to any member of the family. Hence Thérèse , the youngest child, grew up in a home which was a veritable forcing-house of the spiritual life, though full of happiness and warm affection; and by it was moulded to that puritanism and otherworldliness which is characteristic of real Catholic piety. There the conception of earthly existence as a "school for saints" was taken for granted, and the supremacy of religious interests never questioned: all deeds and words, however trivial, being judged by the grief or pleasure they would give to God. Even as a tiny child, she was given a string of beads to count the "sacrifices" made each day. The Martin family lived, in fact, within a dream-world, substantially identical with the universe of mediæval piety. It was peopled with angels and demons, whose activities were constantly noted; its doors were ever open for the entry of the miraculous, its human inhabitants were the objects of the Blessed Virgin's peculiar care, every chance happening was the result of Divine interference. For them this universe was actual, not symbolic. Their minds instinctively rejected every impression that conflicted with it; and its inconsistencies with the other -- perhaps equally symbolic and less lovely -- world of our daily life were unperceived. The most bizarre legends of the saints were literal facts; all relics were authentic, andmost were full of supernatural power. The Holy House of Loretto, the face of St. Catherine of Bologna still marked by the kiss of the Infant Christ, found in them willing and awestruck believers. Yet these crude symbols, thus literally understood, became for them the means of a real transcendence. The dominant interests of the home were truly supersensual; a vigorous spiritual life was fostered in it, marked by humility and love, true goodness, complete unselfishness, a courageous attitude towards misfortune and pain.

Thus from birth Thérèse was protected from all risk of intellectual conflict, and surrounded by harmonious contributory suggestions all tending to press her emotional life into one mould. Such a nurture could hardly fail to create either the disposition of a rebel or that of a saint: but there was in Thérèse no tendency to revolt. Her temperament -- ardent, imaginative, abnormally sensitive, and psychically unstable -- inclined her to the enthusiastic acceptance of religious ideas, and even in childhood she showed a fervour and devotion exceeding that of her sisters. When she was still a little girl, the two eldest left home one after the other, in order to become nuns in the Carmelite convent of Lisieux. The departure of the first, Pauline, was a crushing grief to Thérèse , at that time about nine years old; and was apparently the beginning of her own desire to be a nun. She told the Superior of the convent that she, too, intended to be a Carmelite, and wished to take the veil at once. The Reverend

Mother, a woman of kindness and good sense, did not laugh; but advised her to wait until she was sixteen, and then to try her vocation. There is less absurdity than at first appears in this childish craving; for the religious type is often strangely precocious. As the tendency to music or painting may appear in earliest childhood, so the sense of vocation may awaken, long before the implications of this mysterious impulse are fully understood. Thus Elizabeth Catez, afterwards Soeur Elizabeth dela Trinité, determined to be a nun when she was seven years old, and began at this age to govern her inner life. She and Thérèse help us to understand the stories and of the visions and self-dedication of the little St. Catherine of Siena; or those of St. Catherine of Genoa and Madame Guyon, who both wished at twelve years old to enter a religious order. We are faced in all such cases by the strange phenomenon of accelerated development: strongly marked in the case of Thérèse, who undoubtedly had, in spite of the great simplicity of her nature, a real genius for the spiritual life.

She had, too, and in a marked degree, the peculiarly sensitive psychic organization which is observed in many of the historic mystics. A long and severe nervous illness had followed her sister's departure for the cloister. It was cured by a form of auto-suggestion for which many parallels can be found in the history of adult religious experience; though few in that of children of her age. This incident Thérèse has described in her memoirs with great clearness and honesty. At a crisis of the sickness, when she was reduced to utter misery and weakness and tormented by hallucinations and fears, her three sisters came to her room and knelt before the statue of the Blessed Virgin, praying for her cure. The sick child, praying too as well as she could, suddenly saw the statue take life and advance towards her with a smile. Instantly the prayer was answered, her pains and delusions left her, and she was cured. The " vision " being told -- and of course accepted at face-value as a supernatural grace -- marked Thérèse from this time as a privileged soul. It certainly indicated in her an abnormal suggestibility, comparable with that which is revealed by the somewhat similar incident in the life of Julian of Norwich, and was not without importance for her future development.

The religious transformation and exaltation so often experienced in adolescence is seen in Thérèse in its mostintense form. It was initiated when she was thirteen by another nervous illness, apparently brought on by a morbid brooding on her own supposed imperfections -- the spiritual ailment well known to religious directors as "scrupulosity" -- and it was from this period that she afterwards dated the beginning of her real spiritual life. The childish determination to become a Carmelite had now grown in strength, and when she was fourteen she broke to her father her own violent consciousness of vocation; a certitude which nothing could shake. Her inner life was at this time astonishingly mature. She was not a prig, but a sensitive and affectionate little girl; yet her autobiography is full of sayings which surprise us by their depth and wisdom, when we remember the age of the child who thought and said them. By the constant practice of small renunciations, self-denial was now habitual to her; for it was by that which she called the " little pathway" of incessant but inconspicuous sacrifices and kind deeds, and not by any abnormal austerities or devotions, that her character was formed. Though perfectly free from all spiritual pride, she was, moreover, quite certain of her own communion with the Divine order, and of the authority of the impressions which she received from it.

" En ce temps-1à, je n'osais rien dire de mes sentiments interieurs; la voie par laquelle je marchais etait si droite, si lumineuse, que je ne sentais pas le besoin d'un autre guide que Jesus . . . je pensais que pour moi, le bon Dieu ne se servait pas d' intermediaire, mais agissait directement."

These are bold words for a young girl who had been reared in the most rigid provincial piety, and had been taught to distrust private judgment and regard her director as the representative of God. In them we see the action of that strong will, power of initiative and clear conception of her own needs and duties, which redeem her often emotional religious fervour from insipidity. It is true that she can and does express that fervour in the sentimental language whichis the least attractive element in French piety. The sense of a special relationship and special destiny which more and more possessed her, far exceeded her powers either of realization or of expression; and unfortunately impelled her to describe herself as the "fleurette," the "petite fiancée," even the "jouet" of Jesus, and to note in too many casual happenings evidence of "les delicatessen du bon Dieu pour moi." Yet we cannot forget that similar declarations, equally offensive to modern taste, abound in some of the greatest historical mystics, and that their full unpleasantness is only mitigated to us by the quaint and archaic phrases in which they are expressed. Whilst no doubt these declarations represent the invasion of human desires and instincts into the field of spiritual experience, its natural craving for protection and personal love; they also witness to the mystic's intense personal consciousness of close communion, a consciousness which far transcends the poor vocabulary and commonplace symbols through which it must be told.

Therefore we cannot dismiss Thérèse Martin as a mere victim of religious emotionalism, because her mental equipment is inadequate to her spiritual experience. When, moreover, we remember the amazing vigour and tenacity of purpose with which, when barely fifteen, this gentle and home-loving child, driven by her strong sense of vocation, planned and carried through a lifelong separation from the father she adored and the world of nature she loved, we are bound to acknowledge in her an element of greatness, a strong and an adventurous soul. With a certitude of her own duty which nothing could shake, Thérèse interviewed on her own behalf the Superior of the order, who snubbed her, and the Bishop of the diocese, who was kind but prevaricated with her; demanding from them permission to take the veil at once, instead of waiting till the usual age of twenty-one. Further, being taken by her father to Rome with a party of French pilgrims, when they were all received by the Pope she hadthe courage to address him directly -- although the priest in charge of the pilgrimage forbade it -- and asked for his support. The end of it was that she at last convinced the authorities of her special vocation, and was allowed to become a postulant in the most austere of all religious orders at the unheard-of age of fifteen.

Her career as a Carmelite was far from being the succession of mystical enjoyments, the basking in divine sunshine, which some imagine the contemplative life to be. She now experienced the common lot of the "proficient " in the mystic way; paying for her religious exaltation by reactions, long periods of aridity, which were doubtless due in part to psychic exhaustion. Then, in addition to the perpetual little sacrifices, self-deprivations, and penances which she imposed on herself, she seemed, as she says, to be plunged in a "terrible desert," a "profound night" of darkness and solitude; and prayer itself became dreary and unreal. "Tout a disparu . . . ce n'est plus un voile, c'est un mur qui s'eleve jusqu'aux cieux et couvre le firmament etoile." But an inner life which was nourished on the robust doctrine of St. John of the Cross could bear this deprivation with fortitude, and make of inward poverty itself a gain. Outwardly, too, her life was difficult. Her superiors seem at once to have perceived in her that peculiar quality of soul which is capable of sanctity; and since it is the ambition of every community to produce a saint, they addressed themselves with vigour to the stern task of educating Thérèse for her destiny. Still a child, sensitive and physically delicate, she was spared no opportunity of self-denial and mortification. Her most trifling deficiencies were remarked, her most reasonable desires thwarted, her good points ignored. When her health began to fail under a rule of life far beyond her strength, and the first signs of tuberculosis -- that scourge of the cloister -- appeared in her, the Prioress, in her ferocious zeal for souls, even refused to dispense the ailing girl from attendance atthe night-office. "Une âme de cette trempe, disait-elle, ne doit pas être traité comme une enfant, les dispenses ne sont pas faites pour elle. Laissez-là. Dieu la soutient." This drastic training did its work. Thérèse had a heroic soul, though her courage and generosity found expression for the most part in small and obscure ways. She has said that she felt in herself the longing to be a soldier, an apostle, a martyr; and within the limits of the cloister, she found means of satisfying these desires. "Elie accomplissait simplement des actes heroiques," said the Superior after her death. Determined, in her own metaphor, to be a "victime d'amour," her brave spirit never faltered in its willing acceptance of pain. She hid her mental and physical sufferings, fought her increasing weakness, ate without hesitation the rough food which made her ill, refused every comfort and amelioration. By this hard yet humble way she rose in a few years to the heights of perfect self-conquest and moral perfection: passing through suffering to a state in which love, and total self-giving for love, was realized by her as the central secret of the spiritual life. "La charite me donna la clef de ma vocation. . . . Enfin, je l'ai trouvée. Ma vocation, c'est l' amour."

In this completed love, stretching from the smallest acts of service to the most secret experiences of the soul, she found -- as every mystic has done -- that unifying principle of action which alone gives meaning to life. In its light all problems were solved, and the meaning of all experiences was disclosed. So Julian of Norwich, fifteen years after her first revelation, was "answered in ghostly understanding: "Wouldest thou wit thy Lord's meaning in this thing? Wit it well, Love was his meaning. Who showed it thee? Love. What showed he thee? Love. Wherefore showed it he? For love. Hold thee therein and thou shalt wit and know more in the same; but thou shalt never know nor wit therein other thing without end." To live in this supernatural charityis to introduce into the world of succession the steadfast values of eternity; hence this quality, so simple yet so difficult of attainment, is the one essential character of the saints. "Pour atteindre a la vie idéale de fame," said Elizabeth Catez, who so greatly exceeded her fellow-Carmelite in philosophic grasp, though not in moral beauty, " je crois qu'il faut vivre dans le surnaturel, prendre conscience que Dieu est au plus intime de nous, et aller a tout avec lui: alors on n'est jamais banal, meme en faisant les actions les plus ordinaires, car on ne vit pas en ces choses, on les dépasse. Une âme surnaturelle ne traite pas avec les causes secondes, mais avec Dieu seulement . . . pour elle, tout se reduite a l' unité."

Thérèse de l'Enfant-Jésus came to this consummation by way of a total and generous self-abandonment in all the daily incidents of life; a love which consecrated " les actions les plus ordinaires." She took as her favourite saint the Curé d'Ars, because "he loved his family so deeply, and only did ordinary things." This was the "little pathway" to the heart of Reality, on which, she thought, all might travel and none could miss the road. "Aux âmes simples, il ne faut pas des moyens compliqués." Though the unquenchable thirst of her ardent nature for more suffering and more love did more than once express itself by way of ecstatic experience, she repudiated all abnormal "graces" and special contemplative powers. "Je ne suis qu' un pauvre petit oiseau couvert seulement d'un leger duvet; je ne suis pas un aigle, j'en ai simplement les yeux et le coeur." Her spiritual practice became simplified as she grew in understanding. In the last years of her life the Gospels were her only book of devotion, and her prayer became "un élan du coeur, un simple regard jeté vers le ciel." Yet the love thus expressed was no mere "divine duet." She was not a victim of that narrow fervour which finds its satisfaction in a vertical relation with the Divine; her religion was of a distinctly social type. "Le zêle d'une Carmelite doit embrasser le monde," she said; and this zeal showed itself, not only in the passionate love she gave to her family, but in radiant affection towards all living beings -- the nuns in the convent, some of whom were extremely tiresome and even unkind, her friends and correspondents in the outside world, the animals and the birds. She always had her eye on her fellow-creatures; she wanted to help them, to show light to them, to save them. The eager service and voluntary mortifications of her life closed with eighteen months of great physical suffering. She died in September 1897, at the age of twenty-four.

Thérèse Martin had lived for nine years within the walls of a small, strictly enclosed convent in a provincial town. This building and its dreary little chapel formed the setting of her religious career. There was nothing impressive in her surroundings, nothing to satisfy those artistic instincts which she certainly possessed, to hint at the poetry and mystery of the spiritual life. Her opportunities of action had been limited on every side; her creative impulse found expression only in the writing of some conventional religious verse, and the record of her thoughts and experiences, composed not for publication, but as an act of obedience to her Superior. Prayer, the teaching of novices, the family life of the community, and a small amount of correspondence with those in the world, were the only channels through which her passionate love of humanity could flow. This record may not sound impressive. Its sequel is amazing. Students of history have often discussed the stages and the circumstances through which a simple man or woman, distinguished only by a beautiful and humble life, has been transformed by the reverence, love, and myth-making faculty of his contemporaries into a supernatural being endowed with magical powers. This transformation has happened within our own time in the person of Thérèse de l'Enfant-Jésus. This young girl, whose life was marked by no bizarre incident, who was brought up in anobscure Norman town, and deliberately shut herself up in a convent of strictest enclosure to remain -- as the " healthy-minded" would say -- buried alive till her death, is now loved and invoked wherever the Roman Catholic church is established. Her short and uneventful life has influenced and comforted countless other lives. Her "cause" has been introduced, and although she is not yet canonized, she is already regarded as numbered among the saints. To visit her grave in the beautiful hillside cemetery outside Lisieux, and watch the endless stream of pilgrims who come on every day of the year from all parts of the world to ask her help, to deposit letters explaining their needs, and lay on her tomb for blessing the clothes of babies or the food of the sick, is to understand what the shrine of a medieval saint must have been like. It is to understand also something of the triumphant power of character, and of the fact that the enclosing of a radiant personality within the cloister is not burying it alive.

Although the whole of her short adult life had been passed behind the high garden walls of the convent, and after she took the veil only the members of her family had seen her -- and this under the most restricted conditions -- yet at the time of her death Thérèse de l' Enfant- Jesus was already known and valued by the whole town. That death was an event of importance, evoking an extraordinary demonstration of affection and reverence. The events which followed it are of deep interest. Here, in our own day, we have the swift rise and diffusion of a cultus exactly similar to those which followed the deaths of the great popular saints of the Middle Ages. Every element is present; the prompt setting up of a pilgrimage, the veneration of the tomb, the distribution of relics -- at the Lisieux convent cards are sold, bearing splinters and bits of straw from the cell of Thérèse -- countless reports of visions, conversions, "supernatural perfumes," and miraculous answers to prayer. The literature of the subject is already considerable, and a journal is published givingdetails of "graces" obtained by her help. The causes which lie behind such religious movements as this are still obscure; but we have in the cult of Thérèse Martin a valuable clue by which to interpret those reported from the past. Her "miracles," in which students of psychic phenomena will find much to interest them, range from the cure of cancer to the multiplication of bank-notes, and even include the restoration of dead geranium-cuttings. Many are obviously explained by coincidence or hallucination, some are admirable examples of faith-healing. But a few, apparently supported by good evidence, seem to defy rationalistic explanation.

The cult quickly lost its local and ultimately its national character. Though French Catholicism rightly claims Thérèse as its peculiar possession, and devotion to her is probably more general in France than elsewhere, yet she is now venerated in every country in the world, and distributes her favours without regard to nationality. Scotland and America in particular have numerous stories of her benevolent intervention, at least as evidential as much that is offered to us by the exponents of spiritualism. Her legend is in active formation, and many picturesque incidents were added to it during the war. She is even said to have appeared at the British Headquarters, and given advice at a critical moment of the campaign. A large proportion of the Catholic soldiers who fought for France probably placed themselves under her protection, and attribute their safety to her care.

A little time before her death, she said to her sister Pauline, "Une seule attente fait battre mon coeur; c'est l'amour que je recevrai et celui que je pourrai donner. . . . Je veux passer mon ciel a faire du bien sur la terre," and again, " Je compte bien ne pas rester inactive au ciel, mon désir est de travailler encore." In these sayings, so unlike in their vigorous activism the conventional aspirations of the devout, we have probably the germinal point of her cultus. It has come to be believed that this simple and loving spirit, who passed from the bodywith so many generous longings unfulfilled, is indeed spending her heaven in doing good; and the deeds attributed to her are just those practical and friendly acts of kindness, through which during life she expressed and perfected her spirit of love.

2. *Lucie-Christine*

THOSE students of mysticism who feel that the purely cloistered type of spirituality, as seen in Thérèse Martin and Elizabeth Catez, is too remote from the common experience to be actual to us, may find something with which they can sympathize and from which they can learn, in the self-revelations of the remarkable contemplative who is known under the pseudonym of Lucie-Christine.

This lady, whose spiritual journal was published in 1912, was a married woman of the leisured class, leading the ordinary life of a person of her type and position. She was born in 1844 and married in 1865. She had five children. At forty-three she became a widow, and in 1908, after nineteen years of blindness, she died at the age of sixty-four. Nothing could have been more commonplace than her external circumstances. On the religious side she was an exact and fervent Roman Catholic, accepting without question the dogmas and discipline of the Church, and diligent in all the outward observances of conventional French piety. Her time was spent in family and social duties, sometimes in Paris, sometimes in her country home; and she appeared to her neighbours remarkable only for her goodness, gentleness, and love of religion. Yet her inward life -- unsuspected by any but her parish priest, for whom her journal was written -- had a richness and originality which entitle her to a place among the Catholic mystics, and often help us to understand the meaning and character of the parallel experiences which those mysticsdescribe. The value for study of a contemplative who is at once so modern and so classic is obvious. This value is increased by the fact that for many years Lucie-Christine knew nothing of mystical literature, and was ignorant even of the names of the spiritual states which her journal so faithfully describes. Therefore in her case unconscious imitation, which accounts for much so-called mystical experience, appears to be excluded.

Her journal -- at present our only source of information -- covers thirty-eight years: from 1870 to 1908. The first twelve years, however, are only represented by fragmentary notes, put together in 1882; when Lucie-Christine, at the suggestion of her confessor, began to keep a detailed record of her religious life. Whatever view we may take of its theological value, this record is certainly a psychological document of the first class. It is the work of a woman of marked intelligence; temperamentally philosophic, and with great intuitional gifts. The short memoir prefixed to the French edition tells us that even as a child she showed unusual qualities; was grave, thoughtful, and to some extent "psychic," being subject to flashes of clairvoyance, and premonitions of important and tragic events. This peculiarity, which she disliked and never spoke of, persisted through life; and its presence in her helps us to understand how the many stories of abnormal power possessed by the mystics first arose.

Her character was by no means of that detached and inhuman type which is supposed to be proper to religious exaltation. She was ardent and impressionable, gave love and craved for it; her qualities and faults were essentially of a lovable kind. She reveals herself in her journal as sensitive, idealistic, and affectionate; somewhat unpractical, very easily wounded, tempted to irritability, and inclined to worry. "The excessive wish to be loved, appreciated, admired by those whom I love," was one of the temptations against which, as a young woman, she felt it necessary to pray:another was the longing for enjoyment, for personal happiness. It was only after eight years of intermittent mystical experience that she learned the secret of inward peace: to "lose her own interests in those of God, and receive a share in His interests in exchange." Though the "activity and practical capacity of Martha" never came naturally to her, she was yet a splendid wife and mother. Even in the years when her inner life was passed in almost continuous contemplation, she never neglected human duties for superhuman joys; but planned and shared the amusements of her boys and girls, wrote and rehearsed the plays which they acted, and watched with care over every detail of their lives.

Her spiritual life developed gradually and evenly. There is no trace in it of any psychic storm or dramatic conversion. She grew up in a religious home, and even in childhood seems to have been attracted to silent devotion or "mental prayer." As a girl she was a vital, impulsive creature, full of eager enthusiasms. That deep, instinctive longing for Perfection which makes one man an artist, another a philosopher, and another a saint, showed itself early in a passionate worship of all beautiful things. " Tout ce que je connaissais de beau me passionnait et entraînait toute mon âme. La première vue de la mer et des falaises m'arracha des larmes. . . . Je ne pouvais trouver l'expression qui traduisit assez ardeur dont le beau enflammait mon imagination, et je ne voyais pas d'inconvénients ces entraînements excessifs; au contraire, je m'y livrais de toute la force de ma volonte. Infortunée, mon âme en revenait cependant avec le sentiment du vide et de l'insuffisance, et c'est alors qu'elle rejetait son activité dévorante sur l'idéal qui lui reservait tant de dangers! Moins altérée du beau, je me fusse peut-être contentée des choses réelles, mais comme le coureur, lancé dans un fol elan, dépasse le but, ainsi mon âme s'élançait vers le beau a peine aperçu et cherchait encore au delâ."

In this important passage we see the true source of Lucie's mysticism. It was the craving for an absolute and unchanging loveliness on which to expend her large-hearted powers of adoration and self-giving, which led her like the Platonists through visible beauty to its invisible source. She had, as she says of herself in a sudden flash of ironic wit, "le coeur assez mal placé pour trouver Dieu plus aimable que le monde, et l'esprit assez étroit pour se contenter de l'Infini"; but it was not until youth was nearly over, and she had been married for eight years, that she found what she sought. One day, when she was meditating as usual on a passage in the Imitation of Christ, she saw and heard within her mind the words "Dieu seul!" -- summing up and answering in one phrase the vague efforts and questions of her growing mystical sense, and offering to the hungry psyche the only satisfaction of desire. As Fox was released from his conflict by the inner voice which cried, "There is one only who can speak to thy condition," so this inner voice, says Lucie (whom it greatly astonished), "fut à la fois une lumière, un attrait, et une force. Une lumière qui me fit voir comment je pouvais être complètement à Dieu seul dans le monde, et je vis que jusque-là je ne l'avais pas bien compris. Un attrait par lequel mon coeur fut subjuguè et ravi. Une force qui m'inspira une résolution genereuse et me mit en quelque sorte dans les mains les moyens de l'exécuter, car le propre de ces paroles divines est d'opérer ce qu'elles disent."

We see at once the complete and practical character of her reaction to the divine; the promptitude with which she makes the vital connection between intuition and act. St. Teresa said that the object of the spiritual marriage was "the incessant production of work." So for Lucie-Christine that sure consciousness of the Presence of God which now became frequent, "clothing and inundating" her as she sat alone at her sewing or took part in some social activity, called her above all to "faire les petites choses du dévouement journalier avec amour"; conquering her natural irritability and dislikefor the boredoms and unrealities of a prosperous existence. "N'avoir jamais l'air ennuyé des autres. Que de fois je manque à ceci avec les pauvres enfants. Vous etes ennuyeux! C'est bien vite dit! Est-ce une amabilité divine? "

More and more, as her mystical consciousness grew, the life of contemplation became her delight; and it was plainly a real trial to be distracted from it for trivial purposes. In company, or busied with household duties, she went for hours with "her soul absorbed, its better part rapt in God." She "tried to appear ordinary," and made excuses if her abstraction was observed; but there are a few entries in her journal which will give pleasure to those who condemn mysticism as an "anti-social type of religion." " Nous avons été nous promener, quatorze. Je remarque que d'aller ainsi avec plusieurs 'Marthes' hommes ou femmes, cela ne fait rien. On laisse discourir, on met un mot de temps en temps, mais, en définitive, on demeure bien libre et l'oraison va toute seule. Mais avec une seule Marthe, que c'est terrible! La tete-a-tete oblige a causer presque tout le temps."

When Lucie wrote this, ten years after her first illuminative experience, she was far advanced in contemplation. She had known that direct and ineffable vision of God "Himself the True, the Good, the Beautiful; all things being nothing save by Him" which is characteristic -- though she knew it not -- of the unitive way: known too the corresponding experience of dereliction, when the door which had opened on Eternity seemed tightly closed. It would be tedious to analyze in detail the rich profusion of mystic states which she had already exhibited: the degrees of contemplation, ecstasies, visions and voices, all the forms taken by her growing intuition of the Transcendent. Many of these can be matched in the writings of the great mystics. Again and again as we read her, we are reminded of Angela of Foligno, Ruysbroeck, Julian of Norwich, Catherine of Genoa, even of Plotinus: yet Lucie-Christine was at this time ignorant of mystical literature,and only in later life found with amazement descriptions of her own experiences in the works of the great contemplatives.

These experiences had a wide range. Some we are justified in regarding as invasions from her deeper self; coming to the rescue of the often distracted surface personality, and correcting the impressions of the outer world by its own intimations of Eternity. Thus, in 1875, she confesses that being particularly worried by a number of people, the Divine voice said to her, "Ma fine, il n' y a que toi et moi." She replied: "Seigneur, et les autres?" The voice said: "Pour chaque âme en ce monde il n'y a que moi et elle, toutes les autres âmes et toutes choses ne sont rien pour elle que par moi et pour moi," and by this timely reminder of the one Reality in whose life she lived, and by and in whom alone all other lives are real, she was recalled to her inner poise.

In assessing the value of this, and many other of her revelations, we have to remember that Lucie-Christine was a fervent and exact Churchwoman. Her belief was literal. She felt no discord between traditional Christianity of the most concrete kind and the freedom of her own communion with God. The fruits of that communion were often expressed by her in theological terms, and the special atmosphere and tendencies of French Catholicism certainly affected the form of many of her contemplations. Thus at one end of the scale her passionate devotion to the Person of Christ, and the fact that her religious practice centred in the Eucharist, sometimes resulted in visions of a distinctly anthropomorphic type. In these, her intuition of God's presence translated themselves into hallucinatory images of the Face of Christ, or of His eyes looking at her; or photisms, which she explained to herself as the radiance emanating from His person. As we all know, such dramatizations of mystical emotion are comparatively commonplace. The elements from which the self constructs them are by no means all of a spiritual kind; and experienced mystics agree in regarding them with muchsuspicion. A careful study of Lucie-Christine's journal forces us to admit, that the deliberate passivity which she cultivated often placed her at the mercy of her instinctive nature; and that its hidden wishes sometimes took a devotional form. To this source, too, we must refer those "obsessions and temptations" -- in other words, uprushes from the lower centres -- by which she was often attacked during contemplation, and also the occasionally sentimental and emotional character of her reactions to the Divine.

These objections, however, do not apply to the remarkable "metaphysical visions" -- sharp onsets of real transcendental consciousness -- in which her innate passion for the Absolute found satisfaction. Then, as she says, God seemed to "put aside all intermediaries between Himself and the soul;" and "bathed and irradiated by the Divine substance "she became "aware of the Divine Abyss," or perceived, as Julian of Norwich did, "the Universe in a point," swallowed up in the simple yet overwhelming sight of God. Here lie, for us, the real interest and value of Lucie-Christine's confessions. She shares with Angela of Foligno and a few other historical mystics the double apprehension of the Divine Nature under its personal and impersonal forms; and as both utterly transcendent to, yet completely immanent in, the human soul. In her descriptions of these visions, this woman unread in philosophy displays a grasp of the philosophic basis of religion which would do credit to a trained theologian. Thus she says "Il n'y a pas, ce me semble, de vue intérieure qui égale celle de l'essence divine. Mon âme était comme environnée de la substance divine en laquelle elle voyait ce caractère essential qui nous est révelé par le mystère de la Sainte Trinité, c'est-à-dire qu'il y a en Dieu l'unite et la distinction, le tout et le particulier, et je sentais combien c'est folie de chercher quelque chose en dehors de lui." Again, "Étant profondement unie a lui dans la Sainte Communion, je vis Dieu en tant qu'il est le souverain bien, et je compris en même temps que le maln'est que la négation du bien, un pur néant. . . . Dans cette vue intellectuelle, je compris aussi combien sera grande la confusion des pécheurs quand ils seront jugés, et qu'ils verront que tout le mal qu'ils ont aimé, préconisé, adoré, se réduit au néant! Avoir aime le néant, avoir veçu pour lui, et perdre pour lui l'Etre éternel!" Here Lucie's view of sin is that characteristic of all mystics; who can seldom be persuaded, however orthodox they may be in other respects, that anything which is not good is real. We remember how Julian of Norwich, also a natural contemplative of philosophic temperament, says, "I saw not sin; for I believe it has no manner of substance nor part of being."

As an analyzer of her own psychological states, Lucie-Christine had something of that genius which St. Teresa possessed in a supreme degree; and she has, perhaps, an added value for us because she speaks not from the past nor from the cloister, but out of the Paris of our own day. We owe to her one of our most vivid descriptions of that apprehension of Eternal Life -- the immersion of our durational existence in the Absolute Life of God -- which Von Hugel regards as the fundamental religious experience. "J' ai observe," she says, "que pendant l'oraison passive et surtout dans l'etat d'union, l'âme perd le sentiment de la durée. Il n'y a plus pour elle de succession de moments, mais un moment unique, et j'ai cru comprendre qu'étant élevée a cet état, l'âme y vit selon le mode de vivre de l'éternité, ou il n'y a point de durée, point de passé ni d'avenir, mais un moment unique, infini." We have again to remember that the woman who wrote this had then no acquaintance with the classics of mysticism. It is her own impression which she is trying to register.

Again, consider this account of the state of divine union as she had known it: "L' âme va prier, elle s' élance pour franchir la distance qui la sépare de l'Infini, et cette distance elle ne la trouve plus! Elle veut aller à vous, mon Dieu, et vous êtes en elle! . . . Perdue en vous, elle oublie elle-même et tout le reste, elle ne sait plus comment elle vit, ni comment elle aime; elle ne voit plus que Vous seul. Encore ne peut elle pas penser qu'elle vous voit et vous adore; car se serait se voir elle-même, et en de tels moments elle ne se voit pas, elle ne voit que Vous. Elle connait et aime par un mode nouveau et incomprehensible, qui est en dehors et infiniment au-dessus de l'exercice ordinaire de ses facultés. Elle sent que l'opération de Dieu a pris la place de la sienne et que c'est Dieu même qui opère en elle la connaissance et l' amour."

This sense of complete surrender to a larger life and greater power, of which love is the very substance and ground, is characteristic of nearly all high mystical experience; and the literature of contemplation would furnish many parallels to all that Lucie tells us of it. In this state, as she says in another place, "the thirst of the spirit is suddenly fulfilled by the Infinite," and "God takes possession of the ground of the soul, without passage of time or feeling of space." Then, the bewilderment and unrest produced in us by the disharmonies of daily life are healed. "Là ou tout raisonnement échoue," she says, in one of her most beautiful passages; "où l'âme est tellement troublée qu' elle ne saurait même expliquer ce qui la trouble, la divine presence paraît, et soudain le vertige cesse et la paix renaît avec la lumière." Consciousness, ceasing more or less completely its normal correspondences with the temporal order, then becomes aware of the eternal and spiritual universe in which we really live.

Such an attitude to Eternity was a marked characteristic of Lucie-Christine's mysticism. Often, it produced in her the complete mono-ideism of ecstasy; and she describes the oncoming, content, and passing of these states with a minuteness which makes her journal a valuable document for the psychologist. Constantly, the intense awareness of the Divine Presence persisted through the many duties and activities of the day; "like a grave and tender note, dominating all the modulations of the keyboard of my exterior life." She isnot afraid to use the most violent metaphors, the most concrete images, in her efforts to express the intensity and reality of this spiritual life that she leads, this divine companionship that she enjoys. "I am nourished by God's substance." "I breathe the divine essence." "The presence of God is so clear that faith is not faith -- it is sight." "The soul plays within God, as within a limitless universe." "The Divine action penetrates and transforms my adoration. It is the Divine Being who thinks, loves, and lives within me." None of the mystics have gone further than this in their claims; but it is significant that nearly all the greatest go as far.

Yet in all this, Lucie-Christine is strictly Evangelical. She was a Christian first, and a mystic afterwards. Though her expressions may seem startling, her mysticism never goes beyond that of St. John and St. Paul; and her most Platonic utterances can be justified by the New Testrnent. But the Pauline and Johannine teachings on the soul's union with Christ are not for her merely doctrinal statements. They are vivid descriptions of states she has personally known, when her consciousness truly penetrated to that "region d'amour, region unique, où l'âme trouve un autre jour, une autre vie, un autre air respirable, où du moins tous ces éléments latents se trouvent manifestés, où Dieu seul apparait, et tout le reste rentre dans l'ombre."

Such a personal and overwhelming consciousness of "the greatness, power, and simplicity of God" -- an all-inclusive unity which the unity of her spirit could comprehend -- was the central interest of her life. She certainly tended to that which Baron von Hugel has called "the vertical relation" with the Divine. Nevertheless, this theocentric existence did not involve either the limp passivity or the spiritual selfishness with which it is sometimes charged. On the ethical side it committed her to a constant moral discipline; for her ardent and impulsive temperament reacted too easily to every externalstimulus. "I must give up pleasure -- never work for my own enjoyment." "My one prayer is, that I may not feel joy and grief so vividly: that I may feel only Thee." This deliberate unselfing and concentration on God so strengthened the fibres of character that she was able to bear with quietness her many personal sorrows, and the long years of blindness -- a bitter cross for that keen lover of beauty -- which closed her life. Yet it did not muffle her in the unattractive folds of "holy indifference." She loved her family devotedly, and felt without mitigation the anxieties and griefs of human life. Her attitude to others was generous and sympathetic. God, she says, gives Himself to us that we may give Him again. His unique light must pass through the soul as through a prism; breaking up into the many colours of word and deed, forgiveness and good counsel, prayer and alms, self-forgetfulness and self-giving. Though exceedingly reserved about her spiritual experiences, which were only known to her confessor, the influence of these experiences was felt by those among whom she lived; and her house was known by them as "the house of peace."

Moreover, her love for the institutional and sacramental side of religion saved her from many of the dangers and extravagances of individualism. It gave her a framework within which her own intuitions could find their place; and a valid symbolism through which she could interpret to herself the most rarefied experiences of her soul. She is an example of the way in which the mystic seems able to achieve the universal without losing or rejecting its particular expression: assimilating symbols of an amazing crudity without in any way impairing her vision of truth. The conflict between that vision and the concrete objectives of popular devotion was ignored by her; as it is generally ignored by practical mystics of the institutional type. She, who had touched the Absolute in her contemplations, was yet deeply impressed by the drama of the Church; by its ceremonies, holy places, festivals, consecrations. Her inner life was nourished by its sacraments. She displayed the power -- so characteristic of Christian mysticism at its best -- of transcending without rejecting the formule of belief as commonly understood; of remaining within, and drawing life from, the organism, without any diminution in the proper liberty of the soul.

Thus, seen as a whole, Lucie-Christine's spiritual life has a richness and balance which reflects the richness and balance of her own nature; for an impoverished or one-sided character was never yet found capable of a fully developed and fruitful mysticism. We see her from girlhood seeking to satisfy her innate longing for reality; urged on the one hand by the artist's craving for perfect loveliness, on the other by the philosopher's instinct for Eternity. When the veil was lifted, and the inner voice said, "God only!" she found at once the reconciliation and the fulfilment of these two desires. The long and varied experience which followed was no more than an unfolding of the content of those words. They revealed to her the Substance of all beauty and truth; shining in that world of appearance which she loved to the last with an artist's passion, yet ever abiding unchanged in that world of pure being which she touched in her contemplations "above all feeling, image, and idea." Because of this double outlook on reality, her mysticism was both transcendental and sacramental. It irradiated the natural world, and also the symbols of religion, with that simple light of Eternity wherein she found "all beauties known and unknown, all harmonies natural and supernatural." Lucie-Christine makes clear to us, as few mystics have done, the immense transfiguration of ordinary life which comes from such an extension of consciousness; when "the veil suddenly drops, God reveals Himself, and the soul knows experimentally that which she knew not before." Her journal is full of passages in which its joy and splendour are described. I take one written in a time of great mental and physical suffering, when the cruel deprivations of blindnesswere already closing in on her, and the two beings she loved best -- her husband and her youngest daughter -- had lately been taken from her by death. " Figurez-vous un pauvre prisonnier au fond d'un cachot renfermé et obscur, voyant tout à coup s'entr'ouvrir la voûte de ce cachot, et par là recevant la lumière du soleil, et aspirant avec force fair du dehors qui lui arrive embaumé des senteurs de la vie et de la chaleur de l' atmosphère resplendissante. Ainsi mon âme s'ouvrait, et buvait Dieu! . . . mon âme aspirait et buvait la vie même de la Trinité Sainte, et se sentait revivre, et n'avait plus aucun mal."

3. Charles Péguy

IN the turmoil and anxieties of the first weeks of the war, few people observed that France had lost upon the battle-field one of the greatest of her modern poets; a fearless and original thinker, a constructive mystic, who exercised a unique influence over the young writers and thinkers of his world. Yet the death in action of Charles Péguy, who was killed on September 5, 1914, at the age of forty-one, removed a striking figure from contemporary literature, and was among the chief intellectual losses sustained by France in the war.

Born in Orleans in 1873, of peasant stock, Péguy had many of the fundamental qualities of the French peasant; the sturdy independence, the frugal tastes, the untiring industry, the close kinship with the soil. His father was a cabinet-maker; his mother that familiar figure of the cathedrals, the woman who lets the chairs. The great friend of his boyhood was an old republican carpenter with whom he used to talk, and to whose conversation he owed his first political ideas. This heredity and these influences gave to his thought and attitude a character which he never lost. In his mature work we see side by side the result of those two compensating elements in his childish environment; the mingled mystery and homeliness of that medieval and intensely national Catholicism which finds in the French cathedrals its living symbols, the keen sense of social justice, of the need for social salvation, which inspired the popularrepublicanism of the years following the Franco-German war. These characteristics, which afterwards, in a sublimated form, came to dominate his mysticism and gave to it its special colour, its mingling of antique tradition with forward-looking hope, can be traced back to the blend of Christian and of democratic impressions which he received as a child. Perhaps only the son of French peasants could understand and reinterpret as he had done the figure of St. Joan of Arc, the peasant girl who saved France; and whose longing to mend and redeem, at once so practical and so transcendental, linked up the objectives of social endeavour and of faith.

Brought up within the atmosphere of provincial piety, Péguy rose from the elementary school to the lycee; and at nineteen, through his own efforts and his mother's sacrifices, passed from Orleans to the University of Paris. There his vigorous mind and positive character soon made him the centre of a group of students, over whom he quickly obtained influence. There, too, he made the transition almost inevitable for an ardent young man of his world from Catholic orthodoxy to humanitarian socialism: the first stage in his spiritual pilgrimage, and the first attempt to answer that question which underlies all his thought and act, his poetry and controversy -- "Comment faut-il sauver?" These words, which Péguy puts into the mouth of St. Joan of Arc, and shows to us as the mainspring of her actions, define too the secret impulse of his own career. His mysticism was not that of the contemplative, the solitary and God-intoxicated devotee: it was that of a strong-willed man of action, who sees far off the "mighty beauty" and longs to actualize it within the common life. He saw that common life with the eyes of a poet who was also a child of the people; discerning beneath its surface the dignity and the beauty of its antique and simple types -- the spinner and the tiller, the housewife, the mother and the child."Les armes de Jesus, c'est la pauvre famille

> *Les freres et la sceur, les garcons et la fille,*
> *Le fuseau lourd de laine et la savante aiguille."*

But he found in the French socialism of the 'nineties a dry and materialistic spirit; which could not satisfy his passionate idealism, his instinct for a completed life, a universal redemption, that should harmonize soul and body and fulfil their needs. Hence, by a process too gradual to be called a conversion, he grew from humanitarianism into a somewhat anti-clerical, original, yet mediæval and mystical Catholicism; in which those ideals and demands which had dominated his humanitarian period -- the sense of the rights and dignity of mankind, the longing to save, "de porter remède au mal universel humain" -- reappear in a spiritualized form. In Christianity he saw condensed the saving power of Spirit; never letting man alone, but redeeming him even in defiance of his own will, contriving its victories by or in spite of the evils and disharmonies of life. The belief which he achieved -- doubtless fed by childish memories -- was absolute and literal, and most easily expressed itself in medieval forms. Modernism filled him with horror; he desired no attenuation of the supernatural, no reinterpretation of dogma. The faith which fought the crusades and built the cathedrals was that in which he felt at home, and which he believed himself destined to bring back to the soul of France: "Au fond, c'est une renaissance Catholique qui se fait par moi."

Yet his inner life was full of difficulty and unhappiness. There were in him two strains, two warring impulses, to which we must attribute many of the griefs and disappointments of his life: for his great accomplishment both as poet and as founder of the Cahiers de la Quinzaine brought him little personal joy. On one side of his nature he was proud, vehement, combative; full of a destructive energy, an obstinate fanaticism, which found vent in his violent political pamphlets, often expressing with the uncouth vigour of the peasant his uncompromising hates and loves. Though so ardent a Christian, he was neither meek nor gentle. He could never resist giving blow for blow, and by his impatience and intolerance alienated by turns his socialist and Catholic friends. About 1910, having thus quarrelled with most of his associates, he withdrew into a voluntary retirement, in which the spiritual side of his divided temperament seems at last to have had some opportunity of growth. His mystical poems -- all composed between 1910 and 1913 -- show to us the love and exaltation of which he now became capable; the purity of that vision which had inspired his vigorous guerilla warfare against the shams and sordidness of modern life, and which now became the chief factor in his consciousness. Writing in 1912 to his old friend Joseph Lotte, he says," Mon vieux, j'ai beaucoup changé depuis deux ans; je suis devenu un homme nouveau. J'ai tant souffert et tant prié. Tu ne peux pas savoir." The secret of this inner conflict, of the terrible months during which, as he afterwards confessed, he was unable to say "Thy will be done," he revealed to none; but hints of the way by which he had passed may be found in his poems. The mystical certitude which inspires their most beautiful passages seems never to have obtained complete control of his psychic being. The life of prayer and the life of personal struggle persisted side by side, not fully harmonized; and it is doubtful whether he ever achieved that complete surrender to the divine action "in which alone we do not surrender our true selves," which is characteristic of the developed mystic life. "Celui qui s'abandonne ne s'abandonne pas, et il est le seul qui ne s'abandonne pas." It was surely to himself that Péguy addressed this observation, and it represents his own central need. Those profound readjustments of character, that unselfing of the moral nature, which must precede spiritual unification, and so are the only foundations of inner peace, had never been accomplished in him. Like his patroness and heroine St. Joan, he combinedthe temperaments of fighter and dreamer, but he never succeeded in fusing them in one.

We know, too, something of the outward circumstances which added to his difficulties. Married during his agnostic period to a freethinker, his intense respect for human freedom forbade him to force on his wife his own convictions, or even to bring his adored children to baptism against their mother's will. For this refusal he was himself denied access to the sacraments; and hence this impassioned Catholic, for conscience' sake, lived and died out of communion with the official Church. No one will really understand Péguy's position or the meaning of his poems, unless this paradoxical situation, and this constant element of frustration and incompleteness in his experience, be kept in mind. He was in one sense an exile, ever gazing at the beloved country which he knew and understood so much better than many of its citizens. Deeply religious, he lived at odds with his religious world. Capable of the strangest inconsistencies and refusals, though sparing himself nothing of the anguish they involved, he could make on foot a pilgrimage to Chartres to pray for the life of his sick child; yet would not face the struggle necessary to make those children members of the Church in which he believed. "Je ne peux pas m'occuper de tout. Je n'ai pas une vie ordinaire. Nul n'est prophète en son pays. Mes petits ne sont pas baptisés. A la sainte Vierge de s'en occuper!"

Himself, he felt called upon to devote his powers, without distraction, to that missionary propaganda in which the mystical and combative sides of his nature found creative expression, and to which his poetry and much of his prose is consecrated. "Il y a tant de manque. Il y a tant à demander," says St. Joan to the patient nun who seeks to teach her resignation: and here she expresses Péguy's deepest conviction. There is so much lacking that men might obtain of joy and peace and love. Action no less than prayer isneeded; every soul must take its share in meeting the world's need, for we are the accomplices of ill if we do nothing to prevent it. There was never any place in Péguy's eager and restless heart for that "other-worldly" mysticism which achieves the love of God at the expense of love of home and fellow-men; for religion in his view was an affair of flesh and blood, not of pure spirit -- not merely transcendental, but concrete, national, fraternal, even revolutionary. On this side his mysticism represents the spiritualization of that activist philosophy which was coming into prominence in the formative years of his life, and could not fail to exert a powerful influence on him.

Both as mystic and as patriot, he had the reformer's passion: a measure, too, of the reformer's violence and intolerant zeal. He worked for a sweeter and a saner world, a restoration to man of his lost inheritance. The modern France, he felt, was wrong. It had lost its hold upon realities; mistaken its professors and scientists for apostles, its codes and systems for truth, its political institutions for liberty, the "triumphs of civilization" for perdurable goods. It had lost freshness, naivete, hope: had sacrificed beauty and joy for an imaginary progress and comfort. In the place of the ancient types of human worth, the primitive yet august figures of parent and child, craftsman and tiller of the soil, it had produced the bemused victim of modern education "avec sa tête de carton et son coeur de bazar." In this perversion of life and cultivation of the second-best he saw the "unversal evil," which poisons the sources of human happiness. Yet behind and within it Péguy, visionary and optimist, discerned the possible restoration of good; mankind brought back into contact with the real and eternal world. He saw his beloved France ceasing to be "un peuple qui dit non," and becoming, by intensity and harmony of action and vision, "une race affirmative." He looked past shams, pretences, and bad workmanship to a heaven that should contain notonly people but things: "Dans le paradis tel que je le montrerai, il n'y aura pas seulement des âmes; il y aura des choses. Tout ce qui existe et qui est réussi. Les cathedrales, par exemple. Notre Dame, Chartres, je les y mettrai."

It was such a restoration of humanity to the wholesome and beautiful life for which it was made, that he had at first sought in socialism; and the earlier numbers of the Cahiers de la Quinzaine, of which he was the founder and editor, reflect this faith. He saw socialism then in its ideal aspect, as a triumph of justice and love: a reasonable career offered to the whole race. For this triumph, this reordering of the common life, he never ceased to work; but a deeper experience taught him that it could not be effected by any change imposed on society from without, or any readjustment between man and man. The readjustment needed was that between man and God; a change of heart, a rearrangement of the values of life effected from within, which should make possible the complete spiritualization of existence. Therefore

it was that Péguy became, in his last and most creative period, a Christian mystic of an original type; an ardent missionary, who opposed the intellectualism, materialism, and individualism which France of the early twentieth century mistook for progress, by a propaganda which was anti-intellectual, nationalist, and profoundly Catholic. It is to this period

that his poetry and much of his most vehement prose belongs. All is didactic in intention; but is saved by its author's wit, sincerity, and remarkable imaginative genius from the usual fate of those who try to turn art to the purposes of edification. The prose is largely controversial, and inevitably suffers to some extent from this: for Péguy was violent and sometimes unjust when attacking the errors and follies of the time, and had at his disposal an astonishing power of mockery, irony, and scorn. Yet even here, his instinct for beauty constantly asserted itself: and in the midst of some biting attack upon "progressive" politics or modernisttheology, we get an abrupt invasion of loveliness which transports us to the atmosphere of his poems. These poems fall into two groups: first, the three Mystères which he wrote for the 500th anniversary of the birth of Jeanne d'Arc, "la sainte la plus grande après Sainte Marie," and which deal with her spiritual preparation for the saving of France; La Charite de Jeanne d'Arc (1910), Le Porche du Mystere de la Deuxieme Virtu (1911), Les Saints Innocents (1912). These are all written in unrhymed irregular verse; a verse so indefinite in construction that it is often indistinguishable from rhythmic prose. They consist chiefly in long meditative

discourses, alternating between the extremes of homeliness and sublimity, and put into the mouths of Jeanne and of Madame Gervaise, a Franciscan nun to whom she tells her problems and her dreams -- an apt device for the conveyance of Péguy's own religious and patriotic gospel. They were followed by three volumes in rhymed duodecasyllabic verse, which he called Tapisseries: Sainte Genevieve et Jeanne d'Arc (1912), Notre Dame (1913), and Eve (1914), perhaps his finest and most sustained single work.

When we examine these poems in order, we find that we can trace in them the development of a consistent philosophy of life: for, like most of the convinced opponents of intellectualism, Péguy was a profound thinker, relying to a far greater extent than he would ever have confessed on the ungodly processes of a singularly acute mind. The deliberate simplicity of diction, the assumed ingenuousness of attitude are deceptive, and conceal a deeply reasoned view of the universe.

> *"Je n'aime pas, dit Dieu, celui qui pense*
> *Et qui se tourmente et qui se soucie*
> *Et qui roule une migraine perpetuelle."*

This is not the doctrine of the charcoal-burner; it is the doctrine of the experienced philosopher, bitterly conscious of the limitations of the brain. The foundation of his creed is the essentially mystical belief, so beautifully expressed in Eve, in the solidarity of the Universe. As humanity is one and indivisible, so too the human and the divine cannot be separated. "Nous sommes solidaires des damnés éternels," he said when he was twenty: and in his posthumous work Clio, he reiterates the same truth. "Jésus est du même monde que le dernier des pécheurs; et le dernier des pécheurs est du même monde que Jésus. C'est une communion. C'est même proprement cela qui est une communion. Et à parler vrai ou plutôt a parler réel il n'y a point d'autre communion que d'être du même monde." The spiritual and eternal world, then, is not something set over against the natural order; but is closely entwined with it, the neglected element of reality, which alone can make human existence dignified and sweet.

> *"Car le surnaturel est lui-même charnel*
> *Et l'arbre de la grâce est raciné profond*
> *Et plonge dans le sol et cherche jusqu' au fond*
> *Et l'arbre de la race est lui-même éternel.*
> *Et l'éternité même est dans le temporel*
> *Et l'arbre de la grace est raciné profond*
> *Et plonge dans le sol et touche jusqu' au fond*
> *Et le temps est lui-même un temps intemporel."*

What he realizes and points out, therefore, is not some distant transcendental life and reality, divorced from our normal, flowing, changing life and reality. Rather he insists on the beauty and nobility, the deep spiritual quality of this immediate life; the supernatural character of nature itself, when seen from the angle of Christian idealism. The Blessed Virgin is herself:

> *"Infiniment céleste*
> *Parce qu'aussi elle est infiniment terrestre."*

In Christianity, with its incarnational philosophy, its balanced cultivation of the active and the mystic life, its sacramental touch upon all common things, he sees the only perfect expression of this principle; the only power capable of embracing and spiritualizing the whole of the rich complex of existence. Determined to bring home to his fellow-countrymen, on the one hand, the concrete and objective nature of this Christian life, on the other, the simplicity of soul necessary to those who would understand it, he rejects all attempts at religious philosophizing or symbolic interpretation. His treatment of theology is characterized by a deliberate homely literalness, a naive use of tradition, which was intensely exasperating to his agnostic and Modernist critics; and which may be found distasteful by some religious minds, unable to realize the intimate connection between gaiety and faith. To others it will seem that, alone amongst modern writers, he has recaptured the mediæval secret of familiarity combined with adoration: of a love, awe, and vision, a pro found earnestness, which yet leave room for laughter. His picture of God is shamelessly anthropomorphic. ("Je suis honnête homme, dit Dieu; droit comme un Français.") Yet it is full of grave beauty, of the sense of fatherhood, the mystical consciousness of the Divine desire. Revealed religion is God's Word, and therefore means what it says. "Jésus n'est pas venu pour nous dire des amusettes," says Madame Gervaise to Joan of Arc.

The faith which Péguy wished to restore to France was not the religious rationalism of the modernist: still less the morbid, aesthetic fervour of Huysmans. It was the homely everyday faith of the past, the humble yet assured relation with the supernatural order, the courage and hope which is rooted in tradition and is wholly independent of intellectual subtleties. "La foi est toute naturelle, toute allante, tout simple, toute venante" -- the great and simple affirmation. The perfect type of this faith is not the world-weary convert, but the healthy unselfconscious child; and the child, for Péguy, is the most holy and most significant figure in the human group. "C'est l'enfant qui est plein et l'homme qui est vide." Only in the child and in those untarnished human beings who retain their childlike simplicity of heart do we see unspoilt humanity: only in the child do we see incarnate hope. "J'éclate tellement dans ma création," says God, "et surtout dans les enfants."

> *"On envoie les enfants à l'ecole, dit Dieu.*
> *Je pense que c'est pour oublier le peu qu'ils savent.*
> *On ferait mieux d'envoyer les parents a l'école.*
> *C'est eux qui en ont besoin*
> *Mais naturellement it faudrait une école de moi*
> *Et non pas une école d'hommes."*

The tenderness and charm of those passages in which he celebrates the importance and sanctity of childhood, its innocence, its capacity for growth, its virginal outlook, its freshness and power of response, place him in the front rank of the poets who have treated this most difficult subject, and constantly remind us of Blake:

> *"Comme leur jeune regard a une promesse, une secrète assurance*
> *intérieure, et leur front, et toute leur personne.*
> *Leur petite, leur auguste, leur si révérente et révérende personne. . . .*
> *Heureuse enfance. Tout leur petit corps, toute leur petite personne,*
> *tous leurs petits gestes, est pleine, ruisselle, regorge d'une espérance.*
> *Resplendit, regorge d'une innocence*
> *Qui est l'innocence même de l'espérance."*

This hope, the childhood of the heart, is to Péguy the most precious of human qualities, and the one in which man draws nearest to an understanding of the Divine Idea. Jesus is "the man who has hoped," and the Christian assault, which is the assault of hope, can alone make a breach in the defences of eternity. It is "the faith that God loves best"; the beginning of liberty, the growing point of the eager spirit of life. Faith beholds that which is: Charity loves that which is: Hope alone beholds and loves that which shall be. Faith is static; hope dynamic. Faith is a great tree; hope is the rising sap, the little, swelling bud upon the spray.

"La peite espérance

Est celle qui toujours commence " -- the persistent element in all effort and all change. She deceives us twenty times running; yet she is the only one of our leaders who never deceives us in the end. She gives significance to human toil, beauty and meaning to human suffering, reality to human joy. In one of his most beautiful verses, he describes the crowning of humanity with this living, budding diadem of hope.

> *"Comme une mère fait un diadème de ses doigts allongés, des doigts conjoints et affronts de ses*
> *deux mains fraîches*
> *Autour du front brûlant de son enfant*
> *Pour apaiser ce front brûlant, cette fièvre,*
> *Ainsi une couronne éternelle a été tressée pour apaiser le front brûlant.*
> *Et c'était une couronne de verdure.*
> *Une couronne de feuillage."*

Moreover, "cette curieuse enfant Espérance " is the motive-power of the spiritual order too. God Himself hopes for and in man: has placed His eternal hope in man's hands, and given to him, along with the gift of liberty, the terrible power of frustrating or achieving the purposes of Divine Love.

> *"Le plus infirme des pécheurs peut découronner, peut couronner*
> *Une espérance de Dieu."*

Such a freedom is the very condition of spirituality; for faith, hope, and charity are not servile virtues, but heavenward-tending impulses of the free soul, activities of the will. Here lies their value; since only in true love, voluntary service, deliberate choice, can the possibilities of human nature be fulfilled:

> *"Toutes les soumissions d'esclaves du monde, ne valent pas un beau*
> *regard d'homme libre."*

Therefore, for the author of this gospel of freedom and hope, the course of salvation takes an exactly opposite course to that described by Huysmans and his school. The typical soul for Péguy is not the "twice-born" exhausted andfastidious sensualist Durtal, driven at last to seek reconciliation by his overwhelming sense of sin. It is the "onceborn" simple and ardent peasant child, Joan of Arc; brought straight from the sheepfold to serve the heroic purposes of God.

> *"Tenant tout un royaume en sa ténacité*
> *Vivant en plein mystère avec sagacité*
> *Mourant en plein martyre avec vivacité*
> *La fille de Lorraine à nulle autre pareille."*

The typical experience is an experience of growth, freshness, novelty; action rightly directed, and a vision which perceives beauty and dignity in the antique and homely labours of the race. The cultivator of the earth and the rearer of children, the faithful priest, the strong and loyal soldier -- of these is the kingdom of heaven. Of these and by these the old France was built up; and through these ideals and virtues, and the national saints in whom they are expressed, the new France may be saved. With Huysmans in our mystical moments we are usually inside a church, assisted by incense and plain-chant of the best quality: with Péguy, we are in the open air, in the market garden, or in the nursery. There his poetry, in Francis Thompson's beautiful image, "plays at the foot of the Cross." Even the Holy Innocents in heaven are playing at bowling hoops with their palms and crowns. "At least, I think so," says God, "for they never asked My permission."

> *"Tel est mon paradis . . . Mon paradis est tout ce qu'il y a de plus simple."*

Side by side with Péguy's spiritual gospel, or rather entwined with it, goes his practical and patriotic gospel. Since for him the whole of life was crammed with spiritual significance, he saw in the patriotic passion a sacrament of heavenly love, and in earthly cities symbols of the City of God. Hence nationalism was to him, as to Dostoevsky, essentially religious, and Joan of Arc -- "Une humble enfant perdue en deux amours,

L'amour de son pays parmi l'amour de Dieu"

was the perfect saint, fusing the two halves of human experience in one whole. These two aspects of love he could not separate, for they seemed to him equally the flowers of a completed life. Even God, he thought, would find it difficult to decide between them.

> *"Dans une belle vie, it nest que de beaux fours,*
> *Dans une belle vie it fait toujours beau temps.*
> *Dieu la déroule toute et regarde longtemps*
> *Quel amour est plus cher entre tous les amours.*
> *Ainsi Dieu ne sait pas, ainsi le divin Maître*
> *Ne sait quel retenir et placer hors du lieu*
> *Et pour lequel tenir, et s'il faut vraiment mettre*
> *L'amour de la patrie après l'amour de Dieu."*

This mystical patriotism was his great gift to the mind of France; and it was to her regeneration that his work was really consecrated. It was the ideal France, the "eldest daughter of God," which claimed his devotion and inspired his finest verse. She is the creative nation, planter of gardens and sower of seeds, the nation which turns all things to the purposes of more abundant life:

> *Ici, dit Dieu, clans cette douce France, ma plus noble création,*
> *Dans cette saine Lorraine,*
> *Ici ils sont bons jardiniers. .*
> *Toutes les sauvageries du monde ne valent pas un beau jardin français.*
> *Honnête, modeste, ordonné.*
> *C'est là que j'ai cueilli mes plus belles âmes."*

Péguy saw France in the laborious and heroic past, with her ancient traditions of culture, liberty, and order: patient, scrupulous, diligent, tending her seedbeds and weeding her fields -- for good work was always in his eyes the earnest of a healthy soul. He hoped for her in the future: a future to be conditioned, not by the progressive character of her political institutions, but by her freshness, her eternal youth; above all, by her spirit of hope."Peuple, les peuples de la terre te dirent léger

> *Parce que to es un peuple prompt. . . .*
> *Mais moi, je t'ai pesé, dit Dieu, et je ne t'ai point trouvé léger*
> *O peuple inventeur de la cathédrale, je ne t'ai point trouvé léger en foi.*
> *O peuple inventeur de la croisade, je ne t'ai point trouvé léger en charité.*
> *Quant à l'esperance, il vaut mieux ne pas en parler, il n'en a que pour eux."*

Owing everything to the love and industry of his mother and grandmother -- for his father died before his birth -- it was natural that Péguy should find in faithful and laborious womanhood the ultimate types of human truth and goodness. Two such types appear again and again in his poems, as living symbols of the national soul: St. Geneviève, "vigilante bergère, aieule et paroissienne," whose prayer and fortitude saved Paris, and, above all, St. Joan of Arc, "enfant échappée à de pauvres familles," in whom the dual love of God and man, carried into vigorous action, availed to change the history of France. In the three Mystères which he wrote in her honour, he extols the three qualities in which he found the secret of St. Joan's holiness, significance, and power; her ardent charity, her unquenchable hope, the childlike innocence of her soul. Charity, the passionate longing to help and save, urged her to rescue France from its miseries. "Il y a tant de manque, il y a tant a demander." In this profound sense of ill to be mended, her mission, and in Péguy's view the mission of all Christians, takes its rise. Hope, the ever-renewed belief in a possible perfection, "invisible et immortelle et impossible a éteindre," gave her courage to obey her Voices and strength to perform apparently impossible acts. Because she was a child at heart, with a child's unsullied outlook, simplicity and zest its entire aloofness from the unreal complications of adult existence -- she had an assurance, a freshness, a power of initiative, which carried her through and past the superhuman difficulties of her task:Ce grand général qui prenait des bastilles

> *Ainsi qu'on prend le ciel, c'est en sautant dedans,*
> *N'était devant la herse et parmi les redans*
> *Qu'une enfant échappée à de pauvres families. . . .*
> *Elle est montée au ciel ensemble jeune et sage*
> *A peine parvenue au bord de son printemps*
> *Au bord de sa tendresse et de son jeune temps*
> *A peine au débarqué de son premier village."*

St. Joan thus appears as the supreme example of the practical mystic; rooted in the soil, and agent of that saving force which will never rest until it has resolved the discords of man's life and inducted him into the kingdom of reality. She is for Péguy not only the redeemer and incarnate soul of France, but also, in her spirit of prayer and her militant vigour, the leader and patron of all those initiates of hope who "seek to mend the universal ill."

> *"Heureux ceux d'entre nous qui la verront paraître*
> *Le regard plus ouvert que d'une âme d'enfant,*
> *Quand ce grand general et ce chef triomphant*
> *Rassemblera sa troupe aux pieds de notre maitre."*

It is easy enough to exhibit Péguy's defects, both literary and temperamental. Among the first we must reckon his tiresome mannerisms and apparent absence of form, his digressions and lapses into the didactic, his exaggerated love of repetition: the way in which his verse, in such a poem as Eve, seems to advance by means of passionate reiterations, stanza after stanza, like the waves of one tide, distinguished only by the smallest verbal changes. On the temperamental side we must acknowledge his intractable arrogance, a complete want of sympathy with his opponents' point of view, something too of the morose distrustfulness of the peasant: faults which persisted side by side with his real mystical enthusiasm, for his nature never completely unified itself. On one side a spiritual poet, on the other side he was and remained to the last a violent and often cruel pamphleteer: carrying on against both private enemies and public movements a guerilla warfare in which he seemed to himself to be like his patroness, fighting the cause of his Voices and of right. As with most poets who are also missionaries, apostolic zeal sometimes got the better of artistic discretion. In the fury of his invective against the folly, priggishness, cowardice, and love of comfort of the modern world he seized any image that came to hand; sometimes with disconcerting effect. No other poet, perhaps, would have dared to introduce cachets of antipyrine into his indignant catalogue of our weaknesses and crimes. Yet, as against this, what other poet of our day has achieved so wide a sweep of emotion; has revealed to us so great and so earnest a personality? When we consider his range, the tender simplicity of his passages on little children, the sublime Hymn to the Virgin and Address to Night in La Deuxieme Vertu, the solemn yet ardent celebration of "les armes de Jésus" -- suffering, poverty, failure, death -- in La Tapisserie de Sainte Genevieve; and Eve, with its alternate notes of irony and exaltation, its exquisite concluding rhapsody on St. Genevieve and St. Joan of Arc, the "two shepherdesses of France " -- then we forget the sermons and the diatribes, and we feel that the world lost in Péguy a great Christian poet. He died, as we maiy be sure that he would have wished to do, in defence of the country which he so passionately loved: and a strangely poignant interest attaches to those verses in his last published work which he devotes to the "poor sinners " redeemed by this most sacred of deaths:

> *"Heureux ceux qui sont morts pour la terre charnelle,*
> *Mais pourvu que ce fût dans une juste guerre.*
> *Heureux ceux qui sont morts pour quatre coins de terre.*
> *Heureux ceux qui sont morts d'une mort solennelle . . .*
> *"Heureux les grands vainqueurs. Paix aux hommes de guerre.*
> *Qu'ils soient ensevelis dans un dernier silence.*
> *Que Dieu mette avec eux dans la juste balance*
> *Un peu de ce terrain d'ordure et de poussiere."'Que Dieu mette avec eux dans le juste plateau*
> *Ce qu'ils ont tant aimé, quelques grammes de terre.*
> *Un peu de cette vigne, un peu de ce coteau,*
> *Un peu de ce ravin sauvage et solitaire. . . ,*
> *"Mere, voici vos fils et leur immense armée.*
> *Qu'ils ne soient pas jugés sur leur seule misere.*
> *Que Dieu mette avec eux un peu de cette terre*
> *Qui les a tant perdus et qu'ils ont tant aimée."*

www.ingramcontent.com/pod-product-compliance
Lightning Source LLC
Chambersburg PA
CBHW031223090426

42740CB00007B/684